PAYING ATTENTION:

Critical Essays on Timothy Findley

Edited by

ANNE GEDDES BAILEY

and

KAREN GRANDY

ECW PRESS

We acknowledge the support of the Canada Council
for the Arts for our publishing program.
This book has been published with the assistance
of grants from the Ontario Arts Council.

CANADIAN CATALOGUING IN PUBLICATION DATA
Main entry under title:
Timothy Findley : paying attention

ISBN 1-55022-367-4

1. Findley, Timothy, 1930-   – Criticism and interpretation.
I. Bailey, Anne Elizabeth, 1963-   . II. Grandy, Karen Joy, 1964-   .

PS8511.I38Z93 1998   C813'.54   C98-931405-7
PR9199.3.F52Z93 1998

Cover design and artwork by Guylaine Régimbald.
Imaging by ECW Type & Art, Oakville, Ontario.
Printed by AGMV Marquis Imprimeur, Cap-Saint-Ignace, Quebec.

Distributed in Canada by General Distribution Services,
30 Lesmill Road, Don Mills, Ontario M3B 2T6.
Distributed in the United States by General Distribution Services,
85 River Rock Drive, Suite 202, Buffalo, New York 14207.

Published by ECW PRESS,
2120 Queen Street East, Suite 200,
Toronto, Ontario M4E 1E2.
www.ecw.ca/press

PRINTED AND BOUND IN CANADA

TABLE OF CONTENTS

ACKNOWLEDGEMENTS

The editors would like to acknowledge and express our gratitude to ECW PRESS, especially for the support and advice given to us by Robert Lecker throughout this project.

We would also like to note and state our thanks to our fellow contributors, whose enthusiasm and generous participation in the collaborative process enriched the individual essays and the collection as a whole.

It has been a pleasure to join in critical conversation with you all.

Introduction

ANNE GEDDES BAILEY and KAREN GRANDY

IN 1995, when ECW Press included Timothy Findley in the *Canadian Writers and Their Works* series, Lorraine York began the review by suggesting that Findley is an observer of the twentieth century. Having lived through two-thirds of the century and having examined its major historical moments in his many works of fiction and drama, Findley is indeed a writer concerned with his time and place, and how that time and place have been shaped by the events and myths of the last 100 years. His novels and plays, for example, return to the First World War, the Second World War, the Holocaust, Hiroshima and Nagasaki, and the Cold War. His cast of characters includes people of varied racial, ethnic, and class backgrounds, different sexual orientations, multiple ages, and divergent political stripes, and, of course, a number of animals and birds, so powerfully characterized that they seem as real to Findley's readers as Wallis Simpson or Sir Harry Oakes. Several characters step out of the pages of famous literary works, most written in the last 100 years. Now, as we near the end of the twentieth century, it is appropriate to focus our attention on Findley, since his work provides us with such a rich standpoint from which to review, examine, question, and interpret the culture, politics, myths, and history of our contemporary society.

The millennial metaphor, however, should not imply that the end of the century signals a simultaneous end to either Findley's writing or its critical importance. Indeed, throughout this volume, we hope to suggest the opposite: that Findley's contribution to our under-standing of literature and human culture is continually refreshed with each new novel and play, and that critical reexaminations of his oeuvre constantly add important dimensions to that understanding, which, Findley's works suggest, should be under continual recon-struction. As many critics over the years have noted, Findley's works imply, above all else, that it is the practice of interpretation, the act of making meaning, that is crucial — it is when interpretation and meaning become fixed that the "end" needs to be anticipated and feared.

As York notes in her review of Findley's work, it was not until the publication of *The Wars* and Findley's receipt of the Governor General's Literary Award in 1977 for that novel that serious criticism of his fiction began to appear. In 1981, *Canadian Literature* published the first, and to date only, special issue focused upon Findley; that volume was devoted largely to *The Wars*, although John F. Hulcoop's article laid the groundwork for reconsiderations of Findley's earlier novels and short stories. In the 17 years that have followed, many reviews, articles, and interviews have appeared in various journals, ranging from those interested in Canadian literature to others devoted to narrative theory and postcolonial issues.[1] A significant body of Findley scholarship has developed in New Zealand and Australia, and, more surprisingly perhaps, in Germany. York discerns a number of critical directions that have developed over the last 17 years, beginning with close textual analysis, but then quickly moving on to a primary focus upon the structure and style of his novels. Meaning, critics soon discovered, is slippery in Findley's fiction, leading to postmodern and poststructural questionings of the construction of history, identity, and truth as a way of critiquing the often oppressive social and political forces that determine public knowledge. Out of these postmodern questionings grew a number of studies of Findley's politics, outlining his feminism, environmentalism, pacifism, anti-imperialism, and anticonsumerism. York ends her critical overview in *Canadian Writers and Their Works* by calling for further study of Findley's short fiction and drama, and by urging critics to examine more thoroughly the humorous and performative elements everywhere apparent in Findley's work.

The substantial body of Findley criticism outlined by York stems not only from Findley's obvious popularity among readers — the number of weeks Findley has appeared on best-seller lists attests to this — but more importantly from the complexity of his work. Delighting readers with gripping plots and a dramatic flare for both the humorous and the tragic, Findley's works, at first glance, may appear to be more surface than depth. However, as will become evident over the course of this collection, in bringing the surface, the gesture, the literary figure to the fore, Findley raises important aesthetic questions concerning literature's function, as both arti-fact and social agent, within the events of the twentieth century.

Examinations of Findley's returns to the period of European fascism, for example, illustrate his complicated moral and ethical position, as his narrators and characters, who are themselves often artists or artist-figures, navigate their way through the paradox of their stated antifascist stance and their covert fascist desires. Indeed, many of the following articles focus upon just such moral and ethical ambivalence, evident in both the structure and theme of Findley's novels; although ambivalence has often been noted in Findley's work, only recently has it become the main subject of criticism. Through this focus, critical returns to narratological, historical, allegorical, and generic approaches to Findley urge us to reread and reevaluate earlier studies of his work. Findley's fictions and dramas, as the following articles illustrate, are simultaneously critical of and complicit with mythic and allegorical structures that tend to end in violence and death. This paradox, although at times frustrating for the reader, ultimately allows Findley to explore the ethical and aesthetic dimensions of desiring both our actual end and representations of that prophesied destruction.

Our aim from the conception of this collection to its completion has been to pay attention to the complexity of Findley's work — as Hulcoop, taking his cue from Findley, urged new readers of Findley to do in 1981. By paying attention, we hope to provide readers and scholars of Findley with original perspectives on his work. We have invited and commissioned new articles from established, influential Findley scholars and from others known to be doing graduate research on his work. We include material on both the lesser known works, such as the short fiction and drama, and novels such as *The Butterfly Plague* and *The Last of the Crazy People*, and the major novels. We also include some of the first articles to be published on both *Headhunter* and *The Piano Man's Daughter*. Significantly, several of the articles come out of the many doctoral dissertations now centred on Findley (either in part or in whole). Perhaps acting upon York's lead in calling for further examination of the performative and theatrical aspects of Findley's fiction and drama, many of these articles draw upon theories of performance, highlighting the construction of race, gender, and identity through national and mythic paradigms, on the one hand, and through personal memory, on the other. Karen Grandy, for instance, considers these issues in Findley's drama, ironically a genre often ignored by Findley's critics even though the "performance" of identity and self is emphasized through the performance on stage. As we hoped, the work by established critics illustrates the ways in which rereading Findley continually rewards the experienced critic with new ideas and arguments.

As we have already mentioned, several of the following articles return to issues that have interested Findley's critics from the start. However, these returns are not repetitions, but instead add other interpretative layers and significance to earlier readings, readings that, we have been constantly reminded, are open to critique and revision. As a result, Tom Hastings's historical contextualization of the mythic underpinnings of *The Wars*, for example, will force readers to reevaluate the anti-imperialist stance of Findley's most famous "Canadian" novel. Other articles in this collection examine issues that have been noted but not closely considered. For instance, Catherine Hunter delves into the theoretical implications of a narratological tic that many others have only briefly remarked upon — that of the double beginning. Similarly, Lorraine York critically examines what others have too often taken for granted in his fiction: Findley's sympathetic and humanistic representation of the racial and ethnic other. Heather Sanderson focuses upon Findley's sophisticated analysis of fascist aestheticism, reconsidering Findley's critique of fascism through the theory and practice of allegory. In this way, her article reveals how the act of interpreting Findley's highly self-conscious narratives challenges many of the very theories his fictions invite us to use as we read.

The task of ordering the essays in this collection was not an easy one, difficult not because we could see no way in which the articles might go together but because there are so many different and interesting ways in which they illuminate, contrast, connect with, and diverge from one another. Although we encourage readers to draw connections of their own, we have chosen to emphasize three main areas: narrative, myth, and performance. While many critics have examined the narratological implications of Findley's historical novels, few studies have considered his manipulation of other fictional and generic structures, as do the first three essays in our collection.

Our collection begins with an essay on Findley's openings. In " 'I Don't Know How to Begin': Findley's Work in the Sixties," Catherine Hunter examines the anxiety and violence of narrative beginnings manifest in Findley's first short fiction, his first novel, *The Last of the Crazy People*, and "The Paper People," an early script written for television. Hunter highlights a pervasive ambivalence toward narrative in these works, which shows a desire to tell, and thereby order and interpret experience, in conflict with an anxiety about telling, evident in the large narrative gaps and the stammering, violent openings and reopenings. She traces the source of this anxiety both to a healthy respect for the potentially dangerous power of narrative and, more significantly, to the nostalgic desire for what she labels the "unnarratable" story, a desire that simultaneously sets narrative in motion and is itself ruptured by the inevitable violence and corruption of narrative.

As Hunter observes, *The Last of the Crazy People* begins as it ends. Marlene Goldman, in the second essay in this volume, draws on this scene of obliterating destruction to launch her discussion of *Headhunter* and apocalyptic and prophetic fiction. In "The End(s) of Myth: Apocalyptic and Prophetic Fictions in *Headhunter*," Goldman demonstrates this novel's incorporation and secularization of the standard elements of the apocalyptic paradigm: recursive literary intertextuality; warnings and signs of catastrophic, imminent self-destruction; a visionary narrator with a transhistorical, panoramic perspective; and a small community of the faithful elect, who battle the corrupt, demonic forces at work, and in power, in their society. Goldman argues, however, that Findley's novel both draws on and critiques the apocalyptic model, and might also be read in the tradition of preexilic prophetic writing. Most notably, *Headhunter* eschews the notion of a postapocalyptic paradise, with its attendant lack of responsibility to reform the here and now. Furthermore, she observes, the novel undermines a clear boundary between good and evil — the elect and the demons — and between fiction and reality. *Headhunter* calls us to pay attention to world and word as inextricable constituents of each other.

As Anne Geddes Bailey contends near the end of her article, "Finding Lily: Maternal Presence in *The Piano Man's Daughter*," if *Headhunter* warns of the danger of mistaking the word for the world, then *The Piano Man's Daughter* offers a new, maternal relation between word and world that might reshape narratives of absences and ends. Grounding her argument in the psychoanalytic model of intersubjectivity theorized by Jessica Benjamin, Bailey contends that Charlie Kilworth's story of his own and his mother's life includes the presence of his mother as subject rather than her absence, in contrast to traditional linguistic and narrative models of development that objectify and silence the mother. In recognizing the presence of his mother, Charlie's narrative reflects the intersubjective relationship

5

that exists between them. At the same time, Lily's experience of mothering is a complex blend of natural regeneration and cultural production, blending which parallels the paradoxical space of inter-subjectivity: a space that allows for her own and Charlie's simultaneous objectivity and subjectivity, being and nonbeing, independence and dependence, while not endangering each other's autonomy. This contrasts sharply with the traditional, oedipal shape of the bildungs-roman, which depends upon the silencing of the mother not only for the autonomy of the individual but also for the very functioning of language and narrative itself.

The focus on parental imagery continues in the first essay of the second section, Tom Hastings's " 'Their Fathers Did It to Them': Findley's Appeal to the Great War Myth of a Generational Conflict in *The Wars*." However, Hastings focuses less upon narrative shapings and more on the mythic dimensions of Findley's fiction. Hastings's article begins with a search for the "fathers" whom Findley, in *Inside Memory*, identifies as war mongers and rapists. Hastings argues that the "fathers" whom Findley refers to are the parents of the generation of young men who fought in the First World War, and that Findley, in both *Inside Memory* and *The Wars*, invokes a myth of generational conflict that presents the First World War as "a dirty trick played by the older generation on the younger." Hastings notes the pervasive presence of this myth in British war and postwar literature, explaining its consolatory effect on a nation emotionally and economically devastated by the war. He argues that Findley's adoption of this myth, together with the dearth of Canadian references or Canadian historical context, marks *The Wars* as belonging to the British literary tradition. The limits of this generational myth, which rests on an unstable father/son binary, are highlighted in Hastings's essay, as is the paradox of employing an inherited literary myth in a work about a war that marked Canada's emancipation from the binding limits of its colonial inheritance.

We move from First World War generational myth to fascist myths and allegories in the Second World War with the next essay, Heather Sanderson's "(Im)Perfect Dreams: Allegories of Fascism in *The Butterfly Plague*." Sanderson discusses *The Butterfly Plague*'s exposure and critique of fascist allegorization as limiting, fixative, and destructive in its assumption of a perfect, natural correspondence between surface and essence. Sanderson also shows, however, that Findley himself employs allegory throughout the novel; for example, he parallels Nazism's glorification and imposition of its own definition of bodily perfection with Hollywood's obsession with the same. Yet, argues Sanderson, Findley's resistance to allegorical meaning-making is paradoxically evident in his very employment of allegories that are deliberately unstable, excessive, and incoherent. Thus, she identifies the "central moral message" of the novel as a warning against the always destructive and doomed practice of attempting to realize mythic dreams.

In concert with Sanderson's argument that Findley both uses and subverts allegorical meanings in *The Butterfly Plague*, Peter Dickinson's article, " 'Running Wilde': National Ambivalence and Sexual Dissidence in *Not Wanted on the Voyage*," examines how myths of new worlds, nations, and sexuality are subverted by an ambivalence that haunts the space of allegory. Drawing on Homi Bhabha's notion of "the meanwhile" — a space in which minority voices emerge within discourses of nationalism — and Jonathan Dollimore's definition of "sexual dissidence" — which also operates " 'betwixt and between' . . . dominant and subordinate cultures, groups, and identities" — Dickinson argues that Findley's allegorical version of the Flood highlights these "in between" spaces and discourses. *Not Wanted on the Voyage*'s anachronistic narrative and Findley's use of the alternative narrative viewpoints of Mottyl and Mrs. Noyes are both slightly askew to Noah's vision of the new world, creating a space between the dominant discourse and its margins. Most important, though, is Findley's representation of Lucy, seeped in camp vernacular and cross-dressed as a geisha. She, like Oscar Wilde in his creation and "taking on" of the role of Salome, crosses and destabilizes sexual and national boundaries, and in doing so demythologizes Noah's (and by extension Judeo-Christian culture's) dominant new world myth.

As both Dickinson and Sanderson note in their articles, Barbara Gabriel's earlier work began the task of reading Findley's fiction through theories of gender and performance, and Gabriel continues this work in the first essay of our third section, which is focused upon performances in Findley's fiction and drama. In " 'The Repose of an Icon' in Timothy Findley's Theatre of Fascism: From 'Alligator Shoes' to *Famous Last Words*," Gabriel provides a reading of Findley's second novel of fascism traced over his teasing original title for the manuscript. The "alligator shoes" are those of Harry Reinhardt, the Nazi thug whom Mauberley desires masochistically and who will turn out to be his murderer. Gabriel argues that studies of the novel to date have tended to divide meaning production from structures of desire and in doing so overlook the importance of Mauberley's sexuality. In fact, she suggests, examination of his desires leads "to a much wider analysis of the way in which power operates in the social field: mediated by iconic figures who focus cultural discourses and desires in discrete historical moments." By revealing theatrical and cinematic encodings, this essay shows the influence of Jean Genet's *The Balcony* on what Findley himself called "the repose of an icon."

"Performed and Performing Selves in Findley's Drama," by Karen Grandy, also brings questions from performance theory to the works Findley wrote to be performed — his plays. Grandy's examination of *Can You See Me Yet?*, *The Stillborn Lover*, and *The Trials of Ezra Pound* focuses on Findley's treatment in these works of the controversial crux of performance theory: the acting or enacted self. Findley's adaptation of memory play and tribunal play models, Grandy suggests, allows him to explore memory, sexuality, and sanity as performative acts. Taken together, these plays adopt and then move beyond the conventional extremes in the debate about the performing self. *The Stillborn Lover* presumes an essential, transcendent self; *Can You See Me Yet?* denies the existence of such a self; *The Trials of Ezra Pound* posits a self that emerges from, rather than transcends, performance — that is, a performed *and* performing self. These various positions have ramifications for drama with a component of social criticism, which Grandy's essay also considers.

Performance of another kind is the central concern in the final essay of this collection, " 'A White Hand Hovering over the Page': Timothy Findley and the Racialized/Ethnicized Other." Lorraine York draws material from nine novels, two collections of short stories, and his writer's memoir, *Inside Memory*, to support her comprehensive discussion of representations of racial and ethnic otherness through-out Findley's work. York examines the construction of race and ethnicity as cultural and critical performance in Findley's texts. She highlights the ambiguous complexity of Findley's adoption of racial myths that are simultaneously affirmative and diminishing, such as the recurrent figures of the protective, maternal black maid and the eroticized, unattainable, exotic, racial other. York notes Findley's humanist call for identification and reconciliation of difference, and she draws attention to the problematic issue of cultural appropriation that some critics argue is inherent in such a stance. She points to Findley's presentation of his own ethnicity — WASP — as hybrid-ized construction, particularly in *The Piano Man's Daughter*, as encouraging evidence of his ongoing, conscious exploration of his own assumptions and representations of sexual, racial, and ethnic difference and identification.

In conclusion, we should point out that much of this collection has evolved through collaboration. All contributors were asked to read, comment upon, and then integrate some aspects of other contributors' work in their own articles. Collaboration is, we think, a most appropriate method through which to study and critique Findley's fiction and drama, because throughout his work meanings that are derived from communal sharing and equitable exchange of vision are the meanings that are the least destructive and oppressive. We need only think of the community below decks aboard the ark, Lily Kilworth's field of connections between herself, the natural world, and her family, or Lilah Kemp's collection of unlikely "Marlows" to find confirmation of this communal ethic/aesthetic. Conversely, we need only remember Noah's dictatorial commandments, Captain Leather's unreasonable but inviolable refusal to free the horses, or Rupert Kurtz's authoritative control over the desires of his "clients" to realize the dangers of too closely cherished individualism, on the one hand, or institutional authority, on the other. Of course, as Findley's work also suggests, to lose oneself in the group also has its dangers — both Cassandra Wakelin and Lily Kilworth meet their fiery deaths in the arms of their friends. So it is, we hope, with a balance between individual insight and the communal production of meaning that we have gathered our separate pieces into this collection on the work of Timothy Findley.

NOTE

[1] For a detailed summary of Findley criticism, see York 81–87.

WORK CITED

York, Lorraine M. "Timothy Findley and His Works." *Canadian Writers and Their Works.* Fiction Series. Vol. 12. Ed. Robert Lecker, Jack David, and Ellen Quigley. Toronto: ECW, 1995. 69–120. 12 vols. 1981–96.

PART I: NARRATIVE

"I Don't Know How to Begin": Findley's Work in the Sixties

CATHERINE HUNTER

"I DON'T KNOW HOW TO BEGIN . . .," says the narrator in the opening sentence of "About Effie," the story that begins Timothy Findley's career as a writer of fiction. The statement may seem paradoxical, but in retrospect it seems prophetic, for it thematizes a difficulty with beginning that continues in Findley's work for the next thirty years. The openings of his works often seem to signal anxiety over the task of beginning to write. It is therefore interesting to turn to works that Findley composed in the sixties, as he began to write for a living. His early short fiction, his first novel, *The Last of the Crazy People*, and an early television script, "The Paper People," all manifest intense and fascinating forms of narrative anxiety.

The term "narrative anxiety" does not refer here to some uncertainty on the part of the living, breathing man named Timothy Findley. Rather, it refers to the movement of the narrative itself. As theorist Peter Brooks has argued, it is possible, and illuminating, "to see the text itself as a system of internal energies and tensions, compulsions, resistances, and desires" (xiv). He points out that the opening of a narrative signifies, or "gives the illusion" of being, the moment at which narrating begins (103), regardless of when author first put pen to paper. In Findley's fiction, that moment is often in hiding, obscured by naïve narrators, by apparent hesitation, or by violence. As I will argue, these three narrative practices can be read as the manifestation of a strong ambivalence about the telling of stories.

One of the earliest signs of narrative anxiety in Findley's work is his use of naïve narrators. The openings of his narratives are often linked with a loss of innocence, and in his early work this loss is often imaged through the figure of a troubled adolescent whose fall from childhood constitutes the narrative movement. "About Effie" is the first in a series of early narratives concerned with sexuality, mental illness, and violence — issues that later become the focus of

Findley's major works. In the early fiction, the investigation is tentative; the narratives circle around these concerns, portraying them in "About Effie," "Lemonade," and "War" (all collected in *Dinner along the Amazon*) through the eyes of children who can never get close enough to the story to tell it whole, and thus these narratives are marked by silences and gaps. The adults in these stories engage in a conspiracy of silence about the frightening things that are happening in their families — parents who refuse to be parents, people who drink themselves into oblivion, shoot themselves, drive their cars off cliffs. From the adult point of view, these are unspeakable acts that must never enter the discourse of society. Perhaps the adults are attempting to protect the children, to keep them innocent. But the prolonged innocence is double edged. It builds up unbearable tension, generating an insatiable desire to break the silence. The stories of these families must be told — and the desire to tell them is embodied in Findley's children. Yet without a language in which to speak, they don't know how to begin. In this way, the boys in Findley's early fiction serve as a sort of buffer for the narrative, distancing it from the core of the story, which it both desires and fears to tell.

A second sign of narrative ambivalence is that Findley often seems to begin his novels hesitantly, with scenes that are repeated later in the book. As Laurie Ricou has said, *The Wars* "opens stammering" (129). *Famous Last Words* and *Not Wanted on the Voyage* seem to stammer also, with a series of false starts. *The Last of the Crazy People* opens in medias res, at the moment just before Hooker Winslow opens fire. Like other Findley novels (*The Wars*, *Not Wanted on the Voyage*), its prologue provides partial narration of a painful scene that occurs much later in the novel, and its following chapter immediately jumps backward to "begin" the story again at an earlier, and more peaceful, point in time. In terms of Findley's literary craft, such prologues are highly successful, hooking the reader immediately and setting up great suspense. But the split beginning also seems to signal ambivalence, suggesting that the narrative doesn't entirely want to begin.

The third, and most dramatic, sign of ambivalence is the repetition, in novel after novel, of a story that begins with blood, pain, fire, or death. This series of violent beginnings suggests that violence itself is the impetus, the "irritation," as Brooks puts it (103), that gives rise to narration. It also suggests that beginning — particularly the beginning of writing — is a form of violence. Almost every Findley novel starts with violence, and the opening scenes often depict the

14

human figure split, disfigured, or destroyed. *The Butterfly Plague* begins with a decapitation; *The Wars, Not Wanted on the Voyage,* and *The Piano Man's Daughter* all begin with the evocation of fire; *Famous Last Words* begins with a suicide; *The Telling of Lies* begins, as all good mysteries do, with a murder; and *Headhunter* begins with the most intriguing split of all, as Joseph Conrad's Kurtz doubles himself and emerges from the pages of *Heart of Darkness* to begin a bloody campaign of terror in futuristic Toronto. Although there are numerous explanations for these violent beginnings (marketing among them), it seems to me that on the whole they signal a conflict that seems to arise from anxiety about translating story into narrative.

It is interesting to speculate on the possible reasons for this anxiety. Perhaps, most obviously, we can say that Findley's apparent distrust of stories stems partly from an awareness of their pervasive power to shape our lives. For example, his later fictions clearly express a distrust of narrative explanation for madness and difference. Characters who attempt to explain aberrations through narrative structures (Noah, Dr. Potter, Kurtz) create disastrous consequences for the people around them. Several critics, including two who have contributed to this volume of essays, have focused on Findley's apparent ambivalence toward specific types of stories. For example, Marlene Goldman examines Findley's engagement with the structure of apocalyptic narratives, arguing convincingly that *Headhunter* "paradoxically signals the imaginative tenacity and the untrustworthiness and limitations of a full-blown apocalyptic vision — a vision that represents transformation as absolute destruction" (34). And Lorraine York examines Findley's engagement with the construction of narratives of racial identity, arguing that his participation in this construction paradoxically performs "the cultural work both of critique and of repetition or echoing of hegemonic discourses" ("White Hand" 203). Both critics reveal through their analyses that Findley's attitude toward storytelling is far from simple. As Goldman points out, *Headhunter* presents us with "the idea that we cannot help but narrate our lives and that we are all caught in the grip of a host of plots" (49); therefore, "stories represent the collective unconscious of the culture that we have inherited, and we ignore them at our peril" (51–52). The telling of stories, it seems, is fraught with danger. Yet Findley clearly desires to tell them, for a complete rejection of the power of narrative would, of course, consist merely of silence.

Perhaps, however, the danger lies not only in the consequences of specific stories but also in the act of narration itself, which begins, as

Brooks puts it, "when story or 'life' . . . demands narration" (103). Throughout this essay, I will maintain the distinction between the terms "story" and "narrative" as defined by Gérard Genette: story is the "signified," and narrative is the "signifier"; story is the "narrative content," and narrative is the "statement, discourse or narrative text itself" (27). In other words, story refers to *what* Findley tells us, whereas narrative refers to *how* he tells it. Narrative anxiety about beginning seems to stem from the desire to keep story out of the realm of narration, as if the story could remain unnarratable, somehow preserved or protected from becoming narrative. But why?

The concept of an unnarratable story is an impossible paradox. It is important to note that this entity exists only as the object of a desire that can never be fulfilled. The desire for the unnarratable story is always nostalgic, always looking back to a golden age that never was. Although narratology separates story from narrative, and I use this convenient distinction constantly, the two are inextricable. Story cannot exist without narrative any more than narrative can exist without story. The unnarrated story is the dream of a story uncorrupted by narration. It is also the very story that would, if it could, put an end to narration. It is the dream of a self innocent of division, confident of its own coherence.

The beginning of narration is dangerous because it marks the place where writing, with its play of *différance*, will rupture the desire to believe that either story or self can exist in a self-identical, cohesive, uncorrupted form. Because writing appears to split signified from signifier, thought from word, intention from meaning, Jacques Derrida uses writing as a metaphor to investigate this split. The sign, or trace, marks the operation of difference, in which "the completely other is announced as such — without any simplicity, any identity, any resemblance or continuity — within what is not it" (47). Writing is the site where the split is announced, the place where the dream of self-presence is destroyed.

The "violence" of writing, Derrida concludes, violates only that which has already been violated. Writing seems violent because it occasions the "loss of the proper, of absolute proximity, of self-presence, in truth the loss of what has never taken place, of a self-presence which has never been given but only dreamed of and always already split, repeated, incapable of appearing to itself except in its own disappearance" (112). Self-presence, says Derrida, is "only dreamed." But with what persistent and forceful desire has that dream been forged! It is a desire whose traces are, in fact, writing. (For there

16

is nothing outside writing, as Derrida never forgets, nothing "that one can call alien at once to writing and to violence" [127].) Findley's narratives seem driven by the desire to forge that dream again and again, and at the same time they seem driven by the conflicting desire to rupture that dream.

Thus, Findley's texts display an ambivalence toward self and story — both a nostalgic desire for stable absolutes and a desire for the fragmentation, or even destruction, of them. It is not necessary here to condemn nostalgic desire (as Derrida often seems to do) and to privilege as more realistic the conflicting desire to destroy the illusion. I am not taking sides in the conflict. Rather, I am interested only in examining the ways in which this conflict leaves its mark on narrative.

* * *

"I don't know how to begin about Effie . . .," says the narrator, and his statement suggests that it is not only Effie, strange as she proves to be, who causes the difficulty. It is the story itself: *I don't know how to begin "About Effie."* The story of Effie, a maid with peculiar delusions, is narrated by the young Neil Cable, a character who also appears in "War" (and, years later, in "The Name's the Same" and "Real Life Writes Real Bad," both collected in *Stones*). In all his stories, Neil is a self-conscious narrator, anxious about structuring his narratives, uncertain of his ability to get them right. In "About Effie," Neil, like many of Findley's young male protagonists, sees only the outlines of a story — the puzzling clues and traces left by adult mysteries.

Every encounter with Effie, it seems, is a scene of miscommunication. The first sign of her presence is an inarticulate "noise": "I went in, and there was a shout. Maybe it was a scream, I don't know. But somebody sure made a noise . . ." (83). Effie does not speak immediately but gives Neil "the look that said 'Are you the one I'm waiting for' — and then she sat down and started to cry" (83). Her explanation for her behaviour is vague, to say the least: she is waiting for some mysterious man, or men, who will be heralded by music and thunder, to summon her away to some unspecified place. Neil's attempts to learn more about Effie are thwarted at every turn. His conversations with her consist of a series of interruptions, non sequiturs, and misunderstandings. For example, when Neil asks her to identify the awaited man, she answers without answering:

17

"Him."

"Who's that?"

"There has to be thunder, or he won't come." (86)

Effie promises Neil, "Someday when I know you better, I'll tell you" (88). But that day never arrives. One night, Neil and his mother seem to be on the verge of discovering the answer to the mystery. Hearing music and thunder, they creep downstairs to see Effie watching at the window. Finally, she speaks, but Neil reports, "I don't know what it was because she said it too quietly for me to hear" (91). He and his mother say nothing, turn, and go back upstairs. They lie in bed, thinking about Effie, and their conversation echoes the silence that permeates this whole story:

"Do you know?"

"No. Do you?"

"No." (92)

The story is not only about Effie. As her name suggests, it is about ineffability itself, what cannot be said.

"About Effie" is the gentlest of Findley's tales of childhood encounters with the ineffable. In most of the stories, the young male characters react to the silence around them in dangerous, usually violent, ways. In "War," Neil's anger at his father's decision to go to war is exacerbated by his father's failure to *tell* his son that he was enlisting. In "Lemonade," eight-year-old Harper is emotionally abandoned by his mother, a severely depressed alcoholic who will not leave her bedroom. Neil and Harper attempt to attract their parents' attention by running away. But these attempts fail, and both boys resort to more direct methods. Neil's response is to ambush his father with an arsenal of rocks. Harper gazes up at the window of his mother's bedroom and then suddenly hurls a rock through it, shattering the glass and, apparently, her precarious balance: his mother shoots herself that very night.

Both stories foreshadow Findley's first novel, *The Last of the Crazy People*, in which Hooker's reaction to the silence of his family is to massacre them with a handgun. "Are we crazy people?" Hooker asks his brother (203). "Mother is upstairs and won't come down. You live in the library. Rosetta won't look at me. Iris has secrets. And Papa sits with his back to everything. What does it mean?" (204). At the age of eleven, Hooker is vaguely aware that sexuality plays some part in the mystery of his family's behaviour. His mother's illness is linked to her recent stillbirth; his brother, Gilbert, is accused of fathering an illegitimate child; his father is exiled from his mother's bed. But sexuality is never discussed in this family. Hooker's questions are never answered. Iris, the maid, tells Hooker that he will understand when he's "old enough." In the meantime, "You shouldn't speak on things you don't know about" (54). Even Gilbert, the only one willing to talk, reacts with despair to Hooker's questions about sex: "I don't want you to know. Oh, Jesus — I don't want you to have to know things!" (203).

The boys in "About Effie," "War," "Lemonade," and *The Last of the Crazy People* exist in a preadolescent realm from which they perceive the world of adults through soundproof glass. Nothing is explained to them. Even the kindly maids who care for Harper and Hooker in the absence of their parents refuse to explain or even to speak of that absence, other than by oblique reference. Harper and Hooker are driven, by the tension of the silence around them, to create a narrative logic that will enable the untellable stories of their families to be told. Brooks notes that the most important functions of narrative are that it "demarcates, encloses, establishes limits, orders" (4). This is the desire of the boys in these stories: to place some limits on their experience, to give it some order. Unfortunately, as York puts it, "Both children, in the midst of a domestic war zone, are innocents who misinterpret information they receive" (*Front Lines* 3), and therefore neither boy is able to create an effective interpretation.

Harper envisions a logic in which the redemption of jewellery will equal the redemption of his mother. And Hooker, forced to rely on eavesdropping to get any information at all, is left to draw on his own limited experience to interpret the euphemisms and unfinished sentences that he overhears. From his unsophisticated perspective, the only context in which he can place them is that of "crazy people." And the only ending to the story that he can think of is total destruction, forcing a narrative closure so lethal that it puts an end to the story of his family forever.

These boys begin to break out of their innocence by creating narrative structures. The pain that they experience as they do so suggests a conflict surrounding the genesis of narration. Narrative desire is generated by instances of "narratability," which D.A. Miller defines as consisting of those "instances of disequilibrium, suspense, and general insufficiency from which a given narrative appears to rise" (ix). Narratability is the condition that makes narrative possible by arousing the desires that fuel its momentum. The traditional nineteenth-century novel, of which Miller writes, moves from narratability toward the "nonnarratable" — that "state of quiescence assumed by a novel before the beginning and supposedly recovered by it at the end" (ix). The nonnarratable cannot generate a story; it can only function as closure. Miller's list of nonnarratable events (marriage, death, inquest — depending on the genre) names the things that are lacking in the state of narratability. These events are the objects of desire that will close the discourse by fulfilling desire. But in Findley's fiction, from the very beginning of his career, the object of desire is rarely a specific event, and resistance to closure does not simply take the form of leaving us without telling us what happened next. Rather, the object of desire seems to be untellability itself. The very thing that his narratives desire to tell us about is untellability. They may promise to tell us what Effie is waiting for, why Harper's mother rejects him, or why the Winslows are so repressed, but they never do.

In their efforts both to approach and to avoid certain moments, Findley's narratives move in a way similar to the "narrative discontent" that Miller observes in the nineteenth-century novel. But moments that they fear and desire are not exactly what Miller means by the nonnarratable. I prefer to use the term "unnarratable" because it connotes more than a simple absence of narrative desire. It is a reversal of that state, even a release from it (as in the difference between "not doing" something and "undoing" it). Findley's fiction returns us, again and again, not to quiescence but to lack. Instead of moving steadily toward the nonnarratable, his fictions often end once they have succeeded (through a series of struggles and disruptions) in making their stories *unnarratable*.

Like the boys in his early fiction, Findley continually tries and fails to break the silence on mysterious and taboo subjects. And this is where the desires of story and the desires of narrative intersect: because the ineffable in the story is often taboo, most of the characters avoid it, and the immature boys who seek to penetrate it are incapable of doing so. And what remains hidden by the characters in the story is usually the very thing that is unnarratable. There is, of course, no story that literally cannot be told. Even the highly mysterious areas (madness, sexuality, violence) that Findley explores *can* be spoken of and even explained — most notably by political, psychoanalytic, or religious discourse. But his fiction resists such explanations, desiring to preserve the silence that surrounds these subjects. If the adults in the story were to reveal what is hidden — to create, say, a sociological narrative to explain alcoholism — there would be no story, or at least there would be a very different (and certainly not a Findleyesque) story. In these early works, narratability depends upon the untellable — it is the untellable itself that sets narrative desire in motion.

Neil's story of Effie seems to reach its peak of narratability just when its untellability becomes unbearable; Neil begins at the point where he doesn't know how to begin, as if his desire to shape the story into a narrative were fuelled by his very inability to do so. Paradoxically, the insufficiency from which these narratives arise can never be satisfied, because satisfaction would kill narrative desire, render the story pointless. In a sense, to narrate the story is to "ruin" it. After all, if Neil could really tell us about Effie, then there would be nothing to tell.

Despite the force of the desire to begin, there is an equally strong but opposite desire to resist beginning. In his study *Beginnings: Intention and Method*, Edward Said describes beginning as a point of rupture and loss. He quotes Maurice Merleau-Ponty: "Qu'il soit mythique ou intelligible, il y a un lieu où tout ce qui est ou qui sera, se prépare en même temps à être dit." Merleau-Ponty suggests that there is a "place" where the ineffable resides. Said's comments on this concept touch on the imaginary space that exists, as it were, before the beginning: "Mythical or utopian, this place . . . is probably the realm of silence in which transitive and intransitive beginnings jostle one another. Silence is the way language might dream of a golden age" (73).

This "realm of silence" is the realm of the unnarratable story, and it does seem to represent a golden age, a nostalgic desire for a time before language. It represents, perhaps, a kind of childhood, yet one that can only be desired in retrospect. As Harper in "Lemonade" begins to formulate his plan to break the unbearable silence of childhood, that silence is already becoming a lost, and therefore desirable, thing: "Perhaps he was turning from childhood — although he did not feel it going from him. His sense of loneliness was to determine this, beginning to become the loneliness of an adult, the loneliness defined by remembrance" (34). The break from silence is a break from innocence and wholeness into the criminal and shattered realm of language.

* * *

In *The Last of the Crazy People*, the link between narration and corruption occurs at the beginning. The novel opens during the last moments of Hooker's innocence, just before Hooker finally breaks (and is broken by) the silence of his family and leaves childhood irrevocably behind him. Thus, the beginning of writing is linked to the loss of innocence. Hooker falls from grace at the same time that Findley's story "falls" into discourse.

Parallels to ancient Greek tragedy run throughout much of Findley's work, and *The Last of the Crazy People* is no exception. The narrative movement of tragedy has traditionally been described as a decline from a superior state, culminating in a purging climax that restores some form of order to the world of the text. In Hooker's case, the superior state is the Edenic realm of childhood that Hooker fancies he inhabits before his mother's illness forces him to begin his swift and premature decline toward adulthood. In a parallel movement, the Winslow family, like Faulkner's Compsons, has degenerated from its former status as a respectable patriarchy to that of "a bunch of people everybody thinks is nuts" (91). The Winslows follow closely a long tradition of domestic tragedy, defined in part by the critic Bennett Simon as involving

> first, a sense of terrible warfare within the family, and second, the sense that problems cannot be solved by displacing the issues to outside the family. . . . [T]he family is at risk of destroying itself, either by literally destroying its own progeny or by making propagation impossible, for example, because of intractable warfare between husband and wife. (2)

The Winslows drive one son to suicide and are murdered by another; Jessica is at war with her husband and seems obsessed with the idea of killing babies (109–10). The word *family*, Rosetta says, is "the worst word I know, now" (153).

The novel also follows the tragic pattern in its preoccupation with the untellable. Simon argues that the genre of domestic tragedy is concerned with "thwarted communication, in the frustration and inhibition of telling" (60). As the tragic family of classical drama collapses in on itself, in an incestuous kind of death, it puts an end to all stories of itself that might ensure a kind of immortality: "Narration and child are gagged and killed, and silence and absence communicate the essence of tragedy" (66). *The Last of the Crazy People*, as its title suggests, is the end of the line. There will be no more Winslows — and no more story. "Will anyone remember?" asks

Hooker (191). "Will they talk about her [Jessica]?" Gilbert answers "No" (192).

Inability or unwillingness to talk pervade the novel, and this motif has its roots in another classical tradition. In his play *Can You See Me Yet?* Findley's central character, Cassandra, is named for the mythical prophet to whom no one would listen, and the conflicting desires that shape the myth of Cassandra shape Findley's fiction as well. According to Greek mythology, Apollo's sexual desire gives rise to the paradoxical curse. Apollo and Cassandra make an agreement: she will sleep with him, and in return he will give her the gift of prophecy. But after receiving her gift, Cassandra refuses to fulfil her part of the bargain. Rather than take back the gift, Apollo adds a curse, decreeing that her warnings will always go unheeded. Thus, he inscribes upon her the story of her betrayal, branding her with a double mark — that of his desire and her reluctance. In the structure of the original myth, both the bargain and the revenge impose an economy in which the frustrated desire to tell is linked to frustrated sexual desire. This model of blocked energy works as a way to approach the narrative structure of *The Last of the Crazy People* as well.

Findley's Cassandra is rendered powerless by the painful conflict between her missionary zeal and her inability to attract anybody's attention. Hooker and Gilbert, in *The Last of the Crazy People*, share a similar fate. Hooker remembers his mother's prophecy that he and Gilbert would be silver tongued: "There were two bracelets she always wore, made of silver. One bore Gilbert's tooth marks and the other his own, and the story was that they had teethed on silver and would grow up to speak like kings" (133). But this promise, like Apollo's, is never realized. Both Gilbert and Hooker think that they must warn the family, but they are unable to do so. Hooker is not even certain what it is he wants to tell:

"Something will happen — it will. It will happen."
"What honey? What will?" [asked Iris].
"I don't know," said Hooker. "But it will. Something will."
(152–53)

He knows that the unspoken tension in his family cannot go on forever; like the heat during this hottest summer in memory, it must eventually come to an end. But Hooker cannot say what is going to occur, nor can he imagine any way to stop it. He can only state, over and over, his fearful desire for that final something, that closure.

Within the Winslow family, creative energy is consistently blocked. The world outside the house is never allowed in, except in the form of reified narratives that are never challenged. Despite an apparent tradition of respect for the arts, none of the Winslows is able to create any artwork. The stories that are allowed into the Winslow household play an ominous and oppressive role. Literary texts, songs, television news reports, and biblical scripture embedded in the text all point toward betrayal, revenge, and death, and all import into the novel a strong desire for apocalyptic closure.[1]

Although Hooker is the central character of the novel, it is important to look closely at Gilbert as well. Because Gilbert is a writer, or at least a writer figure, his silence and lack of invention are particularly striking; York has aptly described his unhappy state as a kind of "intellectual stillbirth" (*Front Lines* 7). His many books suggest that he has access to a wide variety of stories, but the books seem only to stifle him. His shelves are full of the classics, including many by writers often romanticized in the popular imagination as tragic heroes: Blake, Byron, Shelley, Keats, Wilde, and Fitzgerald. Gilbert himself displays the romanticized gestures of the poet. True to popular stereotype, he drinks and smokes to excess, suffers from an "illness of the heart" (64), and is misunderstood by those around him. Yet despite his supposedly artistic bent, his literary endeavours are confined mainly to rereading books that he has already committed to memory and copying down other people's words. Lines from the canonized poets continually run through his head. His mind, "where he hoarded so much, so many words, for quoting" (46), is cluttered with memorized phrases that he repeats to the uninterested members of his family or scribbles on the scraps of paper that litter his room. His only "original" writing consists of garbled phrases interspersed with literary allusions (260). In one scene, Gilbert and Hooker play an obviously much-repeated game, in which Hooker reads aloud the titles of books on the library shelves while Gilbert, able to recall whole books with great speed, quotes from or comments on them in capsule form (188–90). The scene is reminiscent of the pathetic joke about the prison inmates who have heard each other's stale jokes so many times that they have invented a system of telling them by number. For Gilbert, literature is not alive with possibilities. It is a closed system, already coded and confined to its place in the stuffy library, "hung with the opaque air of cigarettes and liquory smells" (187), where he will "never let anyone in" (188).

Gilbert views himself as an intellectually and poetically gifted loner, cast adrift in a world of philistines, and his father, Nicholas, seems to have encouraged this romantic view. Nicholas describes Gilbert to Rosetta: "He has a genius for explanations. That's what gets me. He has a marvellous, wonderful — *loaded* — mind. . . . I think, here's someone who will probably write someday, or paint — or create something, and is just waiting now, simply waiting it out. Time. Waiting for the right time" (64). Of course, his mind *is* loaded, but more in the sense that Hooker's gun is loaded than in any potentially creative sense. And he *is* waiting for the right time — he times his suicide carefully so as to put his family in the worst possible light in front of the most possible people. After crashing his car over an embankment, he lies "like Peter crucified, hooked by his feet to the cross of the motor car, his arms spread out in a hopeless gesture" (230). His crucifixion marks him as the slaughtered lamb, sacrificed for the sins of his family.

Gilbert is sacrificed in order to preserve the quiet respectability that Nicholas (erroneously) believes his family enjoys in the community. Although local gossip has it that Gilbert is responsible for the pregnancy of a young neighbour, Nicholas's only concern is that "nothing outright has been said, yet" (118). Nicholas refuses to speak to Gilbert or the girl's family about it. He deals with this situation as he deals with every other family problem: "I don't think we should say anything" (120). Even in his private conversation with Rosetta, the words *pregnancy* and *baby* are never spoken. Sexuality and birth are consistently associated with suffering and shame, whereas silence, like death, is associated with relief. Like the actual baby and mother, who have been spirited away to Jamaica, these words must be suppressed; everything will remain safely in stasis as long as nobody names the disruptive forces in the family.

While Nicholas and Rosetta "discuss" this problem, Gilbert lies in the bathtub rereading passages from Euripides's *Iphigeneia in Taurus* (120–23). The story of Iphigeneia, whose father was willing to sacrifice her life in return for safe passage over the sea, stands as a dramatic parallel to the story of Nicholas's sacrifice of Gilbert in return for smooth sailing in society. The passage that Gilbert reads aloud is a nostalgic remembrance of childhood days in Athens, infused with a longing to return there. Like the rest of the family, he is paralysed by a nostalgic longing to return to the past, which is always imagined as perfect and golden. Nicholas may believe that Gilbert is waiting to create something, but in this story creation equals destruction. Something equals nothing, as any break in the silence leads inexorably to oblivion. Gilbert, like Hooker, knows that "something funny" is going to happen, something that he fears (203). But like Hooker's, his warnings fall on deaf ears. Unable to articulate the untellable, Gilbert chooses suicide as a form of communication, reinforcing the way in which this novel links the breaking of silence with danger and violence.

If breaking the silence is dangerous, then the split narrative at the beginning of this novel seems understandable. The prologue begins with Hooker's preparations for his role as sniper, but it ends before narrating — or even mentioning — the murders. At the beginning of chapter 1, the narrative jumps backward in story time (to the scene of Hooker's relatively peaceful last day of school), as if to avoid the coming slaughter, and the novel proceeds chronologically from this point on, shielding us from the scene of violence.

The beginning of the epilogue returns, briefly, to the last moments of Hooker's innocence, which open the prologue.

> Waiting in the stable, the boy and the cat at last were answered.
> "Hook!"
> It was beginning.
> Hooker drew the box close and opened it. He lifted the revolver up into view before his eyes, and it gleamed for him, oiled and ready, in his grasp. He inserted six bullets. . . . (272)

Hooker opens the (Pandora's) box and loads the gun when he "at last" is "answered." The silence will be broken now. "It" is "beginning," ironically, in the epilogue, for it is the end — the scene of the massacre that the narrative has avoided during all twenty-two chapters of the novel. Meanwhile, the narrative has piled up, along with a considerable amount of suspense, a library of untold stories and unanswered questions. The narrative has taken the length of the novel to be able to begin telling this story of violent destruction. And in the telling, it seems to destroy itself. The novel ends almost immediately, its desire, apparently, abruptly spent, as though the long analepsis has been only a way of delaying its own death.

*   *   *

One early work that has received little critical attention has perhaps the most fascinating beginning of all. This is Findley's television drama "The Paper People," broadcast on CBC Television on 13 December 1967, the same year that *The Last of the Crazy People* was published.

Findley's script begins, like so many of his works, with smoke and flame. In the opening sequence, a life-sized papier-mâché doll is set on fire. The doll sits among a broken bedroom set in the middle of a junkyard, its face reflected in a cracked mirror, indicating perhaps the splitting of the self that occurs when narration begins, and its outline obscured by smoke. This first sequence is shot in black and white. In the second sequence, shot in colour, the camera zooms back to reveal the first sequence as a film being viewed in a screening room. The viewers are artist Jamie Taylor and filmmaker Janet Webb. The scene that they are watching is from Janet's documentary on Jamie and his work. Their discussion of the sequence (minus Findley's stage directions) is terse:

> Janet: Well?
> Jamie: So much for nothing.
> Janet: You don't like it?
> Jamie: I hate it.
> Janet: So?
> Jamie: So burn her again. And this time I want to be there to see you do it right. (68)

The camera then cuts to sequence 3, in colour, in which the doll is burned again, on the same location, this time with Jamie's assistance.

The first sequence of "The Paper People" is deliberately deceptive in its use of smoke to make the doll appear human to the viewer. Findley's directions read: "the obscuring is sufficient to maintain the illusion that the figure is human" (67). The use of black-and-white film increases the illusion. Findley commented on viewing the film that "Whenever the burnings were in colour, you were certain it was a series of dolls being burned, but as soon as it went to black and white they were people" ("On 'The Paper People'" 61). It is also deceptive in concealing its frame (Janet's screening room) from the viewer. The first three sequences take the viewer rapidly back and forth between illusion and reality, art and life, setting up and simultaneously blurring the distinctions between narrative levels. Like the repeating achronic prologues of Findley's novels, the opening sequence of "The Paper People" is doubled. It appears first as a film and then, in sequence 2, as a film within a film.

"The Paper People" further blurs its point of origin by beginning "again" in sequence 3, with the reshoot of the scene. Jamie's desire to "burn her again" and "this time" to "do it right" is seemingly also the desire of Findley's film script, which incorporates Jamie's repetition of the burning. Jamie, in his editorial capacity here, is a metafictional double of the maker/editor of "The Paper People," whose desire to "Do It Again" (the title of sequence 2) is acted out in "Tonya Burned Again" (the title of sequence 3). During this second burning, Janet's cameraperson is reluctant to get too close to the flames, and Jamie grabs the camera in order to shoot the scene himself. At this point, "The Paper People" shifts again into black and white, showing Jamie's point of view through the viewfinder (71). His position is identical here to those of the maker of "The Paper People" and the viewer, who are both thus implicated in his desire to "do it right" by "moving in [toward the fire] to a point of danger" (71).

The opening of "The Paper People," like those of many Findley novels, is structured by split desire. The first opening, it appears, is unsatisfactory — it doesn't get close enough to the fire and must be redone. Like the prologues to *The Wars* and *Not Wanted on the Voyage*, the "prologue" of "The Paper People" must be repeated. The repetition in the three works of a scene of fire suggests a narrative ambivalence about such a scene. These narratives tend to describe a scene of fire, then back away from it, then return to it later, as if unable to touch it yet unable to leave it alone. "The Paper People" suggests that the reason for the return is to narrate the fire more directly, even though this desire is impossible to fulfil. Brooks describes narrative desire as "a desire that never can quite speak its name — never can quite come to the point — but that insists on speaking over and over again its movement toward that name" (61). The "point" that Findley's narratives seem to be moving toward is one of destruction.

The fire itself, what the film seems to desire, signals destruction — both of the self (in the first sequence, where it appears to destroy a human figure) and of artistic creation (in the third sequence, where the "human" is revealed to be a papier-mâché doll). The viewer's identification with Jamie's point of view, as Jamie risks his life to get a closer shot of the fire, suggests that this desire may destroy the viewer as well. Artist, art, and audience all court annihilation when they participate in the making of narrative. Ricou says of *The Wars* that "Findley touches on the possibility that violence obscures story, and storyteller, and even reader" (130). Perhaps, as well, Findley suggests that storytelling itself is a kind of violence: *"Nothing so completely verifies our perception of a thing as our killing of it"* (*Wars* 191). As an artist, Jamie creates and then destroys his sculptures, filming both his creative and destructive processes. This type of performance art can be read as a form of social protest against the reification of art as product, and as such it focuses attention on the dynamics of the artistic process (Mary Jane Miller 51). In Jamie's case, those dynamics suggest that creation equals destruction: his dolls are created for the purpose of being burned — they are born to die. In Janet's case, her desire to get at the real Jamie is thwarted by his secrecy (like a gothic hero, he has a mad wife hidden carefully away). But Janet is also thwarted by the very nature of her documentary desire: the closer she gets to finding out about Jamie's inner life, the closer she comes to destroying Jamie. He recognizes the lethal nature of her project: "You really dig deep — don't you?" he accuses. "I knew you were a born killer the moment I laid eyes on those cold, cold hips of yours" (142–43).

In the case of "The Paper People" as a narrative, creation also equals destruction. The desire to narrate the fires of destruction is thwarted as soon as the narrative begins. The first sequence apparently fails and must be redone. But it is preserved as a sort of prologue to the film. Its failure consists in failing to fulfil the desire to get closer to the fire. Yet even the third sequence, in which Jamie does get closer, is a failure. He must wear an asbestos hood to protect himself. He cannot enter fully into the fire. Neither can the narrative, despite its desire, for of course, like Jamie, the desire would then cease to exist. The hesitant opening of this film is the narrative's protective "asbestos hood," its way of distancing itself from the beginning, which marks the point where its desire begins to die.

Virtually all of Findley's narratives are motivated by the desire to investigate violence, to get closer to the fire, as though the narrative were compelled to return to the scene of some primal crime. This series of beginnings and beginnings again describes the movement of the desire to narrate the unnarratable — and this time to do it right. Nevertheless, the beginning of every narrative is the violent rupture of this desire. At the beginning — the point where story breaks into discourse — this desire bursts into flame.

* * *

29

Narrative anxiety about beginning leaves visible marks on these works from the sixties, manifesting itself in a variety of ways. Findley's naïve characters continually approach yet never arrive at the unspeakable secrets at the hearts of their stories. His narratives hesitate at their openings, as if uncertain how or where to begin to tell their stories. And when narrative comes close to touching the core of the story, the story frequently erupts in violence. The movement of conflicting desires in the narrative may be visible only in its effects, in its traces, but it is perhaps this very conflict that serves to keep narrative desire in play.

Neil Cable, the narrator of Findley's first story, doesn't know how to begin about Effie, because the beginning of his narration is the place where the unnarratable nature of his story will be destroyed. His anxious, hesitant opening reveals the conflict between his desire to preserve the ineffability of his story and his desire to tell that story. As I have argued here, this is a conflict that structures many of Findley's early works. And as I have argued elsewhere (see Hunter 23–71), a similar conflict structures the openings of his subsequent narratives.

Findley's writing seems always to desire the ineffable. His works speak always of the unspeakable, the mysterious and unnamable forces that move his characters, and his narratives, from place to place. And, for a writer who seeks to tell the untellable, the moment when story becomes narrative will always be a moment of danger, for writing is the negation of the ineffable. As soon as Findley's narratives begin to construct the unnarratable story, that story explodes. Yet Findley always begins again. The unnarratable story — that falsehood which is only dreamed — is nevertheless the powerful force that drives the narrative onward. "I don't know how to begin about Effie," says Neil, *"but I've got to."*[2]

NOTES

[1] For an analysis of the influence of these texts on Hooker, see Pennee 20–27. For an examination of the astounding number of these texts that are related to war, see York, *Front Lines* 16–21.

[2] The ideas for this essay were first developed under the supervision of Professor Stephen Scobie at the University of Victoria, during the tenure of a SSHRCC doctoral fellowship, for which I am grateful.

Brooks, Peter. *Reading for the Plot: Design and Intention in Narrative.* New York: Knopf, 1984.

Derrida, Jacques. *Of Grammatology.* Trans. Gayatri Chakravorty Spivak. Baltimore: Johns Hopkins UP, 1976.

Findley, Timothy. *Can You See Me Yet?* Vancouver: Talonbooks, 1977.

——. *Dinner along the Amazon.* 1984. Markham, ON: Penguin, 1985.

——. *The Last of the Crazy People.* 1967. Markham, ON: Penguin, 1986.

——. "On 'The Paper People.' " *Canadian Drama/L'Art dramatique canadien* 9.1 (1983): 60–61.

——. "The Paper People." *Canadian Drama/L'Art dramatique canadien* 9.1 (1983): 62–164.

——. *Stones.* Markham, ON: Penguin, 1988.

——. *The Wars.* 1977. Markham, ON: Penguin, 1987.

Genette, Gérard. *Narrative Discourse: An Essay in Method.* Trans. Jane E. Lewin. Ithaca: Cornell UP, 1980.

Goldman, Marlene. "The End(s) of Myth: Apocalyptic and Prophetic Fictions in *Headhunter.*" *Paying Attention: Critical Essays on Timothy Findley.* Ed. Anne Geddes Bailey and Karen Grandy. Toronto: ECW, 1998. 32–55. Also published in the *Timothy Findley Issue.* Ed. Bailey and Grandy. Spec. issue of *Essays on Canadian Writing* 64 (1998): 32–55.

Hunter, Catherine. "Desire and Disruption: Narrative Structures in the Fiction of Timothy Findley." Diss. U of Victoria, 1991.

Miller, D.A. *Narrative and Its Discontents: Problems of Closure in the Traditional Novel.* 1981. Princeton: Princeton UP, 1989.

Miller, Mary Jane. "An Analysis of 'The Paper People.' " *Canadian Drama/L'Art dramatique canadien* 9.1 (1983): 49–59.

Pennee, Donna Palmateer. *Moral Metafiction: Counterdiscourse in the Novels of Timothy Findley.* Toronto: ECW, 1991.

Ricou, Laurie. "Obscured by Violence: Timothy Findley's *The Wars.*" *Violence in the Canadian Novel since 1960.* Ed. Virginia Harger-Grinling and Terry Goldie. St. John's: Memorial UP, 1981. 125–37.

Said, Edward. *Beginnings: Intention and Method.* New York: Basic, 1975.

Simon, Bennett. *More than Kin, Less than Kind: Psychoanalytic Studies of Tragic Drama and the Family.* New Haven: Yale UP, 1988.

York, Lorraine M. *Front Lines: The Fiction of Timothy Findley.* Toronto: ECW, 1991.

——. " 'A White Hand Hovering over the Page': Timothy Findley and the Racialized/Ethnicized Other." *Paying Attention: Critical Essays on Timothy Findley.* Ed. Anne Geddes Bailey and Karen Grandy. Toronto: ECW, 1998. 201–20. Also published in the *Timothy Findley Issue.* Ed. Bailey and Grandy. Spec. issue of *Essays on Canadian Writing* 64 (1998): 201–20.

The End(s) of Myth:
Apocalyptic and Prophetic
Fictions in *Headhunter*

MARLENE GOLDMAN

The dreams of apocalypse, if they usurp waking thought, may
be the worst dreams.

— Frank Kermode (108)

IN TIMOTHY FINDLEY'S FIRST NOVEL, *The Last of the Crazy People*
(1967), an eleven-year-old boy becomes convinced that the end of
the world is fast approaching. His belief in the world's imminent
destruction is instilled by the prophetic visions of a drunken servant.
In her booming voice, she tells him, "No one knows, 'cept they knows
it's coming. Arm'geddon. . . . Like for a moment it's gonna be real,
real, terrible, hon. . . . But for those of us in this perdition *now*, it
will surely be bless'd relief . . ." (98–99; first ellipsis in original).
The power of the apocalyptic narrative works on the child's imagination. At the end of the novel, the boy, Hooker Winslow, realizes
the prophecy by gunning down his entire family, transforming the
narrative of the end of the world from a fantastic biblical fiction into
a tragic lived experience.

What are readers to make of this tragedy? Is it simply the result of
an insane conflation of the biblical fiction and the text's reality? Or
does the text imply something far more disturbing, namely, that
apocalyptic dreams have a way of resisting strategies of containment,
of blurring the boundaries between art and life?

Similar eschatological concerns appear in subsequent works, including *The Wars* (1977), *Famous Last Words* (1981), and *Not
Wanted on the Voyage* (1985). However, in *Headhunter* (1994), the
focus of this study, the narrative invokes virtually every facet of
the apocalyptic paradigm. I would argue that, rather than remain
complicit with the paradigm, *Headhunter* calls into question the quest
for transcendent revelation. Whereas the protagonist of *The Last of
the Crazy People* acts out the apocalyptic plot to its grisly conclusion,

in *Headhunter* a significant number of characters, although caught up in the apocalyptic plot, challenge and ultimately subvert the full-blown apocalyptic perspective, which calls for the destruction of the world in favour of the world to come. Although *Headhunter* seems at times to convey an uncompromising apocalyptic vision, it simultaneously counters this radical vision with a more earthly and historically oriented perspective. As a result, the novel never fully embraces the apocalyptic perspective; ultimately, it champions a perspective with strong ties to preexilic prophetic eschatology — a prophetic perspective that stresses humanity's responsibilities in the here and now.

Although the relationship between prophetic and apocalyptic eschatology remains the subject of much critical debate, for our purposes it is sufficient to recognize a basic difference between the two. As a number of biblical scholars suggest, prophetic eschatology involves a revelation to the *entire nation* of the divine plan, which the prophet translates into "the terms of plain history, real politics, and human instrumentality," a plan that will "be effected within the context of [the] . . . nation's history and the history of the world" (Hanson 11). Although prophetic and apocalyptic eschatology share an essential vision of restoration, apocalyptic eschatology is "the mode assumed by the prophetic tradition once it had been transferred to a new and radically altered setting in the post-exilic community" (10). Apocalyptic eschatology is characterized by a religious perspective that focuses on the disclosure of an esoteric vision of the divine plan to an *elect group*. In apocalyptic narratives, the prophet no longer translates the vision into "the terms of plain history, real politics, and human instrumentality due to a pessimistic view of reality growing out of the bleak post-exilic conditions" (11–12). Simply put, prophetic eschatology addresses the nation and concerns the fate of the nation in historical time. By contrast, apocalyptic eschatology offers a mystical vision to the elect and anticipates the end of human history.

As we approach the millennium, the term "apocalypse" has increasingly come into vogue. As M.H. Abrams observes, it is "often applied loosely to signify any sudden and visionary revelation, or any event of violent and large-scale destruction — or even anything which is very drastic" (*Natural* 41). In suggesting that Findley's narrative invokes an apocalyptic paradigm, I am not referring to this type of broad definition. Instead, both structurally and thematically, *Headhunter* systematically draws on traditional elements of apocalyptic discourse, including its recursive structure, panoramic vision, glaring images of destruction, and depiction of the elect locked in their struggle with the demonic host. By tracing allusions to this discourse, I hope to show how the text paradoxically signals the imaginative tenacity and the untrustworthiness and limitations of a full-blown apocalyptic vision — a vision that represents transformation as absolute destruction.

Structurally, apocalyptic literature rewrites the past in order to forecast the future. In its attempt to show how past, present, and future are bound together in a single unity, this literature relies on a densely intertextual format. As critics have repeatedly observed, the last book in the Bible, the one explicitly called Revelation, is intricately recursive; that is, it "represents the present and future by replicating or alluding to passages in earlier biblical texts, especially in Genesis, Exodus, the Old Testament prophets, and the apocalyptic visions in Daniel" (Abrams, "Apocalypse" 9). As critics have noted, many passages are "simply translated from the Hebrew Bible, and in addition, there are more than 300 references to Daniel, Isaiah, Second Isaiah, Jeremiah, Ezekial and Zechariah" (Cohn, *Cosmos* 212).[1] The allusive nature of the text led one critic to describe Revelation as "a jigsaw puzzle in which nearly all the pieces are torn away from their contexts" (Bloom 1).

In keeping with this distinctive feature, Findley's novel signals its recursive structure immediately: *Headhunter* opens in the Metro Toronto Reference Library. Seated on a bench, the schizophrenic ex-librarian Lilah Kemp reads Conrad's *Heart of Darkness* and accidentally conjures up the horror-meister Kurtz from page 92, setting him loose in the streets of Toronto. Retooled for the times, Kurtz has become a modern-day headhunter, a "shrink" who wields seemingly limitless power as head of his empire, a psychiatric institute.

Right from the start, the novel posits a mysterious link between Kurtz and a group of catatonic children at the Queen Street Mental Health Centre. The trauma suffered by these children constitutes the enigma at the heart of the text. Following Kurtz's escape, a host of characters (including Charlie Marlow), based on familiar figures from canonical texts, make their appearance in Findley's work. As one might expect, the task of uncovering the root of the children's trauma falls to Marlow.

In light of the abundant allusions to Conrad's novel, the initial scene, which establishes *Heart of Darkness*, with its critique of imperialism, as a primary intertext, can be taken as emblematic. Like its biblical predecessor, Revelation, Findley's apocalyptic novel constitutes a reference library. In addition to its debt to Conrad's novel, *Headhunter* relies heavily on two other classic works, Fitzgerald's *The Great Gatsby* and Flaubert's *Madame Bovary*, one of the founding texts of modernism.[2] Not all of *Headhunter*'s literary allusions are as overt and intricately developed as these. Often the novel makes only a fleeting reference to a canonical work; the title of a book or the name of a character usually suffices to signal the connection to a well-known intertext. Early on, for instance, readers learn that Lilah marches around the city pushing a baby carriage. Under the blankets is a copy of *Wuthering Heights*. Later on, readers are introduced to Dr. Shelley, a psychiatrist who conducts sadistic experiments involving animals. The name forges a connection with Mary Shelley and her gothic novel *Frankenstein*. This link is reinforced by a comment made by an important character in Findley's novel, Lilah's beloved teacher, Nicholas Fagan, the learned professor of literature from Trinity College, Dublin.[3] Lilah recalls that, in one of his lectures, Fagan proclaimed: "If I were to propose a text for the twentieth century, it would be Joseph Conrad's *Heart of Darkness*. As subtext, I would nominate Mary Shelley's *Frankenstein*" (139). By confronting readers with the barrage of intertextual material — specifically works, such as *Heart of Darkness* and *Frankenstein*, that repeatedly focus our attention on the intersections between dreams of transcendence and technological control — the text both reveals its debt to the allusive structure of apocalyptic discourse and highlights the implications of its persistent hold on the reader's imagination.[4]

In contrast to prophetic writings in the Bible, which deal with a narrower set of temporal events, the ancient apocalyptists offer a vision of history from beginning to end, conveying the impression of temporal unity.[5] As Northrop Frye explains, the creation of this type of panoramic vision is a fundamental characteristic of apocalyptic discourse, and the apocalyptic prophet carefully locates his or her vision "in a near future and just before the end of time" ("Typology" 70). In addition, whereas prophecy confirms that "this world is God's world and that in the world His goodness and truth will yet be justified," apocalyptists promote a more pessimistic view of the world: "their optimism, their hope, is not directed to what history will bring forth, but to that which will arise in its ruin . . ." (Scholem 10). The catastrophic character of apocalyptic redemption manifests itself in signs of terror and decadence — "in world wars and revolutions, in epidemics, famine, and economic catastrophe; but to an equal degree in apostasy and the desecration of God's name, in forgetting of the Torah and the upsetting of all moral order to the point of dissolving the laws of nature" (12).

Turning to *Headhunter*, we can discern the same transcendent temporal perspective and the familiar catalogue of catastrophic signs. In Findley's futuristic universe, the world has "begun to fracture and to fragment, nation by nation," rival gangs of Moonmen and Leatherheads stalk the streets, and AIDS has been joined by another plague, called sturnusemia (34). But the narrator asserts that "Sturnusemia and AIDS were not the only plagues. Civilization — sickened — had itself become a plague. And its course . . . could be followed by tracing the patterns of mental breakdown. . . . Psychiatric case loads, everywhere, carried alarming numbers. Broken dreamers, their minds in ruin. This was the human race" (388). Fagan, the literary critic, confirms this diagnosis and condemns his culture's fascination with disaster:

> *Nothing better illustrates than these two books [Heart of Darkness and Frankenstein] the consequence of human ambition. On reading them again, I fell away from my complacent view that nothing could be done to stop us, and took up my current view that the human race has found its destiny in self-destruction.* (139)

Despite the gruesome novelty of some of *Headhunter*'s apocalyptic signs, familiar landmarks confirm that the world hurtling toward catastrophe represents a spatial and temporal extension of our own.

For the most part, the characters remain confined to their historical moment. But, like the seer of Revelation, the third-person, extra-diegetic narrator offers the reader proleptic insights, which suggests that he has transcended the world of time and history as we know them. Commenting on people's response to the plague, the narrator states, "Most were sceptical — others were incredulous. . . . The truth was, most eyes would open too late on a world without birds and a city under siege. *But that was not now — that was later, much later, after Kurtz and after Lilah Kemp*" (10; emphasis added). Later, remarking on Marlow's first, misguided impression of Kurtz, the narrator says, "Within weeks, Marlow . . . would laugh at his own innocence. *But that was not now. That was later*" (199; emphasis added). Throughout the text, the catalogue of signs and the dark pronouncements concerning a future known only by our visionary narrator reinforce the novel's reliance on the apocalyptic paradigm. Far from unreservedly embracing apocalyptic eschatology, the novel — by selecting aspects of this discourse and rejecting others in favour of prophetic eschatology — launches its critique. Although the narrator assumes a transcendent position, he does not promote an apocalyptic vision that points beyond the end to a new paradise. Instead, he gestures relentlessly to the nontranscendent destruction of the world. As a result, the absence of the topos of the New Jerusalem, the keystone of the biblical apocalypse, comes to haunt the narrative.[6] In this way, rather than simply mobilize desires for paradise, the figure of the end serves as an imaginative vantage point from which to interrogate Western culture's lethal fascination with apocalypse.

Headhunter often strikes a precarious balance between what Paul Hanson describes as visionary and realistic elements, common to both prophetic and apocalyptic eschatology (30). According to Hanson, the visionary element, more pronounced in apocalyptic eschatology, entails a "vision of a divine order that transcends all mundane institutions and structures." By contrast, the element of realism, a stronger component in prophetic eschatology, involves a concern "with the day-to-day maintenance of those same mundane institutions and structures, and with preserving continuity so as to assure a context for the continued life of the community." As Hanson warns, when separated from realism, the vision leads "to a retreat into the world of ecstasy and dreams and to an abdication of the social responsibility of translating the vision of the divine order into the realm of everyday earthly concerns." Alternatively, when separated from the vision, the realism "becomes a sterile preserver of the status quo which absolutized and eternalized the existing order together with all of its inequities."

This type of oscillation recalls Catherine Hunter's arguments concerning Findley's ambivalence about the act of narration itself. As Hunter says, his texts "display an ambivalence toward self and story — both a nostalgic desire for stable absolutes and a desire for the fragmentation, or even destruction, of them" (17). In keeping with Hunter's observations, I would suggest that Findley's ambivalence has an equally strong impact on his approach to endings. An awareness of his painstaking negotiations between visionary and realistic elements also helps to explain why *Headhunter* rejects the apocalyptic indifference to social responsibility yet consistently draws on apocalyptic discourse.

The text's reliance on a visionary narrator is only one of the many elements borrowed from apocalyptic discourse. In addition to offering a panoramic temporal structure and glaring images of destruction, as noted earlier, apocalypses are characterized by the private, transcendent content of their visions. Whereas Jewish messianism addresses the entire nation and sets forth images of natural and historical events through which God speaks, apocalyptic prophecy is revealed solely to the individual, and its declarations involve "special 'secret' knowledge gained from an inner realm not accessible to every man" (Scholem 5). One critic goes so far as to describe the knowledge contained in Revelation as "deviant" because it is gained by "esoteric means apart from larger communal, institutional validation" (Thompson 181). Although this "deviant knowledge" is based on personal revelation, the possibility of considering this revelation to be "a partisan, idiosyncratic view of the world is minimized by the narrative style" (178).

In *Headhunter*'s realistic displacement[7] of apocalypse, the biblical prophets' sacred visions have become the property of secular spiritualists and schizophrenics such as Lilah Kemp and Amy Wylie.[8] Just as Revelation's narrative style prevents the listener from dismissing the information on the ground that it is idiosyncratic, Findley's narrative likewise controls and transforms the reader's response to the character's visions. For example, most readers initially reject Lilah's fantastic claim that she has released Kurtz from *Heart of Darkness*. But their reaction to Lilah is tempered and manipulated by the text in at least two ways. First, the narrator's dispassionate treatment of Lilah's condition undercuts a measure of the readers' scepticism. Second, and more important, after this opening scene, readers learn that the man who stood before Lilah in the Metro Toronto Reference Library is indeed Kurtz. The narrative's matter-of-fact validation of her vision (and others that follow) dissuades readers from interpreting her illness as a disease that generates nonsensical visions. Instead, the text portrays her madness, which connects her to a myriad of famous persons from the past and literary characters, as a visionary gift *"for cutting through time"* (365). Although her visions constitute "deviant knowledge," in accordance with the apocalyptic paradigm, they are nevertheless accorded legitimacy, and Lilah herself is subtly identified as a member of the elect.

The concept of the elect has its roots in the Old Testament belief that the Jews are the chosen people, and it is common to prophetic and apocalyptic eschatology. As Norman Cohn observes, in the parent of apocalyptic, the Book of Daniel, one can recognize "the paradigm of what was to become and to remain the central phantasy of revolutionary eschatology" (*Pursuit* 4). Daniel's prophecy refers specifically to the elect, termed "the Saints of God":

> The world is dominated by an evil, tyrannous power of boundless destructiveness — a power moreover which is imagined not simply as human but as demonic. The tyranny of that power will become more and more outrageous, the sufferings of its victims more and more intolerable — until suddenly the hour will strike when the Saints of God are able to rise up and overthrow it. (*Pursuit* 4)

In *Headhunter*, as we have seen, the sacred scriptures are refigured as the secular canon of Western literature. Those who have faith in its wisdom are the elect, whereas the apostates desecrate and forget their "Torah." Again, although *Headhunter* invokes the idea of the elect, a distinction must be drawn between preexilic, prophetic notions of the elect — which include the entire community — and postexilic, apocalyptic views of the elect — which constitute a small and privileged subset of the community. In prophetic eschatology, as Hanson explains, the suffering of the endtimes was understood to "have an effect on the entire nation, including those who were the oppressors, for through repentance and purification the nation would once again be made whole" (396). In apocalyptic narratives, no hope exists for a national repentance that could lead to purification; there would only be "a bloody purge whereby the wicked would be exterminated, leaving those who were destined to be recipients of the salvation to come" (396).

With her "evangelical passion for literature" (*Headhunter* 11), Lilah represents the contemporary incarnation of the Saints of God. Like a priestess welcoming initiates into the temple, in her role as librarian, she eagerly turns toward the "bright unwritten faces of the young," enjoining them to "Read! Read! Read!" (364). Rather than preach to an isolated, elite group, Lilah, in keeping with the preexilic prophetic tradition, addresses the entire community and implicitly suggests that a sacred encounter with literature potentially awaits anyone. Despite her passion, Lilah considers herself a mere student, a humble disciple, whereas Fagan, whose "voice was the voice of English literature itself," is a god (40, 266).

Fagan, who is clearly a member — if not the leader — of the elect, consistently describes the function of literature using language that recalls the rituals of religious worship. In the New Testament, toward the conclusion of his sermon on spiritual gifts, Paul describes the way in which prophets should ideally conduct a service of worship, which includes, among other things, the singing of hymns and the procla mation of apocalypses. Prophets can use one of several forms of worship: a prayer, a hymn, a revelation, or even a teaching (1 Cor. 14.26, rev. standard ed.). According to Paul, every prophet should be permitted to give his revelation, so that all may learn and all be comforted. As far as Fagan is concerned, literature itself constitutes a hymn or song that offers comfort and instruction. At one point, Lilah recalls him telling her that *"A book is a way of singing. . . . A way of singing our way out of darkness. The darkness that is night — and the darkness that is ignorance — and the darkness that is . . . [fear]"* (138; second ellipsis in original).[9] The link that Fagan implicitly draws between literature and religious worship is reinforced when Lilah visits the university bookstore on College Street, which once served as the home of the Metro Toronto Reference Library. She walks "[r]ound and round the islands of shelves . . . with a measured pace, reciting the titles under breath, as one might utter prayers in a cloister" (270). Drifting through her mind is a phrase uttered by her teacher — a playful allusion to a famous Shakespeare quotation. But Fagan's alteration infuses the phrase with spiritual overtones: *"All the words are prayers . . . and all the men and women merely pray-ers . . ."* (271; ellipses in original).

Lilah and Fagan are not alone in their reverence for literature; others, including Marlow and Amy, join the ranks of the elect. Marlow, who has met Fagan at Harvard, finds him to be an enthusiastic supporter of his use of literature as a tool in psychiatric research (365). On the whole, however, a devotion to literature is not sufficient to qualify one for membership. In Findley's novel, the criteria for inclusion are also abstract and humanitarian: the elect differ from the apostates on the basis of the former's willingness to rage against a corrupt empire that dismisses culture as well as pressing environmental and social concerns in favour of a ruthless pursuit of economic gain. The desire to safeguard art from the degrading commodification of culture in the West and the concomitant disgust for empires that privilege profit above all else forge the strongest link between *Headhunter, Heart of Darkness*, and Revelation.

In his study *The Book of Revelation: Apocalypse and Empire*, Leonard Thompson counters the prevailing view of the apocalyptists as a desperately oppressed minority. He argues that John writes, not as a beleaguered outcast, but as "a true cosmopolitan," who is nevertheless unequivocal in his negative attitude toward Asian society and the empire (5). According to Revelation, the political order of Rome is "wholly corrupt, belonging to the Satanic realm," and the economic order "belongs to the same corrupt realm" (Thompson 175). Buying and selling require the "stamp" of the beast (Rev. 13.16–17, rev. standard ed.). Thompson goes on to explain that, "In contrast to the writings of Paul or to 1 Peter, the seer of Revelation rejects any recognition of the empire as a godly order. In both style and content the writer of the Book of Revelation sets his work against the public order" (192).

The same rage against a corrupt empire informs *Headhunter*'s primary intertext, *Heart of Darkness*, which charts the exploitation of the Congo by Belgium's King Leopold II. Conrad, in his essay on the subject, describes the Belgian Empire's activities in the Congo as the "vilest scramble for loot that ever disfigured the history of human conscience and geographical exploration" (187). According to one critic, Conrad's work "is not merely a reflection of the modern temper; it is an active revolt against it" (Erdinast-Vulcan 19). In keeping with the rejection of empire in Revelation and *Heart of Darkness* — a rejection that is not restricted to social outcasts — the members of Findley's elect include characters from all walks of life. What they have in common is not so much their status as outcasts (Marlow can hardly be described as marginalized) as their rage and the belief that they have been chosen to battle against a decadent and brutal social order.

Using the familiar language of election and images of a Manichean struggle, Lilah claims responsibility for overthrowing the demonic power. Two days after she releases Kurtz, she clutches the shoes of Peter the Rabbit, her talisman, and offers up the following prayer:

> *Dear shoes. . . . I require some news of Kurtz. I have released him out of* Heart of Darkness. *He has disappeared and I am afraid. Kurtz, if he puts his mind to it, can destroy the world — and only I can prevent him. I have been chosen to be his Marlow — and must begin my journey — but I don't know where to start. . . . (39; second ellipsis in original)*

Unlike Lilah, who embraces her mission, the "real" Marlow only reluctantly assumes the job of uncovering Kurtz's nefarious use of experimental drugs on children — drugs that render them the pliant victims of their fathers' perverted appetites. In keeping with Lilah's outlook, Marlow views his task as a battle (499). And he continues to invoke martial imagery when he describes Fagan's attitude toward society. According to Marlow, Fagan rejects pessimism in favour of "the stabilizing influence of his anger. He fought back. He drew a bead with his aging eyes and fired at human pride and wilful ignorance — not with a fusillade, but with a single bullet" (381).

In the case of Amy Wylie, the battle between good and evil becomes an all-out war against reality. A schizophrenic poet, Amy crusades on behalf of the animals slaughtered in a misguided attempt to prevent the spread of the plague. According to her sister, Amy is "never at rest — never making peace with reality. War was more like it" (346). Along the same lines, Marlow's colleague, psychiatrist Austen Purvis, also distinguishes himself as a soldier in the war against reality. In a skirmish with Dr. Shelley, "overly fond of somnificating her patients," Purvis yells, *"We are not here to drag [the insane] . . . willy-nilly back into our world! We are here to drag our perceptions forward into theirs!"* (189). Unable to win his fight, Purvis shoots himself, but before he dies he enjoins Marlow to continue the war against the tyrannous power and save the children (402). The motley crew of Findley's elect would not be complete without Orley, the black maid in the Berry household, whose innocent husband was shot by police. Ever since the incident occurred twelve years ago, Orley has nurtured rage at social injustice. Her rage is "still a source of satisfaction. She had vowed that she would foster it until the day she died — and up until now — including now — she had succeeded" (240).

Taken together, Findley's elect wage war against the oppression and exploitation of groups marginalized by society. But, in contrast to fully developed apocalyptic eschatology, they do not anticipate that their struggle will end in earthly destruction and secure the salvation of a privileged elect. Instead, in keeping with prophetic eschatology, they fight so that suffering on Earth will be eradicated; the restored community will exist not in heaven but in the historical realm. As I mentioned earlier, however, the narrative maintains a delicate balance between prophetic and apocalyptic eschatology. Although the text stresses the need to ensure continuity, particularly the continuity of the literary archive, the prophetic tradition shifts toward the apocalyptic in the novel's depiction of the chaotic and immoral force bent on destroying the community.

In apocalyptic literature, the righteous anger of the elect is inevitably directed against an enemy personified by the Antichrist. In the

Book of Daniel, he appears in the prophet's dreams as a king who "shall exalt himself, and magnify himself above every god" (11.36, rev. standard ed.). He "shall wear out the saints of the Most High, and shall think to change the times and the law; and they shall be given into his hand for a time" (7.25). According to Daniel, the false god's dominion "shall be taken away, to be consumed and destroyed to the end" (7.26). In Revelation, the figure of the Antichrist reappears as a pseudomessiah who is once again "allowed to make war on the saints and to conquer them" (13.7). Like Satan, the Antichrist is typically portrayed as a gigantic embodiment of "anarchic, destructive power" (Cohn, *Pursuit* 20).

When Lilah discovers that the man whom she conjured up directs the Parkin Institute, she knows that she has unleashed the Antichrist. After reading the marble panel outside his door, she concludes, "Rupert Kurtz was God" (53). Like the biblical force of evil, Kurtz exalts himself. In his infamous research paper, he boasts: *"We psychiatrists . . . must necessarily appear to the mentally ill as being in the nature of gods. We approach them with miracles up our sleeves. 'Save us!' they cry — and we do . . ."* (603; second ellipsis in original). To clarify the difference between good and evil, between true and false gods, the text juxtaposes Fagan and Kurtz.[10] Each man has his followers; Lilah's devotion to Fagan is mirrored by Julian Slade's affirmation of Kurtz's divine status. By Kurtz's own admission, the bedevilled Slade — a schizophrenic, moribund artist — was "something of a disciple as well as a patient" (265); "He believed — naïvely — in what Kurtz was doing at the Parkin," and Kurtz found it "exhilarating" to have "a believer at his feet" (265–66). Fagan likewise attracts believers and espouses a quasireligious view of literature (138). In contrast to Fagan's communal orientation and his insistence on the need to escape fear, Kurtz adores Slade's art — whose subject matter is always terror — precisely because it "verified his fears" and "informed him that fear was wonderful" (102). Not surprisingly, Kurtz's favourite painting, a canvas filled with mutilated male bodies, is dubbed "a depiction of hell" (455). Rather than join Fagan's choir, Kurtz remains isolated, mesmerized by his disciple's masterfully executed "hymn to violence" (203).

Like his fictional predecessor, Findley's Kurtz knows no bounds in his quest for his transcendent empire. In pursuit of this goal, he sanctions the activities of the pedophiliac Club of Men and willingly sacrifices children to their fathers' carnal desires. What Kurtz and the Club of Men do not understand or simply choose to dismiss —

and this is made clear in the text — is that children are the future.[11] By agreeing to their deaths, Kurtz assumes the apocalyptic stance of the postexilic visionaries, who dismissed the claims of all earthly institutions and structures and abdicated completely from any social responsibility.

In the end, Marlow learns that Kurtz's corrupt nature was shaped by his own tortured relations with his sadistic father. All his life, Kurtz wanted to please an utterly selfish man whose "criterion . . . was money — not achievement," but his father "simply laughed at . . . [his] efforts. Laughed at them, and died still laughing" (620). In its relentless depiction of the abuse and, in some cases, the murder of children by their parents, *Headhunter* once again draws on the traditional apocalyptic paradigm, in which the world is seen in terms of a mortal struggle "waged by good parents and good children against bad parents and bad children" (Cohn, *Pursuit* 69). In the popular eschatology of the Middle Ages, the elect saw themselves as good children. Their leaders perceived themselves as incarnate gods who combined the fantastic images of the divine father and his son, the risen Christ. In reward for following the Messiah, the elect shared in their saviour's supernatural power (71). As Cohn explains, in opposition to the "armies of the Saints, and scarcely less powerful than they, there appears a host of demonic fathers and sons" (71). The concern for good children left at the mercy of bad parents remains a long-standing motif in Findley's corpus.[12] In *Headhunter*, it assumes mythic and apocalyptic proportions.

The battle between good and evil is integral to prophetic and apocalyptic eschatology. As Abrams suggests, apocalypse is "a chiaroscuro history, in which the agencies are the opponent forces of light and of darkness and there is no middle ground between the totally good and the absolutely evil" ("Apocalypse" 11). In apocalypse, the "consummation of history will occur, not by mediation between polar opposites, but only after their extirpation of the forces of evil by the forces of good" (11; see also Scholem 6). However, as I have been arguing, Findley mobilizes apocalypse in order to defuse it, and ultimately he promotes a community-oriented vision characteristic of prophetic eschatology.

One effective way to challenge the apocalyptic paradigm is to reveal the permeable boundary between the elect and the demonic host. This blurring of boundaries is perhaps most evident in an episode featuring Charlie Marlow. In this scene, he feels alienated while attending a dinner party in honour of Nicholas Fagan. Part of his discomfort stems from the ostentatious show of wealth and power at the party. But he is also uncomfortable because his host and hostess have likely not read any of the expensively bound paperbacks in their library. Initially, Marlow ponders whether it matters that they are not readers, and he tries to dismiss the importance of reading by reminding himself that books are just "cultural artifacts and, if found in some vault a thousand years hence, could probably not be deciphered" (380). At one point, he asks himself "what it was that drove him to think so badly of people who had found a way . . . to live without the support of books. To live, in their way, entirely without the support of culture" (380). Gradually, however, he gives way to despair and admits to feeling "deeply uncomfortable" — a feeling that is linked to "the fact that he was a snob, an elitist and — against his wishes — a believer in that most dangerous of concepts, the concept of men and women who were superior" (380).

On one level, Marlow's preoccupation with the waning of high culture and his belief in superior men and women can be linked to the biblical faith in the elect. But his views also relate to the late-nineteenth-century European belief in the powers of superior individuals. Carlyle's "hero" and Nietzsche's "superman," in conjunction with the writings of Vilfredo Pareto, Gaetano Mosca, and the movement known as the Action Française, directly influenced modernist writers such as Yeats, Lewis, Pound, Eliot, and Lawrence. Like Marlow, these writers believed that the masses required the guidance of a higher, responsible, conscious class (Harrison 27).

Findley is well aware of the implications of these views. Earlier novels, including *The Butterfly Plague, Famous Last Words*, and *Not Wanted on the Voyage*, underscore the connection between apocalyptic discourse and the visions of heavenly perfection that inspired totalitarian movements in the first half of this century.[13] From his research on modernism, Findley is likewise familiar with the apocalyptic sentiments of poets such as Pound and Yeats. As Kermode points out, Yeats, in anticipation of the end of his age, "filled his poems with images of decadence, and praised war because he saw in it . . . the means of renewal" (98). Perhaps Kermode puts it best when he says, "What we feel about these men at times is perhaps that they retreated into some paradigm, into a timeless and unreal vacuum from which all reality had been pumped" (113).

The links between this strain of modernist elitism and Marlow's belief in the concept of superior men and women remind us of the difficulty of drawing a neat division between good and evil. Even

45

benevolent men such as Marlow err on occasion and maintain views that other people, with a more practical and sinister bent, have used to justify holocausts of one kind or another.[14] Viewed in this light, *Headhunter* demonstrates that, like it or not, we are all caught up in the apocalyptic plot. This realization dawns on Marlow at the end of the novel, when he tries on a gang member's abandoned glove. After placing the glove on his left hand — the sinister hand — Marlow thinks, *"We all could be Moonmen. . . . My hand in this glove — a perfect fit. Kurtz, too, in all of us. All of us in Kurtz"* (622). In his study of apocalypse, Thompson likewise argues that, for all its apparent Manichean divisions, Revelation conveys the indeterminacy between good and evil.[15]

Marlow's identification with the Moonmen and with Kurtz signals his awareness that apocalyptic pessimism concerning existing structures and institutions, together with desires for radical change, is not restricted to crazed, evil individuals. At issue in the novel is not the longing for and vision of perfection so much as the implications of severing this vision from the realm of everyday morality. Whereas *The Last of the Crazy People* demonstrates the translation of apocalyptic discourse into reality, *Headhunter* contests the view that the existing order is so tainted that it cannot be redeemed and that the new order must be preceded by the extermination of all that went before.

In the end, what separates Fagan's group from Kurtz's entourage is merely the latter's more fervent and active embrace of the apocalyptic paradigm and its promise of radical transformation. For instance, at the opening of Slade's exhibition, Kurtz encounters Griffin Price. The wealthy owner of a host of factories churning out souvenirs, Price makes a mockery of art and culture; in the novel, such behaviour is a sure sign of the mark of the beast. Price, who fancies "himself as something of a social critic," seizes the opportunity to expound his theory that "The human race needs another Mengele to bring it up to date" (87). He goes on to explain that, when he was visiting his factory in Prague, he stood in the glassworks and had the following vision:

> There were all these men with mechanical buffers polishing, polishing bits of crystal. Turning them, turning them, making them perfect. And I thought: *if only we could do that to ourselves; shape ourselves that way.* . . . [M]y vision was that we are ready for another version of the human race. The final

honing. . . . And this is where you come in — the king of psychiatry. I mean — if there are new forms of human beings, then it follows there must be new forms of madness. (87–88)

Although Kurtz does not "want to commit himself" to what Price is saying (87), from his subsequent behaviour it becomes clear that he shares Price's vision.

Kurtz has his own radical plans for the human race. Later, in his office, which looks over the campus of the University of Toronto, he attests to his faith in the imminent end of the world, and he mocks so-called intellectuals for their inability to come to grips with radical, apocalyptic change: "Naming. Defining. Quantifying. Quantumizing. Everyone preparing for the past to repeat itself — as if the past was a continuum and that now did not exist. . . . *And when the past has been defined, . . . not one of them will have the courage to say: it is over*" (209). Kurtz expresses similar views at the close of the novel. On his deathbed, he refers to the present as being a *"long-dead civilization"* (615). Gesturing to the world below, he encourages Marlow to hasten its destruction:

> *It is all changed now. . . . There will be a new social contract. . . . All those fires beyond the windows. . . . There is nothing down there for us, Marlow. Not any longer. Go out and light more fires. If everyone did that, we would have the stuff of a new world ready for the making. . . .* (615–16; final ellipsis in original)

Kurtz's faith in the radically new — as opposed to restoration or renovation — aligns him with apocalyptic thinkers such as Price. But these men omit a fundamental aspect of the eschatological vision, namely, the recognition that the final condition of humankind and the world rests on the idea that "history is a *moral* process, with a goal toward which it is moving" (Salmond 734; emphasis added). By stripping their visions of any vestige of morality, the narrative sharpens the focus on the dangers of an unqualified attraction to the formal, aesthetic elegance of beginning, middle, and end that served as a beacon for fascism. In this way, readers are reminded of the disasters that potentially ensue when apocalyptic dreams are projected onto the world.

As Paul Ricoeur explains, the projection of this narrative onto the world — the translation of a theological narrative structure to a historical-political model for praxis — is facilitated by the fact that in the Bible the end of the world and the end of the book are concurrent:

> the idea of the end of the world comes to us by means of the text that, in the biblical canon received in the Christian West, at least, concludes the Bible. Apocalypse can thus signify both the end of the world and the end of the book at the same time. This congruence between the world and the book extends even further. The beginning of the book is about the beginning and the end of the book is about the end. (23)

In his study of narrative, Ricoeur discerns a gradual transformation of the apocalyptic paradigm; as he explains, crisis now replaces the end (24). In the contemporary novel, he argues, one can best observe "the decline of paradigms . . . the ruin of the fiction of the end" (24).

By contrast, Kermode, who likewise sees a shift from end to crisis, maintains that humanity cannot do without apocalypse. He argues that its elegant linear form fulfils an incontrovertible human need to see the world as ordered and meaningful. Novels, he suggests, must have beginnings and ends "even if the world has not" (138). By telling lies, novels convert the otherwise meaningless chaos of existence into meaningful patterns (135). These lies only get out of hand, according to Kermode, when people lapse into literary primitivism and treat fictions, which are consciously false, as if they were empirically true; thus, "the world is changed to conform with a fiction, as by the murder of the Jews. The effect is to insult reality, and to regress to myth" (109). Although he maps the intersections between the apocalyptic visions of the modernists and fascist ideology, Kermode intimates that this was merely an unfortunate lapse and that what is needed is simply a more vigilant policing of the border between reality and fiction.

It is at this point that Kermode's theory and Findley's novel part company. Although *Headhunter* affirms Kermode's view of literature as a vital lie, it erodes the very foundation of his argument: his assumption of a clear-cut boundary between reality and fiction. For Lilah, literature and life are indistinguishable. As noted above, she wheels *Wuthering Heights* around in her buggy and treats it as her child. She is schizophrenic, but readers learn, to borrow Kurtz's words, that there is nothing "in the wide world of madness that was not the property of sanity as well" (102). Her behaviour, then, merely exaggerates our acceptance of the everyday interpenetration of art and life.

In an effort to distinguish the *as if* of fiction from the *is* of reality, critics such as Kermode look to literature for concordance and a disingenuous assurance of simplicity — the lie of apocalypse. But Findley's text emphasizes that this vision of the boundary between art and life — in which fiction can be identified and contained, thereby neatly ridding the world of fiction — is itself a fiction.[16] To borrow Fagan's metaphor, books may be a way of singing, but they do not always offer simple harmonies. This view is confirmed by Marlow, who uses literature as psychotherapy. He believes in literature's "healing powers — not because of its sentiments, but because of its complexities." As he says, "No human life need ever be as knotted as Anna Karenina's life had been . . ." (186). Rather than simplify the chaos of life, Marlow implies, books offer us complexity. The impulse to pit the complexity of life against the reductiveness of art is likewise undercut by Fagan's view of literature. As Fagan explains, the *"characters drawn on the page by the makers of literature . . . are distillations of our thwarted selves. We are their echoes and their shadows"* (138).

Readers' awareness of the permeable membrane between fact and fiction — an awareness that precludes faith in a simple "cure" for the spread of apocalyptic dreams — becomes even more apparent when Findley makes an appearance in his own novel. He pops up as the character "Timothy Findley," a writer who is Marlow's patient. "Findley" complains to his psychiatrist that most people spend their time lying (203). Here we have a fictional representation of a real-life author insisting that people (in fiction and/or everyday life) make a habit of lying. The episode confronts readers with the paradox of the Cretan liar. But there is no need to wiggle through the logical convolutions to recognize that "Findley's" reflexive appearance and his comments underscore the idea that we cannot help but narrate our lives and that we are all caught in the grip of a host of plots, which, like language itself, existed before we were born.[17]

The insistence on our complicated and inextricable connection to apocalyptic discourse may well be the primary revelation conveyed by the novel. As Cohn and other critics point out, the apocalyptic paradigm, since its inception, has been repeatedly projected onto history; to pretend that we have outgrown it is foolish and dangerously myopic. Precisely because we have inherited this plot, hope lies not in rejecting the paradigm but in working through it and exploring less radical alternatives, such as prophetic eschatology. Findley's text intimates that part of the process of working through our obsession with apocalypse involves reinterpreting the term, which has traditionally been identified with the promise that fiction will be stripped away and truth revealed.

The root meaning of the word *apocalypse* suggests an unveiling (*apo* [from or away], *kalupsis* [covering] from *kalupto* [to cover] and *kalumma* [veil]). As Douglas Robinson suggests, in this sense the apocalypse becomes "largely a matter of *seeing*; and what one sees by imagining an apocalypse depends chiefly upon how one conceives of the veil" (xiii). If we perceive fiction as a veil obstructing a revelation of the truth or a transcendent realm, then the impulse will be to try to tear it away. The futility of tearing away the veil becomes apparent in the scene in which John Dai Bowen tries to take a photograph of Emma Berry's perfect face, which she hides behind her veil (103). Although he manages to take a picture, the text clarifies that the perfection he captures on film, far from God's handiwork and the truth, is actually the handiwork of her husband, the famous surgeon, Maynard Berry. After Emma was burned in a fire, the surgeon refashioned her face, without her permission, according to his desires. This episode suggests that tearing away the veil will disclose not the truth but merely human notions of perfection, which are repeatedly inscribed onto the world and people's skin. By emphasizing the futility and destructiveness of this gesture, *Headhunter* demonstrates that we are far better off if we recognize the veil's constructed nature and play with its potential to serve as a screen or mirror.

This alternative is highlighted in the scene in which Kurtz asks his friend and patient Fabiana Holbach to write an essay in answer to the question "Who do you think you are?" She begins the essay by insisting that there can be no unveiling of an essential truth because identity itself is nothing more than a fiction — a performance. As she says, "It's a drag act — men pretending to be men — women pretending to be women — but only the artists will tell us that. The rest of us cannot bear the revelation" (341). Rather than continue the futile search for this essential identity, Fabiana turns her attention to the boundary between art and life and criticizes others (save her friend, the writer) for not doing the same, for not interrogating, essentially, the nature of our inventions:

> The whole damn world is a mirror. But no one sees anyone else. We only — all of us — see ourselves — AND TURN

AWAY. . . . My writing friend has looked in the mirror and what he sees is the whole world staring back. And he has the gall to say: that is not me — it's you. (341)

In the end, rather than author the truth about herself, she gives Kurtz a fiction — an insightful sketch of herself composed by her "writing friend" (342). Although Fabiana invokes the traditional image of art as a mirror, her use of the metaphor proves more complex than the standard interpretation of "reflexive" fiction as a mirror, the surface of artifice that reflects a freestanding reality apprehended by a coherent, stable, and knowable self.

In contrast to those critics who argue for the utter separation between the word and the world, relegating reflexive fiction to the funhouse of art for art's sake, Findley's novel repeatedly undermines attempts to separate world and word. By self-consciously foregrounding that narratives or, to use a semiotic model, "code systems" — textual or otherwise — shape knowledge, *Headhunter* denaturalizes apocalypse's entrenched codes and the knowledge that apocalypse helps to constitute and demonstrates that the paradigm can be challenged. At the end of the novel, Fabiana, who has loved Kurtz all along, asks Marlow if Kurtz mentioned her before he died. Marlow replies, "Yes . . . He wanted me to tell you he was sorry" (621). In accordance with the conclusion of *Heart of Darkness*, Marlow tells Kurtz's "intended" a lie. But he does not view his behaviour as an unfortunate breach in the wall separating fact from fiction, as an infelicitous leakage of falsehood into truth. Instead, he takes it as a given that people rely on fictions to map out their lives: "*This way, he thought, we write each other's lives — by means of fictions. Sustaining fictions. Uplifting fictions. Lies. This way, we lead one another toward survival. This way we point the way to darkness — saying:* come with me into the light" (622). If, as Marlow claims, people write each other's life by means of fictions, then it is essential to interrogate and rewrite apocalypse. In the process of exploring and challenging the apocalyptic paradigm, the text outlines an alternative vision — one that rejects isolated, transcendent fantasies in favour of the need for responsible action in a communal context.

At the end of the novel, Lilah surmises that no one will believe what has happened. "It's only a book, they would say. That's all it is. A story. Just a story" (625). By this time, however, readers will have recognized that, in Findley's eyes, stories represent the collective unconscious of the culture that we have inherited, and we ignore them at our peril. So long as we deny that Kurtz is in all of us and that we are all informed by eschatological narratives, dreams of apocalypse will continue to usurp waking thought.

NOTES

[1] For a detailed discussion of the biblical allusions in Revelation, see Thompson 50–51.

[2] In a subplot inspired by Fitzgerald's classic work, we are introduced to James Gatz, a mysterious and lonely man who throws lavish parties that never satisfy his longing for a lost love. When Gatz meets Emma Berry, the novel maps a fanciful intersection between *The Great Gatsby* and Flaubert's famous novel *Madame Bovary*. Like her literary predecessor, Emma marries a doctor, a surgeon in this case, but abandons her husband and daughter and compulsively engages in a series of doomed liaisons, which culminate in her affair with Gatz.

[3] Nicholas Fagan's name first appears in the short story "Hello Cheeverland, Goodbye," in Findley's first collection, *Dinner along the Amazon*; Fagan's comments on John Cheever in *Essays and Conversations* are used as an epigraph. Fagan reappears in *The Wars*. At the conclusion of the novel, we are given a quotation from the Irish essayist and critic: "the spaces between the perceiver and the thing perceived can . . . be closed with a shout of recognition. One form of a shout is a shot. Nothing so completely verifies our perception of a thing as our killing of it" (191). The name Nicholas Fagan may also allude to the work of Charles Dickens — a combination of the title *Nicholas Nickleby* and the character Fagan from *Oliver Twist*.

[4] Aspects of the novel are also drawn from Findley's earlier short stories, specifically "What Mrs Felton Knew," "Hello Cheeverland, Goodbye," and "Dinner along the Amazon."

[5] For more information on the temporal perspective of apocalypse, see Charles; and Scholem ch. 1.

[6] The realization of the new world is also omitted in Findley's retelling of the story of Noah's ark. *Not Wanted on the Voyage* concludes with an image of the ark seemingly doomed to an eternal voyage.

[7] Frye uses this term to discuss the technique of adjusting "formulaic structures to roughly a credible context" (*Secular* 36).

[8] This metamorphosis seems all the more apt in the light of George Bernard Shaw's description of the Book of Revelation as "a curious record of the visions of a drug addict which was absurdly admitted to the canon under the title of Revelation" (qtd. in Thompson 4).

[9] In his portrayal of Fagan's passion for singing, Findley draws from his own corpus. In *Not Wanted on the Voyage*, Mrs. Noyes is famous for playing

her "favourite favourites" (175). When her beloved cat, Mottyl, sings her death song, the subject of her "litany of praise and sorrow" is the "last whole vision of the world before it was drowned" (333).

[10] Their mutual status as gods is playfully compared in the episode in which Kurtz invites his friend Fabiana Holbach to attend the dinner in honour of Nicholas Fagan. At first, she is overwhelmed and declines. When Kurtz asks for an explanation, she replies, "He's a god, Rupert" (266). Smiling, he replies, "Well, you've been sitting here with me this last while — and I'm a god. Or so you say. According to Slade" (266).

[11] The metaphorical connection between children and the future is established early on when Amy's sister Olivia debates whether or not to abort her foetus. During her visit with her mother, Olivia longs to tell her "about the child — wanting to reassure her there was — or could be — a future" (26). At the end of the novel, Olivia decides to keep the baby, and the text juxtaposes the Club of Men's shout of death (596) with Olivia's affirmation of life and the future (602).

[12] See Tom Hastings's exploration of this motif in *The Wars* in his article in this volume.

[13] See Heather Sanderson's article in this volume for an analysis of these issues in *The Butterfly Plague*.

[14] Marlow's fallibility is evident on several occasions: Marlow is completely mistaken about his wife's vicious character; his first impression of his secretary, Bella Orenstein, is likewise wildly inaccurate; and he transgresses the doctor-patient boundary by falling in love with Emma Berry.

[15] The narrator of *Famous Last Words*, Hugh Selwyn Mauberley, conveys the same idea when he insists that Ezra Pound is not solely to blame for inciting fascism: "It will be somebody's job to pull him down and say he was the cause of madness; thus disposing of the madness in themselves, blaming it all on him. 'We should never have done these things,' they will say, 'were it not that men like Pound and Mussolini, Doctor Goebbels and Hitler drove us to them. . . . Missing the fact entirely that what they were responding to were the whispers of chaos, fire and anger in themselves" (77).

[16] In his introduction to Kermode's *Poetry, Narrative, History*, Harold Schweizer points out the epistemological compromises in Kermode's system. As he explains, in "The Sense of an Ending" Kermode's referential assumptions concerning the "real" and "reality" constitute "unacknowledged miniature fictions" (21).

[17] Ironically, whereas Findley climbs into his own fiction, destabilizing the narrative paradigm, he portrays another character, the black woman named Orley, disappearing from his text. Fed up with the way that white authors portray blacks — "Black — with a white hand hovering over the page. All the pages of her life written by a white hand" — Orley decides, "From now on, I will write myself" (592). Clearly, Findley realizes that his

is simply one more "white hand hovering over the page." By allowing Orley to escape his fiction, he signals that it is time to question and perhaps even relinquish the "right" to represent marginalized groups. True to her word, Orley never appears in Findley's text again. This episode deftly counters Kermode's assertion that, in the novel, there can be no "just representation" of human freedom because, if a character were entirely free, he or she "might simply walk out of the story" (138). See Lorraine York's article in this volume for a detailed discussion of Findley's representation of race.

WORKS CITED

Abrams, M.H. "Apocalypse: Theme and Romantic Variations." Bloom, ed. 7–33.
———. *Natural Supernaturalism: Tradition and Revolution in Romantic Literature*. New York: Norton, 1971.
Bloom, Harold. Introduction. Bloom, ed. 1–5.
———, ed. *The Revelation of St. John the Divine*. Modern Critical Interpretations. New York: Chelsea House, 1988.
Charles, R.H. "Apocalyptic Literature." Hastings.
Cohn, Norman. *Cosmos, Chaos, and the World to Come: The Ancient Roots of Apocalyptic Faith*. New Haven: Yale UP, 1993.
———. *The Pursuit of the Millennium*. London: Secker, 1957.
Conrad, Joseph. "Stanley Falls, Early September 1890." *Heart of Darkness*. 3rd ed. Ed. Robert Kimbrough. New York: Norton, 1988. 186–87.
Erdinast-Vulcan, Daphna. *Joseph Conrad and the Modern Temper*. Oxford: Clarendon, 1991.
Findley, Timothy. *The Butterfly Plague*. Rev. ed. Markham, ON: Penguin, 1986.
———. *Famous Last Words*. Toronto: Clark, 1981.
———. *Headhunter*. Toronto: HarperCollins, 1993.
———. *The Last of the Crazy People*. New York: Meredith, 1967.
———. *Not Wanted on the Voyage*. Markham, ON: Penguin, 1984.
———. *The Wars*. Toronto: Clark, 1977.
Frye, Northrop. *The Secular Scripture: A Study of the Structure of Romance*. Cambridge: Harvard UP, 1976.
———. "Typology: Apocalypse." Bloom 69–72.
Hanson, Paul D. *The Dawn of Apocalyptic*. Philadelphia: Fortress, 1975.
Harrison, John. *The Reactionaries: Yeats, Lewis, Pound, Eliot, Lawrence: A Study of the Anti-Democratic Intelligentsia*. New York: Schocken, 1967.
Hastings, James, ed. *A Dictionary of the Bible*. New York: Scribner, 1898. 5 vols.
Hunter, Catherine. " 'I Don't Know How to Begin': Findley's Work in the Sixties." *Paying Attention: Critical Essays on Timothy Findley*. Ed. Anne

Geddes Bailey and Karen Grandy. Toronto: ECW, 1998. 13–31. Also published in the *Timothy Findley Issue*. Ed. Bailey and Grandy. Spec. issue of *Essays on Canadian Writing* 64 (1998): 13–31.

Kermode, Frank. *The Sense of an Ending*. New York: Oxford UP, 1967.

Ricoeur, Paul. *Time and Narrative*. Vol. 2. Trans. Kathleen McLaughlin and David Pellauer. Chicago: U of Chicago P, 1985.

Robinson, Douglas. *American Apocalypses: The Image of the End of the World in American Literature*. Baltimore: Johns Hopkins UP, 1985.

Salmond, S.D.F. "Eschatology." Hastings.

Scholem, Gershom. *The Messianic Idea in Judaism and Other Essays of Jewish Spirituality*. New York: Schocken, 1971.

Schweizer, Harold, and Michael Payne. Introduction. *Poetry, Narrative, History*. By Frank Kermode. Oxford: Blackwell, 1990. 1–28.

Thompson, Leonard. *The Book of Revelation: Apocalypse and Empire*. New York: Oxford, 1990.

Finding Lily:
Maternal Presence in
The Piano Man's Daughter

ANNE GEDDES BAILEY

ALTHOUGH WE ARE ALL BORN OF MOTHERS, they have played an almost negligible role in Western literature. Indeed, once the birthing scene is over, the mother often dies, leaving evidence of her having lived only in the child left behind. This plot, as Marianne Hirsch points out in her book *The Mother/Daughter Plot: Narrative, Psychoanalysis, Feminism*, is hardly surprising when we realize that the mother is missing from Western culture's central psychoanalytic, mythic, and narrative models. In reality, of course, mothers do exist and are present to their children, but as Adrienne Rich so ably shows in *Of Woman Born: Motherhood as Experience and Institution*, it has not been in the interests of patriarchy to give mothers a legitimate voice or access to the channels of power. Instead, patriarchal institutions, ranging from the medical establishment to the family, have sought to alienate children from their mothers, and mothers from themselves, in order to consolidate the powers of fathers and of men in general through the denigration and devaluation of the women who have the biological power to bear them.

Many feminist theorists, Nancy Chodorow and Dorothy Dinnerstein among them, have sought to revise Freud's account of psychological development to account for the gender differences in daughters and mothers. However, their analyses fail to bring the mother into focus because they remain entrenched within classic psychoanalytic models. They also concentrate only on the perspective of the daughter, a perspective that denies mothers subjectivity and agency in the mother-child relationship. In contrast, Jessica Benjamin, in her book *The Bonds of Love: Psychoanalysis, Feminism, and the Problem of Domination*, while acknowledging the influence of Freudian models upon current understandings of sexuality and gender, offers a new interpretation of psychological development, called intersubjectivity, that accounts for the role of the mother *as mother* rather than only as an object of her child's desire or renunciation. Timothy Findley's

The Piano Man's Daughter also brings the mother to our attention and in doing so revises the conventional narrative patterns of the bildungsroman. Reading Findley's novel through Benjamin's theory, we can begin to discern a possible alternative to the patriarchal, oedipal silencing of mothers.

Ede and Lily Kilworth, however, mark a departure in Findley's representations of motherhood. Throughout his other novels, mothers suffer great physical, mental, and emotional pain. Many mothers, such as Jessica Winslow, Mrs. Ross, Eloise Wylie, and Barbara Berry, are either unable to connect with their children or have children taken from them, losses that cause their descent into drink and often into madness. Their inability to connect with their children is usually a result of an enforced maternity in which they become vessels for babies and helpmates for husbands. Without the crucial freedom to choose to mother, these mothers can only rebel by rejecting their children, by thrusting them out, as does Mrs. Ross her son Robert, into a world that does not include mothers and that will not acknowledge the price of such rejection upon these mothers' psyches. Those mothers in Findley's fiction who have chosen to mother are often punished for loving their children, especially children considered inferior and worthless by their fathers. Mrs. Noyes, for example, is relegated to the lower decks of the ark because she refuses to stop nurturing her children or the animals. She also loses her deformed son and later Lotte because of Noah's brutal attempt to preserve the illusion of his paternal "purity." Hannah must also bear Noah's deformed child in great pain, isolated from other women, and is then forced to throw it overboard like other human waste. The number of stillborn babies and miscarried foetuses in Findley's fiction, like Hannah's ape-child or Eloise's "perfectly formed" son preserved in a specimen jar (*Headhunter* 26), signals that something has gone seriously wrong with reproduction and mothering.

That Findley so consistently brings mother's pain and social oppression to our attention reveals his commitment to feminist concerns, concerns that have been noted by various critics, most thoroughly by Lorraine York and Donna Palmateer Pennee. However, Findley's representation of mothers is also troubling. Although his works often show the limitations placed upon women in general and mothers in particular, many of his female characters only gain thematic meaning and importance by exhibiting maternal behaviour — behaviour that is often imagined as natural. This is most apparent in the characterization of Mrs. Noyes, who, as the central character of the "female" side of the story taking place below the decks of Noah's ark, comes to represent an ideal mother, who nurtures and loves even those beasts and demons who terrify her. Mrs. Noyes and her charges are united in the body of the ark and are "rocked together in this great, fat cradle on the waters" (*Not Wanted* 250). In *The Wars*, Mrs. Ross also gains thematic power as her connection to Robert becomes increasingly symbiotic and "natural." So powerful is this representation of the connection between mother and child that many critics forget that it is also Mrs. Ross at the beginning of the novel who wanted the same child to kill Rowena's rabbits and through this cruel demand encourages him to enlist. Other mothers are equally tyrannical and spiteful: Vanessa Van Horne's mother, sitting in the supreme court of the Ash Sands Hotel, or Jessica Winslow, who will not open her bedroom door even to her troubled and lonely sons. From these examples, it is tempting to argue that Findley tends to reify mothers into either monsters or angels. Even when his novels bring the lost story of the mother into focus, the portrait of a strong but caring mother can be seen as ultimately reinforcing the patriarchal dualisms that entrap women in the first place. Thus, women are valued for their femininity, demonstrated through nurturing, intuitive, and compassionate qualities at the expense of reason and independence. They also tend to be associated with nature, which is romanticized along with the biological imperatives of motherhood.

However, though the temptation to categorize Findley's women as either "good, natural mothers" or "monstrous, unnatural mothers" is at times easy to succumb to, I contend that the simple equation of mother = nature = goodness overlooks many of the subtle complexities in his representation of mothers. Nowhere is this complexity more evident than in *The Piano Man's Daughter*, a family saga stretching over three generations of mothers. Although the novel focuses on Lily Kilworth's life, we are also given access to most of Lily's mother's life and glimpses into her grandmother's life. This novel is ironically titled, because Lily is *not* the piano man's daughter, refusing either her father's or her stepfather's name and passing, instead, her mother's name on to her fatherless son, Charlie. In fact, as Charlie, the narrator, tells us, what is missing from this narrative is not the mother but the father: "There are so many fathers in this story — my own, Lily's, Ede's — others. Aside from parenthood, they have only one thing in common: their habit of disappearing when you least expect them to" (72). In the absence of his father, Charlie is not lost, as is Pip in *Great Expectations*, but is "found" by his mother (524), who — in her unique vision of the world — teaches her son new ways of telling old stories.

* * *

Both Marianne Hirsch and Margaret Homans observe that mothers in realist and modernist novels are dead, absent, or if present completely ineffectual. Along with this silencing of mothers comes silence about the activity of mothering, so that it appears as though the hero or heroine simply springs fully formed, as does Athena, from the head of Zeus. Both Hirsch and Homans argue that the absence of the mother is not only an indication of a patriarchal blindspot but also the logical result of Freud's interpretation of the oedipal story in his theory of psychological development. In the oedipal model, the mother must be repudiated if the (male) child is to achieve autonomy. This rejection occurs when the child realizes that he is in competition for his mother's love with his father and thus transfers his identification with his mother to identification with his father. At the same time, he realizes that his mother does not have a penis and thus is no longer worthy of identification but is now a possible object of possession through the penis. But, of course, he can never possess the mother, because the father is more powerful and threatens him with castration (the incest taboo). The phallus, then, becomes a sign of both his difference from the mother and his identification with the father, but because he is not actually the same as the father (after all, he cannot have his mother) the phallus attains a symbolic status in that it symbolizes the authority and power of the father and his own desire to both be the father and possess the mother. As the boy successfully resolves the oedipal complex in Freudian terms, he internalizes the father's authority and the incest taboo and replaces the original threat of fatherly violence (castration) with self-control and conscience. Because prolonged attachment to the mother threatens successful resolution of the complex (i.e., autonomy), any residual identification with the mother is usually eradicated through an emphasis on the mother's lack (of a penis) and an idealization of the father's possession of the phallus.

Homans argues that the missing mother is necessary in Freud's psychoanalytic myth, because her absence "makes possible the construction of language and culture" (2). Outlining Lacan's version of the oedipal complex, Homans describes how the phallus, as "the primary signifier," symbolizes not only the child's separation from the mother but also his entry into language, into the world of signifiers. As the child realizes his difference from his mother, he simultaneously discovers a gap between the literal world, experienced between his own body and his mother's body, and the symbolic world of (the father's) language:

> Thus the child leaves behind the communication system he shared with his mother which required no difference, and enters what Lacan calls the "Law of the Father," or the symbolic order, which is simultaneously the prohibition of incest with the mother, the *non* of the father, and the sign system that depends on difference and on the absence of the referent, the *nom* of the father, that complex of signifying systems and laws that make up Western culture. (7)

If the primary signifier is the phallus, then the primary absent referent is the mother. Language "becomes a system for generating substitutes for the forbidden [and absent] mother" (7), and "the symbolic order," argues Homans, "is founded, not merely on the regrettable loss of the mother, but rather on her active and overt murder" (11). If the mother never goes missing, is never metaphorically killed, then there would be no need for narratives in search of the endlessly forbidden and absent referent/mother.

Whereas Homans goes on to examine how female writers experience the oedipal complex differently and thus maintain a unique connection to the literal order, even as they move into the symbolic order, Hirsch tries to move the focus of her argument away from the daughter in an attempt to uncover the narratological perspective of the mother. Hirsch notes that most feminist work done on mothers and mothering still takes the point of view of the child — often that of the daughter in particular — and the mother remains silent. Indeed, she is often actively silenced by a daughter who sees her mother as a metaphor of female powerlessness and submission. Although viewing the mother-child relationship through the daughter challenges the masculine bias of Freud's supposedly universal theory, it fails to acknowledge the subjectivity of the mother: "in her maternal function, she remains an object, always distanced, always idealized or denigrated, always mystified, always represented through the small child's point of view" (167). At the end of her book, Hirsch calls for a theory of "maternal discourse," challenging feminist psychoanalytic and literary communities to search for models that would include the mother as a subject:

What model or definition of subjectivity might be derived from a theory that begins with mothers rather than with children? Can we conceive of development as other than a process of separation from a neutral, either nurturing or hostile, but ultimately self-effacing "holding" background? . . . Similarly, we might ask whether it is possible to conceive of a narrative that does not depend on maternal "othering," on triangulations, on separation and death. We might ask what shapes such plotting might take. (197)

Before imagining the shape of such plotting, we need to either revise or abandon the original, oedipal, psychoanalytic model. Then we may be able to transform the phallic conception of language and narrative that depends upon the absence of the mother.

Jessica Benjamin provides us with such a transformation. Arguing that Freudian-based models of subject formation lead to patterns of (male) domination and (female) submission, she offers an alternative model called intersubjective theory. Basing her theory on infant research done by Daniel Stern in the 1980s, Benjamin begins her radical revision of classic psychoanalysis by suggesting that "the infant is never totally undifferentiated (symbiotic) with the mother" (18). This observation challenges Freud's idea that subject formation occurs through a long process of differentiation from a desirable and dangerous oneness with the mother/other. If the child is already partially differentiated, then "the issue is not how we become free of the other, but how we actively engage and make ourselves known in relationship to the other" (18).

Through this shift in emphasis, the mother is never either initially wholly present or, after separation, wholly absent; she is always both present and absent to her child — she is simultaneously the object from whom the child must differentiate and the subject who confirms his or her successful differentiation. From the beginning, "the other whom the self meets is also a self, a subject in his or her own right" (20), not simply an extension of an undifferentiated self. The mother and her child must mutually recognize *each other* as subjects, an act that "implies that we actually have a need to recognize the other as a separate person who is like us yet distinct" (23). In fact, Benjamin argues, the mother's subjectivity is necessary to the child's successful development:

The mother cannot (and should not) be a mirror; she must not merely reflect back what the child asserts; she must embody

61

something of the not-me; she must be an independent other who responds in her different way. Indeed, as the child increasingly establishes his own independent center of existence, her recognition will be meaningful only to the extent that it reflects her own equally separate subjectivity. (24)

This separateness is discovered not only in the child's difference from the mother but also in the mother's difference from the child — a difference that is paradoxically also an important similarity, because it signals to the child that the one who recognizes him is *a subject like him* and thus capable of such recognition.

Intersubjectivity theory radically revises the subject-object polarity of Freudian-based theories, in which the mother is always only an object of the child's growing independence or, as Hirsch puts it, "a self-effacing 'holding' background." According to Benjamin, if the mother is not allowed her own subjectivity (as she is not within the classical oedipal model and the patriarchal social structure that it sustains), then she is no longer *real* to the child but becomes a figure of a dangerous, regressive state of "undifferentiated infantile bliss" (147). The father, too, becomes unreal and is idealized into the phallus — the repository of goodness — because only the phallus can supply what the mother cannot: autonomy. The result, contends Benjamin, is a hardened polarity between subject and object, which is a gendered polarity in the oedipal model:

> Separation takes precedence over connection, and constructing boundaries becomes more important than insuring attachment. The two central elements of recognition — being like and being distinct — are split apart. Instead of recognizing the other who is different, the boy either identifies or disidentifies. Recognition is thus reduced to a one-dimensional identification with likeness; and as distinct from early childhood, where any likeness will do, this likeness is sexually defined. (170)

If the subject and object are, instead, simultaneous, mutual states, as they are in Benjamin's intersubjective theory, then this splintered, gendered polarity need not take place. Instead, the child can risk connection without fear for his or her self. Why? Because no connection will be perfect; the reality of the other person's distinct subjectivity will intervene and save the child from complete obliteration. Ironically, the freedom to connect is made possible by the simultaneous impossibility of its completion. As Benjamin writes,

This insight allows us to counter the argument that human beings fundamentally desire the impossible absolutes of "oneness" and perfection with the more moderate view that things don't have to be perfect, that, in fact, it is *better* if they are not. It reminds us that in every experience of similarity and subjective sharing, there must be enough difference to create the feeling of reality, that a degree of imperfection "ratifies" the existence of the world. (47)

It is Benjamin's insistence on imperfection and reality that differentiates her psychoanalytic model from others and makes it possible to imagine a maternal discourse (as well as a new paternal one). Intersubjective theory allows for real mothers and fathers who cannot become permanently hardened into mutually exclusive symbols of either independence or dependence. Although the child may continue to idealize both parents *inside* his or her fantasy, an intersubjective relationship with both *outside* that fantasy will always prevent either full identification or full disidentification with either parent. Inside and outside, which in the oedipal model are split, gendered female and male, and thus hardened into an unbridgeable polarity, are now fluid states constantly being readjusted through the interaction of fantasy with reality and vice versa.

If connection and oneness can be experienced without endangering separation and autonomy — are in fact necessary to the development of autonomy — then two important things can occur: first, the child can connect without fearing the loss of his or her self in the object; and second, the mother does not have to become lost to the child as he or she struggles toward autonomy. If autonomy is no longer dependent upon the absence of the mother, but on mutual interaction with her, then we can also revise the mother's plot to include her presence. As a result, intersubjective psychoanalytic theory redefines the oedipal conception of language. Instead of conceiving of language as only a series of substitutions for a referent (the mother) that can never be present, we can conceive of language as it actually works: as a series of substitutions that makes the referent simultaneously absent *and* present. Of course, because language consists of abstract signs, the referent is not fully present in the sign, but neither is it fully absent. If the referent were completely lost to us, then language would not be comprehensible at all. The sign, if it is to be useful at all, must succeed in making what is absent present. Similarly, intersubjective recognition between mother and child depends on a paradoxical balance of presence and absence; because of their similarities, child and mother can be present to one another; because of their differences, they are also absent from each other. As a result, they recognize each other's subjectivity. The mother is never so objectified (and therefore absent as subject or as referent) as to become fully merged into the child's narcissistic fantasies or omnipotence or to become fully alienated by the child's complete disidentification. Similarly, language becomes an instrument of omnipotence only when it eschews its relation with reality. If language cannot accommodate or is not affected by what is other — that is, what is nonlinguistic — then it truly has killed off the mother (the world) and becomes a sign of nothing real, only a sign of its own authority (i.e., the phallus). Linguistic tyranny, then, is connected to the omnipotence of the subject and the destruction of the other.

Unfortunately, intersubjective relations are still not the norm, according to Benjamin, because subjectivity, as defined in most of Western thought, cannot allow for simultaneous objectivity. The autonomous subject can only maintain that subjectivity by eschewing all qualities of the object, or the other. The only possible relation with the object/other is differentiation. Thus, "the self continues to move in the realm of subject and object, untransformed by the other" (195). The need for differentiation has long been a pervasive narrative model. The protagonist — generally male — must disentangle himself from various social relations that threaten his autonomy, and in doing so he discovers his own identity. He is then able to return to the family and destroy his father's (often unjust) authority and replace it with his own (more legitimate, because self-directed) authority or to marry and father his own family. As Hirsch points out, in these conventional narratives the mother must be destroyed or the hero's plot will not be possible.

However, if the need for differentiation depends upon mutual recognition between two subjects, then the narrative can have a much different shape. The protagonist's main task will be not individuation but social interaction, which will not be at the expense of her own subjectivity or plot, as has so often been the case with the mother/daughter plot. Narrative will be driven by negotiation and fluctuation, authority and submission, identity and rejection, ambiguity and paradox. Rather than focusing on the protagonist's struggle for differentiation through the real and/or metaphorical destruction of the other (a movement away from the mother and toward the father), the plot will be propelled by the struggle between (at least) two subjects who interact within an intersubjective space without falling into polarizing patterns of domination and submission.

* * *

As with many other texts about mothers, we come to Lily Kilworth through her child, Charlie. Although, as Hirsch suggests, this perspective does place limitations on the possibility of a complete articulation of maternal subjectivity, *The Piano Man's Daughter* provides fertile ground for an examination of a new maternal discourse. At first glance, Charlie seems to be the typical bastard hero of realist fiction. As he reminds us, there are many similarities between his narrative and his namesake Charles Dickens's *David Copperfield*. However, in contrast to the patriarchal plotting of Dickens's classic, Charlie's story is only indirectly that of his own life; primarily, it is the story of his mother's life. It is Lily's life, not Charlie's, that parallels that of Copperfield (*Piano* 126), suggesting that like him Lily is the "author" of her life. Indeed, although Charlie is the narrator, and thus literally the author, of her life, he tries to grant his mother as much voice and subjectivity as possible by quoting her words, retelling her stories, and rewriting her diary entries. In other words, he tries to allow Lily her own authority while acknowledging that his voice will inevitably enter into his recording of her voice. His preface suggests that, although there were times that he wished he was not his mother's son, he now believes that in writing the story of his mother's life he will also be writing his autobiography: "I look back now from beyond her death, and I know that my life, without Lily's presence in it, would have been no life at all. Not a life, at any rate, I would want to claim" (9). Charlie's life has not evolved *out of* his mother's life but *in concert with it*, and in this evolution we can trace a new mother/child plot based upon an intersubjective narrative relationship.

The Piano Man's Daughter opens with Lily's death. In contrast to conventional narratives, her absence does not free Charlie into language and narrative. As he clearly demonstrates when he details the sources of his narrative, he has already been "in" language and narrative for a long time — in the stories that Lily has told and in her notebooks. It is not only her absence, then, but also, more importantly, her presence in his lived experience and in her sacred objects that provides the motor for his narrative. His reclamation of his mother's presence is not merely the desire to replace the lost mother

65

— in either an oedipal or a Lacanian sense. Charlie does not write to possess her metaphorically through a linguistic phallus. Instead, he uses language to recognize his mother not as a mirror of his own development but as a separate subject with desires and demons of her own.

Charlie's ability to recognize his mother stems from their unusual intersubjective relationship. As in a traditional bildungsroman, his narrative moves forward through time, but the chronological structure does not reveal a conventional movement toward individuation. Instead, his relationship with his mother, from his earliest memories of her until her death, is a constant negotiation between two subjects in which moments of profound communion alternate with terrible and desirable periods of separation. There is certainly no gradual process of "othering" the mother as Charlie grows older — he is always aware of her difference from the beginning, and Lily continues to include him in her "gathering" even until her death. They are both "you and I" to each other as well as "we" (4). Charlie describes his life when he was eight:

> There was little I did not know about the human condition that any child can know, who has been given a loving parent and a place to stand. But I was not just *any* child. I had also been given silence and music — poetry — a unique religion of reverence for life — a profoundly mysterious companion and a sense of being wanted and cared for by someone whose whole concern for me could be defined in a single word: *wonder*. I was also given someone to decipher — someone to protect — someone to ponder. (490)

Now, at twenty-nine, Charlie is still pondering and deciphering his mother. However, that he is still thinking about his mother and his relationship with her does not indicate either an inability to differentiate from her or a desire to return to undifferentiated bliss; rather, it indicates his awareness that his mother always was and still is both intimately connected to him and profoundly distinct from him. What he learns over the course of time is how to live with this contradiction and find it productive rather than stifling, as is generally the case within patriarchal notions of maternal ties.

There are times, though, when Charlie is not able to live with the paradox of intersubjective relations. Lily's illness eventually interferes with their bond. When Charlie stops Lily from killing herself after

Neddy's death, she can no longer recognize him as he is and calls him a *"traitor"* for preventing her suicide (503). "From that moment forward," writes Charlie, "I never met the woman again who had been my constant companion since birth. Instead, I was given the remnants of her — the incohesive remains" (502). When he is sent to boarding school after his mother's hospitalization, he does find safety in conventional, institutional arrangements of society and discovers, to his horror, that while there he repudiates his mother. However, the collapse of their unique relationship does not end in the complete othering of the mother. Rather, as I will argue, Charlie's narrative is his attempt to regain that intersubjective space they once inhabited.

Part of Charlie's success in reclaiming the subjectivity of his mother is his focus upon her uniqueness. This is not a story about all mothers — which, if it was, might give credence to an argument that Charlie simply replaces the real, lost mother with an ideal mother. As Lorraine York astutely notes later in this volume, idealized mothers have appeared before in Findley's fiction in the form of the black maid. As York shows, these surrogate mothers, though offering real comfort to their charges, are, more significantly, racially figured symbols of "strength and maternal protection" (204). In *The Piano Man's Daughter*, Findley's first novel after Orley in *Headhunter* refuses another appearance as a surrogate mother in a white man's novel, Charlie reclaims not an ideal mother but Lily Kilworth, the mother he has. Her specificity is foregrounded because he does not shy away from her mental illness. Here again the content of his narrative does not repeat that conventional subject/object split, evident in most narratives of maturation, but focuses on her struggle to maintain her own subjectivity within a society that refuses to acknowledge her. Throughout her life, Lily struggles with the line between subject and object, absence and presence, inside and outside. Benjamin might argue that her struggle is typical of those who must negotiate the paradox of intersubjective experience, "with its tension between sameness and difference" (49). However, she would also acknowledge the difficulty of living with that tension, especially within a social structure that values individuality and separation over connection and dependence. In a patriarchal, hierarchal world, the process of recognition can often break down, and "the self may resort to asserting omnipotence (either its own or the other's)" (Benjamin 49). Domination and submission, occurring within a culture that figures attachment and oneness as threats to one's self, are ironically falsely conceived as more pleasurable than attempting to come to terms with paradox and simultaneity, even though both domination and submission indicate an actual loss of the self into the other.

Lily discovers the pleasure of omnipotence early in her life: "The first time Lily escaped, she was gone no more than a minute before it occurred to her that, going into hiding, she had found a way to rid the world of others — and to claim it for herself" (*Piano* 127). However, part of the pleasure of the escape in her early childhood is the reassurance that the others still exist and can thus find her. Being found may dispel her feelings of omnipotence, but they are replaced by more pleasurable feelings of acceptance and love. Lily's desire to be found (to be recognized) infuses her worldview. Lily rescues Willa's dolls, "bring[ing] them into the open where their real mother could find them. Or their father" (86). Babies are not conceived but are "found" by their parents (231), as she was once found by Tom and Ede and as Charlie will someday find his daughter. The people in the fire are lost, waiting for Lily to find them, and lonely strangers need her to reassure them that they have been found, recognized as real.

However, over the course of her life, her escapes become less pleasurable and more terrifying. Being found no longer means mutual acceptance and love but enforced submission. Her "whirlwinds" were once an exciting temporary possession, when her mother was there to welcome her back. However, when Frederick puts Lily into hiding, she increasingly fears her whirlwinds because they no longer signal her difference within a mutual relation but now indicate her inferiority to and alienation from her mother, who is not allowed to welcome her back with love. Unable to tolerate ambiguity and uncertainty, Frederick transforms the pleasure of paradox into pain and terror, and Lily breaks down, unable to balance independence and dependence within a world that refuses to acknowledge dependence at all. By the end of her life, being found is no longer imagined as a birth but as a death — the desire to be recognized as separate is finally replaced with the desire to be obliterated in the fire with the others.

As Charlie's narrative progresses, it becomes apparent that his life story, intricately tied to his mother's life story, subverts the traditional male bildungsroman in both content and structure. In contrast to Copperfield's movement away from communion with the mother and toward autonomy from her, Charlie's narrative illustrates an unusual awareness of the predicaments of his mother and his grandmother. His retelling of both Ede's and Lily's lives as women and mothers reveals both an understanding of female desire and experience not normally acknowledged in masculine narratives and an awareness that women are silenced and marginalized by patriarchal institutions. Significantly, his portraits of Ede and Lily do not eschew their sexuality; Charlie is able to represent and legitimize it without also containing it within an acceptable marriage plot. However, he is also aware that both Ede and Lily desire that marriage plot; although he can recognize their sexuality as their own, they know that society cannot and that without marriage their desire has no legitimate place. So, Charlie's narrative maintains a complex, doubled viewpoint: one that makes present what is normally hidden or silenced and that recognizes the structures that make women and mothers invisible. His focus upon Lily's struggle to avoid the destructive polarities advocated by patriarchal notions of autonomy also indicates his desire to change the emphasis upon individuation common in patriarchal narratives in general. Unfortunately, Lily's failure to survive indicates the difficulty of effecting that change within patriarchy. However, the structure of Charlie's narrative, which is driven not by "maternal 'othering' " but by the desire to re-create and repopulate — to *reproduce* — the maternal, intersubjective space of paradox and ambiguity, succeeds in spite of Lily's failure.

* * *

According to Benjamin's theory, intersubjectivity creates a space between mother and child within which the two subjects can be present to one another. Along with physical desires and needs, the infant desires emotional unity with the mother, unity that is achieved through mutual play:

> The mother addresses the baby with the coordinated action of her voice, face, and hands. The infant responds with his whole body, wriggling or alert, mouth agape or smiling broadly. Then they may begin a dance of interaction in which the partners are so attuned that they move together in action. (27)

This mutual play creates a maternal space that is much different than the chora theorized by Julia Kristeva. It is not a prelinguistic place of undifferentiated connection where the child is so blissfully connected to the mother that language is unnecessary; it is, instead, the place of social connection where the child finds pleasure in interactive communion with the mother. Both child's pleasure and mother's pleasure arise from discovering similarity even in an other who is distinct. Intersubjective, maternal space, then, need not be forever absent once the child discovers his or her difference from the mother — as the chora becomes an unattainable, largely suppressed desire. Rather, it is a space that can be re-created in any relation between two subjects who recognize their simultaneous subjectivity and objectivity.

Throughout *The Piano Man's Daughter*, intersubjective spaces are consistently associated with the mother, whereas confining spaces are linked to oedipal triangulation and patriarchal oppression. Two of the most crucial spaces in the novel are the field where Lily is conceived and born and the attic where she is hidden from view. Her confinement in the attic is the logical result of the oedipal narrative into which Ede, and by extension Lily, marry. After her mother's marriage, Lily must accept that "she ha[s] lost her place in the order of Ede's affections" (215), and Ede must shift her primary concern for Lily onto Frederick. Lily, however, short-circuits the movement through the oedipal complex in two ways. First, she refuses to shift her identification onto Frederick, which galls him and threatens to undermine his carefully constructed familial hierarchy. Second, and more importantly, Lily's illness prevents Ede's complete shift of affection and concern for her daughter to her new husband. As a result, Frederick must make the symbolic arrangement inherent within the oedipal model real; he sends Lily away to Munsterfield and then, upon her return, sends her into the attic during all social occasions. The walls and the door of the attic mark her imposed (and in his eyes necessary) separation from her mother. Empowered by his paternal authority over both his stepdaughter and his wife, Frederick forces an irreconcilable rupture between them.

The metaphoric space between Lily and Ede that is finally penetrated and destroyed by Frederick is first experienced in the field at Munsterfield. Repeatedly, this field is the place where mutual recognition is possible, between Tom and Ede, Ede and Lily, Lily and Lizzie, Lily and Charlie, and finally Charlie and Emma. According to Benjamin, the space of intersubjectivity is both defined and made free by the presence of the other. The presence of the mother creates a safe space in which the child has the "freedom to imagine, discover, and create" (126). Paradoxically, her presence enables the child to play as though the mother is absent, to "know [his or her] impulses (drives) as coming from within, to know them as [his or her] own desire" (126–27). When Lily takes Lizzie to the field, she tells him that she longs to "hibernate" there because in that space she can "Be here

— and not be here . . . know things — and not know things" (*Piano* 258; ellipsis in original). It is a space that allows the simultaneous being and nonbeing characteristic of intersubjective communion. When Lily returns to the field with Charlie, it becomes their "haven" and "sanctuary" (434), where they are both isolated from and safe with each other. The fence marks the boundary of their safe space, but it does not confine them as do the walls and the door of the attic. It is, instead, a source of comfort: an "occasional backrest" (434). The space inside the fence seems paradoxically unlimited because, as Lily tells Charlie, within that part of the field the world stretches out in their infinite connection to the ants, birds, and cicadas surrounding them.

These connections, metaphorically enlarging the field while never threatening to destroy its security, symbolize the maternal continuity that sustains Charlie's narrative as a whole. As Charlie reproduces the presence of his mother, he discovers within it the presence of his grandmother and his own "motherhood." Similarly, although Tom Wyatt "penetrates" the field when he makes love with Ede, he and the desire they share are incorporated into a maternal space. The switch from phallic imagery to maternal imagery — "he pressed for entry," and she feels "the sudden presence of him inside her," (41) — illustrates this incorporation. In contrast, Frederick's entry into Ede creates not presence but absence: "he seemed to be raging inside her" and she is left with "nothing" (202). At the end of the novel, Charlie returns to the maternal space of the field. His entry, however, is accomplished not through masculine penetration but through maternal continuity. By the time of his return, he is changed by two important events. First, he writes this narrative and discovers in Lily's presence his own desire to find his child; second, he has been emasculated in the war and thus is no longer capable of penetration. Although a terrible disfigurement, his wound is also a liberation. Without the literal possession of the phallus, he becomes, metaphorically, a mother. In the field with Emma, in a scene that repeats Lily's own conception and birth, the circle is widened to include three new Kilworth mothers: Charlie, Alex, and Emma.

*   *   *

The metaphoric links between the field and motherhood illustrate Findley's tendency to align mothers with nature throughout his fiction. This is a common feminist strategy. If a masculinized discourse of individuation leads to domination of the other, then not only women but also the Earth suffer from that domination. Both women and nature become the repositories of everything that the individual must "shed" if rational autonomy is to prevail against the threat of being "swallowed up" by the irrational other. Woman's most threatening link to nature is her ability to hold the other within her body during pregnancy — a biological fact that makes her the perfect metaphor for a dangerous slip back into undifferentiated infantilism. Many feminist theories, while decrying the biologism of patriarchal notions of femininity and female behaviour, often also seek to revalue the female body and its links to nature through a critique of patriarchal institutions' alienation from and destruction of nature. However, by doing so, many threaten to simply reverse the dualisms inherent within Western intellectual thought. Benjamin argues that this reversal occurs through a mistaken split between what is considered social and what is considered natural. She contends that there is no split; rather, both women and men are "by 'nature' social," and "the repression of the social, intersubjective side of the self" creates a false polarity (80). The result of this false polarity, whether in patriarchy or in feminism, is to relegate the mother to the biological realm — as the vessel who supplies the necessary physical needs of the foetus and infant — and to rob her of the social agency associated with language and subjectivity.

However, if the nature/culture dualism could be perceived in mutuality, as is the subject/object relation in intersubjective theory, then perhaps the mother could be seen to exist simultaneously in both nature and culture. The mother, of course, already exists within nature and culture; in fact, her body is the site upon which the nature/culture debate is best contested. If we see nature and culture as part of one continuum rather than as poles at opposite ends, could we then imagine a maternal discourse that can be both natural and cultural without one subsuming the other? With the growth of patriarchy, as Adrienne Rich shows, motherhood increasingly became a cultural, rather than a natural, notion. She means that the natural processes of pregnancy, labour, and delivery became increasingly masculinized through the introduction of medical procedures and instruments, which alienated the woman from her body. This alienation robbed her of female knowledge and experience, and, along with mothering, birth became an unspeakable event. For women in the 1950s and 1960s, when they were completely anaesthetized during birth, the experience even became unknowable to them. What "naturally" belonged to women — the experience of birth — became the property of a male medical establishment. Men were thus able to devalue women even more, because the one thing that women can do that men cannot — give birth — was reduced to an event not even worth witnessing for mothers, let alone fathers.

In contrast, Lily's birth in *The Piano Man's Daughter* is represented as a completely natural event. Ede labours and delivers purely by instinct, leaving the house, returning to the field of soft grasses and beautiful wild flowers where Lily was conceived, and letting her body guide her through the experience. But how natural is this scene? Any woman who has experienced labour (and any man who has helped her) knows that Ede's experience has little to do with reality. Instead, it is a highly romanticized, idealized representation of birth that more accurately reflects Ede's wish fulfilment — that Lily's birth be as wonderful as her conception, complete with the presence of Tom. However, before we accuse Charlie (and by extension Findley) of idealizing the connection between motherhood and nature, it is important to note that Charlie is clearly aware of the mythical aspects of this version of Lily's birth. Immediately following his recounting of Ede's labour, he deflates the romance of the moment through Liam's supposed reaction when Ede arrives home with Lily in her arms: "you're wearing my boots" (71). But, we are cautioned, even this humorous deflation is all part of the family tale: "Liam's greeting became a part of Lily's legend as it was recounted to me by my grandmother. The field, the harvest moon and Lena, the Jersey cow, were also woven into it. I must have been told about Lena at least a dozen times" (71). In fact, Lily's story is repeated "at least a hundred times" (231), suggesting that Charlie's representation of Lily's birth has much more to do with the family's culture than with nature. It is a story shared between mothers and their children, between Ede and Lily, then between Lily and Charlie, and eventually between Charlie and Emma. It is a story that is revised over time to reflect the wish fulfilment of the listener. Although Ede idealizes the moment in order to reunite with Tom, Lily wants to believe that she was "found" in the field, so Ede changes the story (231). At the end of *The Piano Man's Daughter*, as I have mentioned, Charlie returns to the field with his daughter in order to bring Emma into Lily's presence, and not surprisingly he "finds" Lily there. His choice of ending his narrative "where it began" (540) adds another layer of metaphoric significance to what was originally a natural moment, so that the field is not only the scene of Lily's actual birth but also the place that signals Charlie's success in reclaiming his mother's presence both in the field and in this narrative.

In spite of these cultural reshapings of the scene of Lily's birth, the field is clearly not simply a textual setting but also a natural one. Lily not only connects with her mother and child there but also does so *through communion with* the ants and other insects, birds, animals, and plants that inhabit the field. She instructs Charlie when he is five years old and sits looking at the field with her:

> *Listen*, she said. *The whole world is singing . . .*
> And it was.
> Frogs and crickets. Nightjars. Owls.
> . . . .
> "You hear that, Charlie?"
> . . . .
> "That song — those songs are just the same as what I was telling you about the ants. . . . All songs pass from one to another. . . . And the frogs are saying just the same — except their song is more about place than food [as with the ants]. Not this *taste* is me — but this *place* is me — this bit of grass — this lily pad. This taste — this place — this song." (533–34; first ellipsis in original)

The frogs' song enables Lily and Charlie to transcend the constraints of their lives and commune with a much wider, human and non-human, community that, as Lily says, includes the whole natural world.

As the analysis of the scene of Lily's birth suggests, the simple equation of woman = mother = nature is not possible in this novel. In spite of Lily's profound connection to nature, her own experience of motherhood is also a complex blend of nature and culture. Charlie's conception and birth are, interestingly, for much of the novel, unknowable and unspeakable. Until almost the end of his narrative, Charlie has no idea who his father is. Lily cannot (or will not) remember the scene of his conception — only that he was waiting "there" to be found. We also never hear of his birth; he only comes into the narrative at age three. The absence of any story, of a family legend, creates the impression that Charlie's birth was simply a biological, rather than a social, event — that his conception has no meaning outside its biological effect. Lily just *is* pregnant, and as a result Charlie exists. However, when he finally does hear the story of his conception, the bare naturalism of the nonstory of what he has known is turned on its head. In contrast to the story of Lily's conception and birth, which are remembered as perfectly natural, Charlie's conception is a most unnatural event.

In the days prior to Lily's meeting with Charlie's father, "Lily was playing a game with her identity" (387), pretending to be Elizabeth Barrett Browning. (This, unlike the rest of the story, is part of family legend. As Caroline tells Charlie about Lily's "spell" as Barrett Browning, *"she is turning the pages of her story"* [387].) Lily is only raised out of this reverie by her friend Eleanor, who convinces Lily to abandon one personality for another. She asks Lily to pretend to be her. Dressed as Eleanor, Lily goes missing and is found a couple of days later in the home of a group of artists located near "where Oscar Wilde had been living. . . . Whistler and Carlyle had lived nearby and the district had once been the haunt of Henry James" (407). In this nest of cultural icons, Lily is discovered clinging to the arms of Karl Hess, a musician, whom she is convinced is *"the Great God Pan"* (527), a figure from Barrett Browning's poem "A Musical Instrument." According to Karl, Lily was *"panic-stricken"* (414), and finally, because she would not let go of him, he relented and they had intercourse. This is the moment of Charlie's conception; the textual "field" yields biological results. Lily may believe that she is lying with Pan in a field, but she is actually lying with Karl in an artist's studio.

Lily's belief that Karl is Pan further blurs the line between nature and culture in the story of Charlie's conception. In Barrett Browning's poem, the Great God Pan destroys nature in order to make his reed, but by creating "sweet music" he reproduces nature out of its destruction (qtd. in *Piano* 452). The poem suggests that the cultural domination of nature (imaged through the actions of Pan) makes nature even more beautiful and sweet than in its original state. However, the poem paradoxically suggests that the cultural shaping of nature is also a natural event. The figure of Pan — the god of nature — is, as his body illustrates, a being half conceived in nature and half imagined in myth. Likewise, Lily's sexual intercourse with Karl involves both biological and textual reproductions.

As Eleanor Hess writes to Charlie, Lily lives in a different *"version of the world"*: *"It wasn't the world we live in, you and I. It was the world she was born in — a corner of a field, and a river winding by, with reeds in it"* (527). Lily's world, however, is not simply nature — a field and a river — but also a field created out of a hundred retellings of family legend and a river found in a poem by Barrett Browning.

75

Lily's lifelong struggle to hold the paradox of interdependence is parallelled by her awareness of her simultaneous existence in both nature and culture. Others, caught within the patriarchal polarity that defines humans by their difference from nature, run panic stricken from nature and their place within it. Frederick, for example, attempts to escape nature by erecting another *"natural order of things"* (217), a concept invented by John H. Young in his *Beeton's Household Management*. This unnatural order of things enables Frederick to ignore biological, familial connections, because cultural ones are more "correct" and empowering. Lily, in contrast to Frederick, runs panic stricken *into* nature *and* culture simultaneously when she merges with Karl/Pan and emerges from her panic a *mother*.

* * *

The intertextual blending of culture and nature evident in both Lily's and Charlie's birth stories suggests that the mother is capable of holding both nature and culture in balance. Because the mother is both a natural object that satisfies the physical demands of the baby and a social being who recognizes the subjective needs of her child, she is made conscious of the continuum connecting social and physical realities. Whereas patriarchal discourse values the intellectual over the physical, the abstract over the literal, the mother is unable to escape the biological imperatives of motherhood. One cannot write or speak oneself into pregnancy; nor can one mother without writing or speaking. The recognition of the materiality of bodies — a recognition that mothers cannot escape — changes the mother-child plot from one of strangulation and differentiation to one of openness and flexibility. As Homans, Hirsch, and Benjamin observe, patriarchal models of psychological, linguistic, and narrative development have made the mother's body invisible, and thus subjectivity has been defined as successful and complete differentiation from that body in particular and from nature in general. The mother's body, however, is in reality invisible. If we change our perception and acknowledge the real presence of that body, rather than its metaphorical absence, we must also recognize the mother as subject. With that recognition also comes awareness that the text is not an entity unto itself but that it is dependent upon the body, as the body is dependent upon the text, in the (re)production of meaning.

This recognition, however, creates a theoretical difficulty, if not an impossibility. How can the text incorporate the body while also signalling the body's extratextual excess or reality? Part of the paradox of Charlie's narrative is that his mother is as much absent from the text as she is present in it. The medium cannot actually reproduce her material body; Charlie can only represent it textually through memories that are themselves textual: "the parts I will tell about Lily's family and the men she loved — all these other parts were written in Lily's notebooks, or told to me by others. Told in the way most family stories are told, some with prejudice, some objectively — always a mixture of myth and reality" (7). In effect, Charlie reads the texts of Lily's lives and from those readings re-creates her life in his own memory and narrative. His narrative, then, is not only intersubjective but also intertextual. Lily is not only Charlie's mother; she is also his text — a text that he both reads and writes. This observation could put us back to where we began with the objectification and silencing of the mother. However, because Lily is both real and textual (at least within the diegesis of the novel), she is not wholly equivalent to the text; to some extent, she — like Karl, who both is and is not the Great God Pan — exceeds the text. Thus, Charlie's text is more properly the materialization of the *space* between Charlie and Lily. This textual space is both shaped by and gives shape to them. Charlie may tell his mother's story, and in doing so "give her back her life" (13), but he does so with the recognition of his mother as a subject separate from his perception of her.

This mutuality is metaphorically represented in Charlie's description of old photographs of his mother and family: "Each of these lives is equal in its moment with each of the lives that surrounds it — all of them reaching out together through the camera's lens to meet the common gaze that greets them. *This is me*" (17). The people in the photograph are not being looked *at*; instead, they are reaching out to the person who sees them through time. They demand to be recognized: *this is me*. The looker does not dominate with his or her gaze but *greets* them in recognition of their equal subjectivity. The photograph enables those pictured to be present to the viewer in spite of their absence. Similarly, Charlie's text reproduces the intersubjective space between Charlie and Lily and in doing so hints at the possibility of a maternal model of intertextuality.

Harold Bloom's model of oedipal intertextual relations, outlined in *The Anxiety of Influence*, is by now well known. The young poet must "kill" the older writer in order to carve out a space for himself to write. The crucial element of Bloom's theory, as it is in all Freudian analysis, is differentiation and separation between father and son, between authoritative pretext and revolutionary text. In this model, the older poet exerts almost tyrannical control through his pretext, threatening the younger poet with metaphorical castration. Throughout his fiction, Findley suggests that this oedipal circle connecting father and son is a noose — the texts of this intertextual relation are stories of repression and violence. As Tom Hastings shows in his article on *The Wars* included in this volume, Findley casts the suffering of Robert Ross and his fallen comrades in terms of just such a father-son conflict, using the rape of Robert as the central symbol of fatherly violence. However, as Hastings's article reveals, this generational conflict is a textual one, rather than a real one, implying perhaps that in Findley's mind the oedipal story itself is partially responsible for the violence that ruptures bonds between fathers and sons, especially during war. In *Headhunter*, for instance, Findley examines how texts "father" one another, creating repetitions of violence that empower patriarchal authorities and force women, children, and animals into submission. The repetition of *Madame Bovary* and *The Great Gatsby* are just two examples of how the textual father dominates textual daughters and sons, metaphorically and literally, robbing them of subjectivity and life.

In *The Piano Man's Daughter*, "The Story of Uncle John Fagan" exercises similar paternal control. While imprisoned in his parents' attic, as Lily is later imprisoned by Frederick, Fagan is terrorized by language. God communicates with him, "not in voices, but in writing" (134). The hand of God covers the walls with commands, omens, and threats of punishment. Fagan covers the walls of the attic with red and orange flames — one whole wall depicts the casting of Shadrach, Meshach, and Abednego into the fiery furnace. Within this textual hell, Fagan loses all connection to reality and any sense of self apart from God. His reality is formed only in the texts that surround him; nature exists only as elaborate textual decoration on God's manuscript. Eventually, Fagan enters the text by actually setting the house on fire. Penetration of the text leads not to life, as does Lily's contact with Pan/Karl, but to death.

Throughout her life, Lily fights against "The Story of Uncle John Fagan," because the text of his life threatens to consume hers. Once her family knows Uncle John's story, her illness is predetermined by the preceding text. His story explains her symptoms, actions, and delusions, and we readers fear the outcome of her imprisonment in the attic by Frederick. However, Lily's lived experience is dissimilar to Uncle John's. For example, her first suicide attempt by fire may look like his final act, but it has significantly different causes. Neddy has been killed on the last day of the war, an irony that mocks the ideal of national heroism and duty and, more importantly for Lily, the ideal of love and fidelity. Fittingly, she slips in behind the movie screen — the medium of romance and heroism — and sets fire to the text that sustains such illusions. It is because of the false ideals perpetuated on film that men like Neddy (and Karl) enter the text of war and end up dead. They are also what draw women into marriage and motherhood, only to have their husbands and sons taken from them in war. In contrast to Uncle John, who embraces the *textual* fire, Lily tries to embrace *real* fire in an act of renunciation *against* the text. When she is stopped by Charlie, she is completely broken and gives in to the story of Uncle John Fagan, a story that eventually claims her.

Charlie's intertextual relation to his mother is much different from the destructive one between Lily and Uncle John Fagan. While Charlie is literally castrated by the patriarchal violence of war, he is metaphorically made mother within the textual space between mother and child. His text, as the material effect of intersubjective recognition, is maternal rather than paternal. The circle drawn around texts in this maternal model is fluid and accommodating. It always acknowledges that which exceeds its textual boundaries; thus, the textual does not overwhelm the natural, and the natural does not negate the textual. When Lily and Karl come together, they have sexual and intertextual intercourse. Out of that union comes Charlie. He emerges from both the text and their bodies. Thus, he acknowledges that his narrative is simultaneously under and out of his control. When he begins his narrative, for instance, he has no idea who his father is. The story of his paternity is not his to tell — only Eleanor Hess can tell it and thus change the course of Charlie's life. Because there is constant reciprocity between text and reality, neither becomes dominant, so neither becomes completely objectified by the other. As I have already argued, the field at Munsterfield is both a natural and a cultural space. The family legends arising from the field may give it narrative shape, but they do not make the field unreal. Likewise, Lily may only be "visible" in the textual traces that she leaves behind, and Karl Hess may only be "known" through a poem, but Charlie is the material proof that they once physically existed and shared a physical bond.

The problem remains, however, that Charlie, Lily, and Karl do not actually exist; they are fictional constructs within Findley's novel.

However, it is significant that Charlie's narrative has few metafictional markers. In contrast to *Headhunter*, which — as Marlene Goldman notes — uses intertextuality to criticize our desire for apocalyptic, mythic closure, the conventions of realism in *The Piano Man's Daughter* emphasize literature's relationship to a world external to it and its need to respond to that world. As well, within the diegesis of the novel, there is a difference between what is textual and what is real. For instance, as readers we can determine what actually occurs and what only seems to occur within Lily's mind. Even though the difference between the textual and the real can only be represented metaphorically, this difference remains discernible and important in terms of the novel's contention that nature — and more significantly the mother — cannot be excluded from the cultural production of meaning. If the mother is excluded, then "fatherly" texts such as Uncle John Fagan's biblical hell or Frederick's *Beeton's Household Management* will lead to our collective destruction, which is suggested by the deaths of Charlie's real father and his potential fathers in war.

The Piano Man's Daughter reveals that narrative need not depend upon the mother's absence and does not have to be shaped by masculine metaphors of erection, climax, ejaculation, and death. Rather, narrative and reading can be generated through a series of negotiations between two entities — between mother and child, between narrator and text, between text and intertext, between text and reality. Interesting things happen in the in between rather than in the end, and the end will just bring us back in, as the final scene of *The Piano Man's Daughter* returns us to the field and to Lily, the central presence of the novel.

WORKS CITED

Benjamin, Jessica. *The Bonds of Love: Psychoanalysis, Feminism, and the Problem of Domination.* New York: Pantheon, 1988.
Browning, Elizabeth Barrett. *Selected Poems.* Ed. Margaret Forster. Baltimore: Johns Hopkins UP, 1988.
Chodorow, Nancy. *The Reproduction of Mothering: Psychoanalysis and the Sociology of Gender.* Berkeley: U of California P, 1978.
Dinnerstein, Dorothy. *The Mermaid and the Minotaur: Sexual Arrangements and Human Malaise.* New York: Harper, 1976.
Findley, Timothy. *Headhunter.* Toronto: HarperCollins, 1993.
——. *The Last of the Crazy People.* Markham, ON: Penguin, 1967.
——. *Not Wanted on the Voyage.* Markham, ON: Penguin, 1984.

——. *The Piano Man's Daughter*. Toronto: HarperCollins, 1995.

——. *The Telling of Lies: A Mystery*. Markham, ON: Penguin, 1986.

——. *The Wars*. Markham, ON: Penguin, 1977.

Goldman, Marlene. "The End(s) of Myth: Apocalyptic and Prophetic Fictions in *Headhunter*." *Paying Attention: Critical Essays on Timothy Findley*. Ed. Anne Geddes Bailey and Karen Grandy. Toronto: ECW, 1998. 32–55. Also published in the *Timothy Findley Issue*. Ed Bailey and Grandy. Spec. issue of *Essays on Canadian Writing* 64 (1998): 32–55.

Hastings, Tom. "'Their Fathers Did It to Them': Findley's Appeal to the Great War Myth of a Generational Conflict in *The Wars*." *Paying Attention: Critical Essays on Timothy Findley*. Ed. Anne Geddes Bailey and Karen Grandy. Toronto: ECW, 1998. 85–103. Also published in the *Timothy Findley Issue*. Ed Bailey and Grandy. Spec. issue of *Essays on Canadian Writing* 64 (1998): 85–103.

Hirsch, Marianne. *The Mother/Daughter Plot: Narrative, Psychoanalysis, Feminism*. Bloomington: Indiana UP, 1989.

Homans, Margaret. *Bearing the Word: Language and Female Experience in Nineteenth Century Women's Writing*. Chicago: U of Chicago P, 1986.

Pennee, Donna Palmateer. *Moral Metafictions: Counterdiscourse in the Novels of Timothy Findley*. Toronto: ECW, 1991.

Rich, Adrienne. *Of Woman Born: Motherhood as Experience and Institution*. New York: Norton, 1986.

York, Lorraine. "'A White Hand Hovering over the Page': Timothy Findley and the Racialized/Ethnicized Other." *Paying Attention: Critical Essays on Timothy Findley*. Ed. Anne Geddes Bailey and Karen Grandy. Toronto: ECW, 1998. 201–20. Also published in the *Timothy Findley Issue*. Ed Bailey and Grandy. Spec. issue of *Essays on Canadian Writing* 64 (1998): 201–20.

PART II: MYTH

"Their Fathers Did It to Them": Findley's Appeal to the Great War Myth of a Generational Conflict in *The Wars*

TOM HASTINGS

Findley's "Fathers"

People have been asking me to cut the rape scene and I can't. They don't want it cut because they are squeamish. At least, I trust that isn't why they're concerned. They're concerned, I assume, because they think it will get the book in trouble. . . .

Margaret [Laurence] phoned just yesterday and said: "it would be tragic if something went wrong because you're being pig-headed. . . . Tell me why it has to be there," she said.

"It has to be there because it is my belief that Robert Ross and his generation of young men were raped, in effect, by the people who made the war. Basically, their fathers did it to them."

Margaret said: "yes, I agree with you. But surely that's implicit in the book already. You don't have to *say so*."

But I cannot remove it. As a scene, it is intrinsic — deeply meshed in the fabric of the book as I first conceived it. I cannot cut away its arms and legs — no matter how convinced other people are that the book will stand and function without them.

In the Wilfred Owen poem that Britten uses in the *War Requiem*, the tenor and the baritone sing together — Abraham and Isaac. . . .

Lay not thy hand upon the lad,
Neither do anything to him, the Angel of God commands.
But the old man would not so — and slew his son. . . .
And half the seed of Europe, one by one. . . .

And slew his son and half the seed of Europe, one by one. It *was* rape.
The scene stays.
— Timothy Findley, *Inside Memory* (150–51)

I BEGIN WITH the "fathers": to whom or what does Findley refer when he mentions in his commentary on *The Wars* that it is his "belief that Robert Ross and his generation of young men were raped, in effect, by the people who made the war. Basically, their fathers did it to them"? Who are these "people" whom Findley believes "made the war"? Do the fathers refer to actual historical personages involved in the war, such as Canadian prime minister Robert Borden, British prime ministers Herbert Asquith and David Lloyd George, or German kaiser Wilhelm II? Do the fathers refer to the members of the Canadian, British, French, German, or other national governments; to their military leaders such as Lieutenant Colonel Sir Sam Hughes, Canada's inept wartime minister of Militia and National Defence, British field marshall Douglas Haig, or General Von Falkenhayn, chief of the German General Staff; or to those citizens who supported the war effort? Do the fathers refer metaphorically to historical events such as Germany's declaration of war against France or its invasion of Belgium; to England's declaration of war against Germany, which involved Canada, as a Commonwealth country, automatically in a legal state of war; to the Canadian Parliament's passage of the War Measures Act or Canada's Compulsory Service Act of 1917 and the subsequent "crisis of conscription" that, as Kenneth McNaught suggests (215), so seriously exacerbated antigovernment and ethnic tensions in twentieth-century Canada? Or do the fathers refer to the actual biological fathers of the text's "sons"/soldiers, such as Tom Ross, Robert's father?

That Tom Ross is, for instance, a good man who does not victimize his son (Tom is "the only member of his family who came to see [Robert] buried" [190]), while Mrs. Ross, who demands that Robert kill Rowena's rabbits "BECAUSE HE LOVED HER" (24), drives her son away from his home and into the darkness of war suggests that Findley's fathers are a sociocultural construction and not a biological construction bound by gender. Interestingly, it is a woman and not a man who first links love with violence in *The Wars*, when Mrs. Ross, despite her husband's pleas for leniency, forces her son to become a killer by slaughtering his sister's rabbits. This crucial scene, among others that include Mr. and Mrs. Ross, implies that the actual, biological fathers of the text (Mr. Ross, Mr. Bates, etc.) are not necessarily the fathers whom Findley writes about when he invokes the abusive patriarchal authority of the fathers to represent the slaughter of young men during the Great War. In other words, the father in *The Wars* is not necessarily the same as the fathers in *Inside Memory*.[1]

The Great War Myth of a Generational Conflict

There is a legend about the history of twentieth-century England. Like all legends, it exists in many variants and was the product of many minds. Though it is nowhere written down in its entirety, fragments of it are to be found in many books and it lives on in national memory and the oral tradition. It goes something like this. Once upon a time, before the Great War, there lived a generation of young men of unusual abilities. Strong, brave, and beautiful, they combined great athletic prowess with deep classical learning. Poets at heart, they loved the things of the mind for their own sake and were scornfully detached from the common struggle. . . . When the war broke out, they volunteered for service in the fighting forces and did whatever they could to hasten their training and secure their transfer to the field of battle. . . . Brought up to revere England and to do their duty, they embraced their country's cause and accepted lightheartedly the likelihood of early death. Most of them were killed on the battlefields of Gallipoli, Ypres, Loos, the Somme, Passchendale, and Cabrai. Those who were not killed were mutilated in mind and body. They limped home in 1919 to find that their sacrifice had been in vain. The hard-faced, hard-hearted old men had come back and seized the levers of power. Youth had been defeated by age. (Wohl 85)

To read either *The Wars* or Findley's extensive commentary on it is to find little concrete evidence of exactly who the fathers might be, either literally or symbolically. Robert Ross voluntarily enlists on 15 April 1915 and enters France as a trained officer in January 1916. He mutinies on 16 June 1916, which means that he is actually *in* the war for less than six months. As a novel about the Great War, *The Wars* devotes surprisingly little time to the actual historical people and events of the war and even less time to describing the conditions of battle — unlike, for instance, another novel about the First World War, Erich Maria Remarque's *All Quiet on the Western Front*, which, more than anything else, focuses on the horror of combat. Although a gas attack against the Allied forces at Ypres is described in *The Wars*, a battle scene of any significant detail is not. Furthermore, except perhaps for Mrs. Ross's private objection that her church's celebration of the sons' military duty is barbaric ("What does it mean," Mrs. Ross asks, "*to kill your children*? Kill them and then

... go in there and sing about it! What does it mean?" [54]), there is virtually no sense when reading *The Wars* that Canada's role in the First World War was as conflicted as Canadian historians such as McNaught, Ralph Allen, Desmond Morton, and J.L. Granatstein have suggested it was.[2] Robert Ross's decision to enlist is not, for instance, accompanied by any of the political furore that surrounded Canada's war efforts. As McNaught explains, between 1914 and 1917, uncontrolled inflation increased the cost of living in Canada by two-thirds, causing great hardship for both farmers and urban workers alike. "Neither wages nor the price of farm products kept pace with the spectacular profits of business, and by the end of the war," he writes, "a cumulative mood of disillusionment broke out in massive labour strikes and independent farmer politics" (215). More seriously, McNaught argues, the federal government's unrealistic commitment to maintaining four full divisions on the Western Front, as well as the sharp decline in recruitment throughout 1915 and 1916, meant that Prime Minister Borden was forced to move toward conscription, even though he faced "bitter opposition from organized labour, farmers and most French Canadians" (215).[3]

Such historical information about Canada's role in the Great War is not to be found in *The Wars*.[4] Instead, the text focuses more specifically upon the trials and tribulations of Robert Ross that, for the most part, take place *outside* the realm of military history and *off* the battlefield. The public controversy that surrounded Canada's passage of the Compulsory Service Act, for instance, would not have personally affected Ross because he voluntarily enlisted two years earlier, in April 1915, and mutinied in June 1916, exactly one year to the month before the conscription bill was passed in Parliament. Ross's exit on that date also means that he would not have participated in Canada's greatest military moment of the First World War, the Battle of Vimy Ridge in April 1917, or the historic Battle of the Somme on 1 July 1916, which so devastated both the Allied and German-Austrian forces. Even more curious is Findley's decision to have Ross in the war for the brief dates that he is (January to June 1916) because this period is the one and only time during the course of the war that Canadian soldiers were, for the most part, not fighting at full capacity (or fighting at all). As Ralph Allen explains in *Ordeal by Fire: Canada 1910–1945*, after Ypres, the Canadians "spent most of 1915" and the first months of 1916 "in a holding action" (87). It was not until 27 March 1916 that Canadians again saw action at the Battle of the Mound of St. Eloi during the Loos Offensive. It is within this historical moment that Findley situates the Stained Glass Dugout scenes. Considering that Ross entered the war in January and exited in June, and that the Canadian divisions remained inactive until the end of March, Ross would have been actively engaged in military battle for all of three months. In other words, Ross's home life in Rosedale and his relationship with his mother, the death of his sister Rowena, his military training, his experience at the brothel, his journey across the Atlantic and relationship with Harris, his protection of the horses, and the circumstances of his death — and *not* his experiences on the front — create the primary narrative of *The Wars*. In, for example, one of the text's few and longest quotations about the historical circumstances of the war, the fall of Poland, the collapse of the French force, and the bloody disaster of Gallipoli, all function as mere backdrop to the more significant event of Robert Ross's nineteenth birthday and emergence, chronologically speaking, into manhood:

Robert and his brother officers were not in Kingston long. Every aspect of the war had worsened. Gallipoli had proved to be disaster. The Allies would have to withdraw. The Germans and the Austrians had reached deep into Russia — three hundred miles to the Pripet Marshes. Poland had fallen. Serbia was about to fall. All the Allies could think to do was to change their leaders in the field. Haig replaced French — the Tsar replaced his cousin, the Grand Duke Nicholas — Joffre was thrown the whole of the French Command in a gesture of desperate consolidation. (General French retired to his bed and wrote his King that General Haig was "mad.") All the Field Marshals seemed to be able to do was bicker and politick on behalf of their own reputations. Thousands were dying in battles over yards of mud. From Canada the word went out that thousands more were ready. It was at this precise moment that Robert received his promotion to Second Lieutenant. He was now a fully commissioned officer and ripe for the wars. On 18 December, 1915 the 39th Battery, C.E.F. — which Robert had joined in Kingston — was embarked on the S.S. *Massanabie* in St John Harbour. Three days before, with a bottle of wine provided by Clifford Purchas, he celebrated his birthday. They did this at midnight — singing songs in the latrine, long after lights out. Robert even smoked a cigarette. He was nineteen years old. (47)

If there is an answer to the question of who the fathers are, it is to be found within Findley's claim that an entire generation of young men was abused by an older generation of men during this war. As Findley writes in *The Piano Man's Daughter*, the First World War was "a man's world then" (358). It was "the war that carried off all those young men" (321). Findley's broad appeal to the generational conflict to describe Robert Ross's ordeal explicitly situates *The Wars* within a British (and not, as I will explain, a Canadian) literary tradition of writing on the First World War that, as Robert Wohl so carefully outlines in his impressive study *The Generation of 1914*, created and perpetuated what he calls *"the myth of the war generation"* (104; emphasis added).

According to Wohl, by the winter of 1916 an indelible impression of the war and the generation of men who were fighting it began to emerge in England. This "myth," he writes,

> was born in the trenches of the Western Front among some of the more sensitive officers and men, who had begun to feel a sense of . . . skepticism about the aims for which the war was being fought. It received its confirmation during the battle of the Somme in the summer and fall of 1916, when more than four hundred thousand British soldiers fell in a vain and badly planned attempt to pierce the German defences. On those churned-up and blood-drenched fields the dream of an imminent victory died. So did faith in the wisdom of the General Staff. The fact of mass and meaningless death seared itself on the consciousness of the survivors and was never to be removed. Even final victory could not heal the scar. . . . The men in the trenches felt deceived, abandoned, betrayed. . . . And out of the trauma produced by the shattering of the dream of victory and this estrangement from the civilian population arose a new poetry, and ultimately a new literature, which represented the fate of the English generation of 1914. (94–95)

Since the slaughter of British soldiers had unexpectedly assumed such "alarming proportions" during a seemingly endless war that was supposed to be over in less than a year (over by Christmas 1914 was the common assumption), and since England so desperately needed to "justify the sacrifice of its sons" after the war (91), the belief that the lost soldiers as well as the survivors of the war "had been the victims of a dirty trick played by History incarnated in the evil form of the Older generation" (115) quickly took hold in the minds of the living, and, according to Wohl, the primary thematic of this myth was thus created. Even before the war was over, writes Wohl, "the tragic nature" of this "generation's fate" was forever sealed in the annals of history (115). That the "war had been a dirty trick played by the older generation on the younger, that it had been a 'crime against humanity,' and that it was responsible for most, if not everything, that was wrong with England" (109) had immediate and widespread appeal among surviving soldiers and the British people, for, as Wohl explains, it was the most tangible way that the country could console itself following such an incomprehensible and devastating international crisis.[5]

Unable to point a finger at exactly who was responsible for the deaths of so many young men (England and its allies did win the war, after all), England instead comforted itself by celebrating, indeed romanticizing and mythologizing, the tragedy of its lost youth. (Over 700,000 British combatants died in the war.) In this process, the "Older generation" — or what Findley calls the fathers — does not signify any specific historical person, group of persons, or events. Rather, this popular appeal to an abusive older male figure (e.g., "age," "old men," "older generation," "fathers") refers to the belief among the survivors of the war that, even though England won, the sacrifice of its sons was too great. The myth invokes a discourse of negative paternity as a way of blaming people without having to specify exactly who they are — that is, who is to blame for the slaughter of the sons. Someone, anyone, had to be responsible for the deaths of so many young men.

Although the power of this myth of generational conflict had its most potent expression in the real-life experiences and physical presence of Rupert Brooke, it was most effectively captured in the poetry of Wilfred Owen. As Wohl suggests, it was Owen, as the most influential of the British War Poets, who "provided the theme" of "doomed youth led blindly to the slaughter by cruel age" that would come to define future interpretations of this war (105). In particular, Wohl singles out Owen's poem "The Parable of the Old Man and the Young" as the definitive literary representation of this thematic. Owen's poem reads as follows:

So Abram rose, and clave the wood, and went,
And took the fire with him, and a knife,
And as they sojourned both of them together,

Isaac the first-born spake and said, My Father,
Behold the preparations, fire and iron,
But where the lamb for this burnt-offering?
Then Abram bound the youth with belts and straps,
And builded parapets and trenches there,
And stretched forth the knife to slay his son.
When lo! an angel called him out of heaven,
Saying, *Lay not thy hand upon the lad,
Neither do anything to him.* Behold,
A ram, caught in a thicket by its horns;
Offer the Ram of Pride instead of him.
*But the old man would not so, but slew his son,
And half the seed of Europe, one by one.* (42; emphasis added)

Owen's response to the atrocities of war, like the thematically related responses of the other major War Poets — Siegfried Sassoon, Robert Graves, Isaac Rosenberg, and Brooke — was one of collective outrage and betrayal, and not triumph and glory.[6] As Wohl explains, this particular poem embodies "the essential theme" of First World War literature: "the betrayal of Youth by Age" (115). Considering the epochal importance of "The Parable of the Old Man and the Young," it should not be surprising to discover that Findley would specifically quote from it as a way of representing and encapsulating his own belief that the First World War destroyed an entire age-group of young males. In the quotation from *Inside Memory* that introduces this study, Findley quotes verbatim the lines from Owen's poem that I have emphasized above.[7]

By suggesting that *The Wars* be read alongside these four lines from Owen's poem and thereby explicitly aligning his text with the British War Poets' response to the war, Findley offers a literary and ideological context within which to read *The Wars*. This intertextual reference to Owen not only offers a *thematic* framework (the discourse of negative paternity) through which to interpret the historical crisis of masculinity that lies at the core of this novel; it also offers a way to examine the problematic response of this text as a *Canadian* text to the horror of the Great War.

As Owen's poem and Wohl's critique suggest, the common intellectual response to the First World War in England was angry disillusionment. The same cannot be said of Canada. Indeed, whereas in England the war was generally interpreted around the idée fixe that it was a momentous disaster that signalled the downward spiral of England's previously preeminent position in the world, the opposite was true of Canada's response to the war. Even though Canadian casualties were disproportionately high considering the huge number of officers and soldiers that Canada, with a population of only eight million in 1914, sent to the war, Canadians generally regarded the loss of its men as a tragic cost to be paid on the road to sovereignty and in the name of world peace. Almost one in ten Canadians who enlisted died serving the country. Of the 619,636 Canadians who either enlisted in the Canadian Expeditionary Force as volunteers or were conscripted under the Military Service Act, 59,544 died and 172,950 were wounded in action (Morton and Granatstein 279). In spite of such staggering losses, there was not the obsession with anger that Wohl identifies as the British response to the war. And though Canadians were concerned with the issue of blame, they were far less so than the English. Instead, as Morton and Granatstein suggest in *Marching to Armageddon: Canadians and the Great War 1914–1919*, the Canadian response was one of determination and well-deserved pride, as well as pain:

> Even though Canadians fought as allies of the British, for Canada the Great War was a war of independence. By 1918, the self-governing colony that had trusted its fate to British statecraft was not only committed to speaking with its own voice in the world, it had won on the battlefield the right to be heard. (1)

Canadian success on the European battlefield,[8] not to mention Prime Minister Borden's successful effort to keep Canadian militiamen on service abroad under Canadian rule and not part of the British Imperial Army, as well as Canada's participation at the Versailles Peace Conference and formal entry into the League of Nations, helped Canada achieve the "international status and recognition" that so many thought it now deserved (Morton and Granatstein 246). In *A Military History of Canada*, Morton therefore reiterates his claim that the Great War was "Canada's war of independence" (145).[9]

More importantly, international recognition of Canada as a sovereign nation was also fostered by its enormous achievements at home. Changes to Canadian social and economic systems immediately after the First World War were so momentous and unprecedented that Allen has rightly suggested that this wartime period should be viewed as the point in Canadian history that marks the beginning of the modern Canadian state. "The first war," he claims, "had established Canada as a tough little military nation, precocious and resourceful. . . . And economically and industrially it had grown beyond imagining" (473). "The truth," according to Morton, "was that the war made Canada prosperous" (134). Among other things, during these years the first national tax was introduced; a pension system was created; enforced national registration for men and women and a national health-insurance plan were implemented; the vote was extended to women; the Trans-Canada Highway was built; the federal Department of Health and the Canadian Legion were created; the federal government took over control of most Canadian railways, wheat marketing, and coal distribution; the Canadian automobile manufacturing industry was reorganized; and the size and influence of Canadian workers' unions increased significantly. Because of such sweeping changes, explains McNaught, wartime economic growth gave further weight to autonomist logic. With demands for farm produce and raw materials almost unlimited, Canada moved dramatically away from the threatening depression of 1913–14. During the war, exports of grain and flour doubled in value. Wood, pulp, paper, lumber, meat, livestock, and metals all pushed up export figures to unheard-of levels. Still more important were changing balances within the economy. By the end of the war, Canada was launched as a significant industrial nation (214).

Given the positive economic and social changes that resulted from the Great War, it is easy to see why the official Canadian response to the war was considerably different from the British response. Although the pain of human loss as well as the relatively slow speed of demobilization and the inevitable frustration that accompanied reconstruction meant that a number of returning veterans and remaining civilians would continue to experience some hardship, the end of the war was generally greeted with optimism. Because, as Morton and Granatstein explain, "Canada had the most logical, efficient, and generous repatriation program of any of the Allies" (251), Canada's future after the Great War did indeed look bright.

If the Canadian response to the war did in any way resemble the British response, it did so in that it was also fixated (albeit in a significantly less obsessive manner) on a politics of blame. But whereas the British directed their enormous anger at the amorphous figure of the father, Canadians directed theirs at more tangible targets: in particular, they railed against the merchant profiteers who plundered the public and against self-interested British and Canadian military leaders who, if they did not actually cause the war, prolonged it. According to Morton and Granatstein,

> From mourning, it was easy to move to disillusionment. The pre-war pacifists had denounced the "merchants of death" as manufacturers of war but now their theories explained a terrible reality of profitable devastation. Krupp, Vivkers, Schneider, and other vast armament firms had profited from the war. Generals, too, emerged with little credit from a war that they had seemingly prolonged. The same electorates that had accepted their genius in wartime now felt savagely disillusioned at bemedalled commanders who lived in safety while their orders sent hundreds of thousands of uniformed civilians to their death. A host of voices insisted that victory would have come swiftly and cheaply if Joffre, von Ludendorff, and, above all, Sir Douglas Haig had not been so blindly stupid. (261)

The Canadian electorate had little love for its own military leaders: Sir Arthur Currie, who took over from the unpopular Sam Hughes, was much more popular with Canadian militiamen and the public. Many Canadians especially despised those armament manufacturers who grew rich with the blood of soldiers on their greedy hands. Nevertheless, the target of Canadian wrath remained, like that of the British, the "bemedalled" British and European — and not Canadian — military leaders: Joffre, von Ludendorff, and Haig, as the above quotation suggests. Apparently, Canadians did not view their own government and military leaders — their own older generation of men or fathers — with the same level of disgust and culpability that the British viewed theirs.

Certainly, such savage disillusionment on the part of the Canadian public is not reflected in Canada's literature of the First World War. As Eric Thompson explains in "Canadian Fiction of the Great War," the "first Canadian war novels were . . . more interested in jingoistic patriotism than honest portrayal of life at the front" (84). Captain S.N. Dancey's roman à clef, *The Faith of a Belgian*, a romance of the Great War (1916), for instance, condemns German aggression, while Robert Stead's *The Cowpuncher* (1917) makes what Thompson calls "an opportunistic appeal to the moral fibre of young Canadians" (86); similarly, Ralph Connor's *The Sky Pilot in No Man's Land* (1919) "exploited the sentimental idealism shown towards the War still further by having his young Protestant chaplain die a sacrificial death" (85).

Perhaps the best case of this early Canadian response is, however, Lieutenant Colonel John McCrae's "In Flanders Fields." Unarguably the most famous Canadian (if not the most internationally famous) war poem, it is commonly misread as a prayer for peace. In fact, McCrae's poem was specifically written with a diametrically different goal in mind: to mobilize public support for the war effort. Lines from the last stanza of this 1915 poem, as Morton and Granatstein point out (145), were used with great success to generate investment in the Canadian Victory Bond campaign:

> Take up our quarrel with the foe:
> To you from failing hands we throw
> The torch; be yours to hold it high.
> If ye break faith with us who die
> We shall not sleep, though poppies grow
> In Flanders fields.[10]

The difference between Owen's "The Parable of the Old Man and the Young" and McCrae's "In Flanders Fields," as well as the poetry of the other Canadian War Poets, F.G. Scott and Smalley Sarson, epitomizes the difference between the two nations' literary responses to the Great War. Unlike Owen's poem, which condemns the sacrifice of British youth ("Lay not thy hand upon the lad"), McCrae's poem condones, albeit reservedly, such sacrifice: "If ye break faith . . . / We shall not sleep. . . ." Thus, Keith Richardson is able to read McCrae's poem as "an evocative statement" about the importance of "worthwhile service" and "sacrifice for a higher principle" (480), while Wohl reads Owen's poem as "an angry indictment of the generation of late Victorians who had lightheartedly sent their sons to die on the battlefields of France and Flanders" (107). In other words, to represent the horror of war through the tragedy of lost youth, the literature of the British War Poets (especially Owen's poetry) invokes a generational conflict in which the opaque fathers abuse sons; conversely, the literature of the Canadian War Poets (especially McCrae's poetry) usually avoids such masculine tropes of identification. Considering how Findley appeals to a father-son conflict by explicitly invoking Owen's poem, it seems that *The Wars* (especially if viewed through Findley's own comments in *Inside Memory* about the generational conflict) has more in common with a British than a Canadian literary tradition of First World War writing. This might explain why there are so few Canadian references and so many British references to the war in *The Wars*.

In terms of a Canadian literary tradition, *The Wars* has more in common with later responses to the war, such as Philip Child's *God's Sparrow* (1937), Peregrin Acland's *All Else Is Folly: A Tale of War and Passion* (1929), and Charles Yale Harrison's *Generals Die in Bed* (1930). These war novels, as Thompson explains, resemble Remarque's *All Quiet on the Western Front* and Ernest Hemingway's *A Farewell to Arms* in that they are more "preoccupied with giving as accurate and damning a portrait of war as possible" (87–88). The "hard-hitting realism" (85) of these later antiwar novels dramatically sets them apart from the "jingoistic patriotism" of the earlier novels. As Thompson declares, "Findley's *The Wars* is firmly in the 'tradition' of the genre inaugurated by Acland and Harrison and developed by Child" (92).[11]

Even though *The Wars* was published in Canada in 1977, half a century after the period in which the War Poets, either British or Canadian, were writing, its affinities — both chronological and ideological — lie with the sentiments of the British War Poets of the Great War years. When, for instance, the narrator of *The Wars* refers to the importance of the Battle of the Somme, a battle in which, as Wohl explains, the myth of this generational conflict had its origin, only the slaughter of British soldiers is emphasized. Nowhere mentioned in the unnamed narrator's comments below is the equally horrifying fact that 24,029 Canadian soldiers were also killed in this battle:

> When men and women of Juliet d'Orsey's vintage refer to the "First of July" they inevitably mean the first of July, 1916. It was on that date the Somme offensive was begun. In the hours between 7:30 a.m. and 7:30 p.m. 21,000 British soldiers were killed — 35,000 were wounded and 600 taken as prisoner by the Germans. This is perhaps as good a place as any to point out that Lord Clive Stourbridge, Juliet and Barbara's eldest brother, was one of the Cambridge poets whose best-known work — like that of Sassoon and Rupert Brooke — had its roots in the war. Other poets who were present on the First of July, besides Stourbridge and Sassoon, were Robert Graves and Wilfred Owen. Both Sassoon and Graves have written accounts of the battle. (102–03)

The Wars, as this passage evinces, interprets the First World War through a predominantly British response. The passage also suggests

97

that Findley is well aware of the role that the British War Poets played in the dissemination of this particular interpretation of the war. Although the novel is written by a Canadian and ostensibly concerns a young Canadian officer's experience of the war, Findley's text privileges the British experience of the war over the Canadian.[12] In spite of the fact that Canadians also participated in the Battle of the Somme, such events and dates are only interpreted through British assessments of them. Only British historical facts are presented, and only British literary representations of the war, despite the existence of Canadian literary portrayals of it, including the Somme offensive, are cited.

By recognizing that *The Wars* has more in common with British than with Canadian responses to the First World War, it becomes possible to address a second question about the novel more precisely: if *The Wars* is primarily interested in exploring the historical crisis of masculinity that accompanied the First World War, what masculinity is in crisis and in what history? Findley, I contend, remains staunchly committed to a social constructionist theory of gender identity in his work in that he examines the process through which the military turns boys into men/soldiers, thereby destroying their childhood innocence; this commitment is evident in the range of his texts, from his first publication, *The Last of the Crazy People* (1967), to his most recent, *You Went Away* (1996). In the case of *The Wars*, however, his investigation of the historical and cultural specificity of masculinity during the war is limited by the universalizing tendencies of the British thematic of the generational conflict that he invokes, one in which the fathers are wholly evil and the sons unequivocally suffer — what Wohl calls "the betrayal of Youth by Age" (115). Like Owen and the other British War Poets, Findley's interest in the Great War is, first, thematic and, second, historical/cultural. This explains why Findley places Ross in the war during a period when Canadian forces were inactive: it allows him to focus on this thematic of suffering without being confined by historical circumstances. By representing the experience of the war through this analogy of fathers raping sons — and thus unconditionally appealing to the myth of the war generation through a discourse of negative paternity — Findley confines his reading of the First World War to an explication of the sons' suffering, or "the tragic nature" of that doomed "generation's fate" (Wohl 115), just as Benjamin Britten confines his reading of the Great War in *War Requiem* to a father mercilessly abusing a son. Consequently, whatever interest the text takes in the historical and

cultural temperament of the soldiers' masculinity is one that thematically confirms their experience of suffering.

In *The Wars*, the masculinity in question thus belongs to this
ill-fated generation of soldiers, while the crisis is their inescapable
experience of suffering. The fathers represent anyone or anything
within the realm of the military that causes suffering for the sons.
Indeed, it may even be possible to say that the father of this
generational conflict is less an epistemological category than an
ontological one. "Father" refers to a way of being during a particular
historical moment rather than to an identifiable entity or being.
"Father" signifies the power of the older generation over the younger.
Like the "ancient *patria potestas*" that, as Michel Foucault explains
in the first volume of *The History of Sexuality*, "granted the father
of the Roman family the right to 'dispose' of the life of his children
and his slaves; just as he had given them life, so he could take it away,"
the father that Findley and Owen invoke similarly has the power of
life and death over the innocent (135).

While such a definition of the fathers may sound somewhat
simplistic, the indeterminacy of the term is indispensable to the
thematic of betrayed youth. Indeed, the indeterminacy of the term
"fathers" *is* the essential feature of this thematic. Without its liminal
character, there would not even be a thematic. As the fathers represent
the war itself, their identity is irreducible; it is not possible, as I have
already suggested, to single out any individual entity to blame for the
devastation that the First World War wrought upon a generation of
young men who did not cause the war but, willingly or not, fought
and died in it. By appealing to this trope of an evil older generation
and accusing everyone older than the sons for causing the war, writers
such as Findley and Owen can conveniently assign blame. They avoid
the necessity of having to specify exactly who these older men are
(and, of course, historically speaking, they cannot) and retain the
ability to blame them.

More importantly, Findley, like Owen and Britten, avoids historical
and terminological particularities and instead revels artistically in the
suffering of the sons. By suggesting that everyone except the sons is
guilty of evil during the war, Findley ignores the fathers' own pain in
such a dehumanizing enterprise as war. The strategy permits him to
overlook the sons' culpability in the horror of war as well. These
oversights lead to a virtually unresolvable dilemma in this thematic:
at times it is difficult, if not impossible, to distinguish a father from
a son in *The Wars*. To erroneously position the sons as beyond

reproach while unfairly positioning the fathers as solely responsible for the destruction of this supposedly innocent generation, Findley creates his own imaginary war.

NOTES

[1] The question of where and by whom the masculine role that a soldier must assume is produced, as well as whom the "fathers" refers to, is further complicated when Bates, during battle, approaches the crater and wishes that his father were with him: "he'd rather his father was with him — telling him what to do. . . . He knew that his father would take one look at the crater and tell him not to go" (119). Like Mr. Ross, Mr. Bates challenges the patriarchal ethos of the war that inevitably causes the sons such un-mitigated suffering.

[2] This scene in St. Paul's Church accurately reflects a sad moment of Canada's role in the First World War. As Morton and Granatstein explain in *Marching to Armageddon*, members of the Canadian clergy often "turned their pulpits into recruiting platforms" (27).

[3] Canada's actual involvement in the war is also discussed by McNaught and Allen.

[4] That is not to say that Findley is unaware of the Canadian Expedition-ary Force's role in the Great War. To the contrary, scenes and moments in the text suggest that he is aware of even the most minor of historical details about Canada's experience of, and involvement in, the war. For instance, that Findley includes the scene of a gas attack at the First Battle of Ypres suggests that he knows that the Canadians (along with the Algerians) were the first Allied forces to experience mustard gas during the war; he knows that soldiers did, indeed, urinate into rags and then cover their mouths with them in order to survive the poisonous gas; he accurately describes the intolerable conditions of the mud flats of Flanders; he knows that the first ships to leave Canada for England were horribly overcrowded; and he knows that the Canadian army was, in fact, a "people's army" (36) and that, in the early years of the war, soldiers (as is the case with Robert Ross) often had to provide their own guns. My list could go on and on. Suffice it to say that, as anyone who has read any histories of the Great War would know, Findley's knowledge of the war is remarkable.

[5] As Wohl goes on to explain, the reason why this "myth of a lost generation" is referred to as a *myth* is because that is precisely what it was. The source of the myth has less to do with actual statistics — though British losses were high, they were "not sufficient to destroy a generation" — than it does with the supposed belief that "the best men . . . the purest and noblest . . . had fallen" (113). Wohl effectively dismisses this self-serving belief as "elitist nonsense" (113). The war only felt as if it had destroyed an entire

generation of British youth because so many middle- and upper-class youth — but still not as many as from the lower classes — perished in the war.

⁶ Technically speaking, Brooke was not a War Poet. He died of blood poisoning on his way to Gallipoli in April 1915. Furthermore, most of his poetry (and certainly his most well-known poetry) was, obviously, published prior to the war. Other British War Poets either published most of their poetry during the latter years of the war (Sassoon and Graves) or it was published for them after the war (Owen, who died in 1918). Nonetheless, Brooke is generally regarded as the most famous War Poet. His physical beauty, his celebration of England and the war effort in his poetry and letters, and, most importantly, the tragedy of his early death can, as Wohl suggests, "be said to have launched" the myth of the lost generation (86). For an excellent study of Brooke's life and poetry, see Adrian Caesar's *Taking It Like a Man: Suffering, Sexuality, and the War Poets*.

⁷ Actually, Findley slightly misquotes Owen's poem. The original line "But the old man would not so, but slew his son" from Owen's poem is copied by Findley as "*But the old man would not and slew his son. . .*" (emphasis and ellipsis in original).

⁸ As McNaught explains, the Canadians developed such an excellent reputation as a fighting force during the early years of the First World War that even British prime minister David Lloyd George commented publicly upon their talents.

⁹ In the context of Morton's rather grand claim, it's possible that the official Canadian response to the war was an attempt to compensate for its feeling of being neglected by the international community. There is no doubt when reading Canadian historical accounts of the war that Canada's involvement was underappreciated by the international community, especially the British.

¹⁰ Written during the second Battle of Ypres by McCrae, a doctor who died in 1918, "In Flanders Fields" is considered by many to be the definitive poem about the Great War.

> In Flanders fields the poppies blow
> Between the crosses, row on row
> That mark our place; and in the sky
> The larks, still bravely singing, fly
> Scarce heard amid the guns below.
>
> We are the Dead. Short days ago
> We lived, felt dawn, saw sunset glow,
> Loved and were loved, and now we lie
> In Flanders fields.
> Take up our quarrel with the foe:

To you from failing hands we throw
The torch; be yours to hold it high.
If ye break faith with us who die
We shall not sleep, though poppies grow
In Flanders fields.

[11] The parallels between *The Wars* and *God's Sparrow* are striking. Like Robert Ross, Daniel Thatcher, the protagonist of Child's novel, is a young man from a wealthy Ontario family. He also has a disabled sister whom he adores, and his experience of the war is one of demoralization and destruction. As Child writes of Thatcher and his fellow soldiers' ordeal, "Somehow many of them existed and survived; but they were not the same men afterwards, for they had seen more than death, they had faced corruption of the soul, and despair" (328).

[12] Although it is not within the scope of my analysis to discuss whether or not *The Wars* is a colonial or postcolonial text, I contend that Findley's appeal to this myth of the lost generation and his erasure of the Canadian experience during the Great War, and his celebration of the British experience, open the text to precisely such a question. For an important discussion of Findley's work, especially *Not Wanted on the Voyage*, as postcolonial, see chapter 3 of Ashcroft, Griffiths, and Tiffin. And for analyses of a number of Findley's texts as postcolonial, I also recommend the work of Diana Brydon.

WORKS CITED

Allen, Ralph. *Ordeal by Fire: Canada 1910–1945*. Toronto: Doubleday, 1961.

Ashcroft, Bill, Gareth Griffiths, and Helen Tiffin. *The Empire Writes Back: Theory and Practice in Post-Colonial Literatures*. New Accents. London: Routledge, 1989.

Brydon, Diana. "A Devotion to Fragility: Timothy Findley's *The Wars*." *World Literature Written in English* 26.1 (1986): 75–84.

——. "The Dream of Tory Origins: Inventing Canadian Beginnings." *Australian-Canadian Studies* 6.2 (1989): 25–37.

——. " 'It Could Not Be Told': Making Meaning in Timothy Findley's *The Wars*." *Journal of Commonwealth Literature* 21.2 (1986): 62–79.

Caesar, Adrian. *Taking It Like a Man: Suffering, Sexuality, and the War Poets*. Manchester: Manchester UP, 1993.

Child, Philip. *God's Sparrow*. New Canadian Library. Toronto: McClelland, 1978.

Findley, Timothy. *Inside Memory: Pages from a Writer's Workbook*. Toronto: HarperCollins, 1990.

——. *The Piano Man's Daughter*. Toronto: HarperCollins, 1995.

——. *The Wars*. Markham, ON: Penguin, 1977.

Foucault, Michel. *An Introduction*. Trans. Robert Hurley. New York: Vintage, 1980. Vol. 1 of *The History of Sexuality*. 3 vols. 1980–88.

Lower, Arthur. *From Colony to Nation*. Toronto: Longmans, 1946.

McCrae, John. "In Flanders Fields." *Up the Line to Death: The War Poets, 1914–1918*. Ed. Brian Gardner. London: Metheun, 1986. 49.

McNaught, Kenneth. *The Pelican History of Canada*. Markham, ON: Penguin, 1976.

Morton, Desmond. *A Military History of Canada*. Edmonton: Hurtig, 1990.

Morton, Desmond, and J.L. Granatstein. *Marching to Armageddon: Canadians and the Great War 1914–1919*. Toronto: Lester, 1989.

Owen, Wilfred. *Collected Poems*. Ed. C. Day Lewis. London: Chatto, 1963.

Richardson, Keith. "John McCrae." *The Oxford Companion to Canadian Literature*. Ed. William Toye. Toronto: Oxford UP, 1983. 480–81.

Thompson, Eric. "Canadian Fiction of the Great War." *Canadian Literature* 91 (1981): 81–96.

Wohl, Robert. *The Generation of 1914*. London: Weidenfeld, 1980.

(Im)Perfect Dreams:
Allegories of Fascism in
The Butterfly Plague

HEATHER SANDERSON

TIMOTHY FINDLEY'S SECOND NOVEL is about a "plague" of beauty and dreams, literalized by monarch butterflies that migrate to Hollywood in such numbers one year that they bring death to humans, as well as to millions of their own. The Californian narrative is set in 1938–39, the last year before the Second World War, a conflict whose millions of innocent victims are suggested by the butterflies. The dreams are multiple and conflicting, and the attempts to realize them usually end tragically. Ruth Damarosch is the central dreamer, and my discussion will focus on the ways in which the novel both criticizes and is infected by the love of the ideal that she demonstrates, an allegorical reading practice that the novel identifies with fascism. Although Findley obviously condemns the fascist denial of the real in favour of the ideal, and his own tendency is toward inclusion rather than fascist exclusion, the repetition of images and ideas in this novel is a sign of its own use of allegory. Thus, Findley exposes the fascist manipulation of reality and, at the same time, is complicitous with it in his attempts to direct and control his readers.

Allegory, as Angus Fletcher has defined it, is a form of encoding language: "In the simplest terms, allegory says one thing and means another. It destroys the normal expectations we have about language, that our words 'mean what we say' " (2). Maureen Quilligan further identifies the textual basis of allegory: "allegorical narrative unfolds as a series of punning commentaries, related to one another on the most literal of verbal levels — the sounds of words" (22). She argues that a main focus of allegory is the reader: "allegory appeals to readers as readers of a system of signs" in that the reader is forced to choose between meanings, negotiating the text's "often problematical process of meaning multiple things simultaneously with one word" (24, 26). Citing Fletcher, Quilligan describes allegories as obsessive in their wordplay: "the process of interpretation can go on indefinitely . . ." (22). This obsessiveness is signalled in *The Butterfly Plague* partly in the fact that Findley thoroughly revised and republished the novel seventeen years after the first edition and partly in the disturbing multiplicity of meanings it makes available for the butterflies, its main allegorical figure.

The Butterfly Plague has not received the same degree of critical attention paid to Findley's later work. This might be because the 1969 edition suffered, as Findley admitted in the preface to the 1986 edition, from overwriting caused by grandiose ambitions:

> Every paragraph was twice as long as it needed to be. The characters, not unlike the butterflies, arrived on the pages in droves. The events were about as large as events could get: there were murders, flaming forests, movie making, the Olympic Games and — not to be outdone by a number of other writers writing then — I threw in World War II. (iii)

Although the second edition is much tighter in its writing, it has the same large scope and confusing plethora of symbols as the first, making the book as a whole difficult to discuss, but also suggesting that this excessiveness is deliberate. The mingling of reality and fantasy in Ruth's narrative sections is never fully clarified, and the butterflies themselves are an overdetermined figure, identified with the many and conflicting dreams and dreamers, from the Jews in Europe to the moviemakers in Hollywood, including Letitia Virden and her profascist cohorts, and from the women whose bodies are manipulated in the pursuit of ideals of beauty to the closeted homosexuals. Just as confusing are the possible readings for the novel's use of plague as a metaphor for fascism and the love of perfection, for haemophilia and homosexuality, and even for dreams. The metaphor of infectious disease, carried by Ruth but marking other characters as well, suggests a process of contagion and conflation in the allegory. The repetition of ideas and symbols points to Findley's desire to direct the reader and control the meanings produced by his novel, as Findley admits to Donald Cameron: "My biggest problem as a writer is the fear of not having made a thing clear, and I'll write the same thing into a novel several times so that by the time I've got it said, I've got it said eight different ways, through eight different characters" ("Timothy Findley" 54). In other words, this is also a sign of an allegorist at work. The conflicting meanings generated by the allegory perhaps signal a failure to control his technique, but they can also be interpreted as a refusal to limit the generation of meanings, as the Nazi allegorists in the novel try to do. The excessive quality of allegory as a genre provides a helpful link to Barbara Gabriel's groundbreaking reading of *The Butterfly Plague*. Gabriel argues that the excesses of Findley's novel signal its "gay enunciation" (231), in that it reinscribes gender and sexuality "in figures of theatricality, double-coding, and parody that mark it as camp" (227). Camp is a subversive strategy of reading dominant culture in sites such as Hollywood films, recoding it to enunciate excluded gay meanings. Gabriel points out that earlier readings of this novel have tended to focus attention on some elements at the expense of others, asking, "how can we explain the fact that central characters, as well as whole narrative threads, have disappeared from readings of this text . . . ?" (227), referring to the novel's two homosexual characters, Dolly Damarosch and Octavius Rivi. She argues that the subversive, "transgressive meanings" they generate "operate as narrative *surplus*, figured through strategies that belong historically to gay signifying and performative practices" and that "cannot be recuperated readily to the normalizing frame of Findley's allegory" (229), which is "overdetermined" (228). However, the excess that signals the destabilizing techniques of camp also signals the presence of allegory. The fascist method of allegorical reading is to attempt to fix one-to-one correspondences, to control meaning; in utilizing allegory but offering an unstable and incoherent multitude of meanings, Findley shows both his attraction and his resistance to this fascist aesthetic.

In *The Butterfly Plague*, fascism is both the literal, historical phenomenon of Nazism and a metaphor for a wider range of abusive power relations, of which a central one is gender, in which love and war often become practically indistinguishable. In this sense, fascism can be read as an extreme expression of current gender constructions in its idealization of an aggressive masculinity over a submissive femininity. Other sets of hierarchical relations configured in fascism are race and sexuality. Fascism violently demands the embodiment of ideals of race, gender, and sexuality. It is an allegorical reading practice that mistakes ideal for real and surface for depth, a practice that is destructive in its insistence that the body manifest a legible identity. In the first comprehensive article examining Findley's use of fascism and references to it throughout his writing, David Ingham argues that for Findley fascism is "intimately tied up with the quest for unattainable perfection" (36). It expresses an impossible human striving, evoking Susan Sontag's influential description of historical fascism as a "utopian aesthetics [of] physical perfection; identity as a biological given" (93). Indeed, while discussing the eternal quest for perfection and evils such as Nazism, eugenics, and genocide, which are its extreme results, Findley acknowledges to Graeme Gibson "that terrible thing . . . that I'm convinced we all have inside, our need for perfection which tells us that [the Nazis] had some of the right ideas" ("Timothy Findley" 142). He expresses his abhorrence of fascism at the same time as he acknowledges some complicity with it in that the demand for perfection pivots on love. Love plays a crucial role in fascism; the need to be loved creates the striving for perfection, but the inability to embody the ideal for which love is the reward destroys. The demand for the ideal causes great damage to the objects of such love. And yet, unreasonably, we still want and love perfection. Fascism is the extreme point at which this sadomasochistic love means death.

The primary allegorical correspondence in *The Butterfly Plague* is between Nazi Germany and Hollywood. The myth of the Aryan master race is the subtext of Ruth's chronicle of her trip to Berlin to swim for the United States in the 1936 Olympics, which were used as an international showcase for Nazi Germany; as Gabriel points out, in a novel that makes Hollywood a main setting and makes multiple, parodic references to actual films, Ruth's story, told in the "Chronicle of the Nightmare," evokes Leni Riefenstahl's notorious idealization of Nazi aesthetics in her films *Olympia* and *Triumph of the Will* (237; see also Sontag). The novel compares Nazi race theory, epitomized by Olympic athletes, to the universal love of beauty and physical perfection expressed in the worship of movie stars. Hollywood, based in artificiality and fantasy, and similarly obsessed with perfect bodies, is revealed as more closely aligned with fascist aesthetics than is at first apparent. The novel opens with Ruth fleeing from Germany and her subjection to her husband's theories of eugenics to her family in Hollywood. Showing that both countries share racism and an insistence on ideal images of femininity that are deeply damaging to women, the novel asserts with Ruth that the fascist mentality is not foreign to America. In the flashback chronicle of her experiences, Ruth is educated from her naïveté into knowledge of the horrors in Germany, enabling her to read the dangerous potential in American idealism: "America is not the Nightmare. It will be" (67).

Klaus Theweleit argues that fascism is a mode of the production of reality that fears "independently moving life," and he describes it as "[t]he language of occupation": "the particles of reality taken up . . . lose any life of their own. . . . Reality is invaded and 'occupied' in that onslaught" (215). Findley also depicts fascism as an attempt to annihilate all of nature to produce a perfect, dead artifact, an allegorical process in which things are translated into bearers of a secondary system of meanings. As Walter Benjamin defines it, allegory is the drive to make every part of an object carry a fixed, controllable meaning. It bears a power over objects that is almost sadistic; the hierarchical schema of meaning

> causes life to flow out of [the object] and it remains behind dead, but eternally secure. . . . That is to say it is now quite incapable of emanating any meaning or significance of its own; such significance as it has, it acquires from the allegorist. . . . In his hands, the object becomes something different; a key to the realm of hidden knowledge; and he reveres it as an emblem of this. (183–84)[1]

The Nazi insistence on determining the purity of race from the body's surface shares in this effort to control. The use of emblems that affix a specific identity to the bearer is a sign of allegory; in their visibility, emblems remove any interpretive confusion. The swastika and the yellow star for Jews, both of which figure prominently in Findley's novel, are two of the most infamous examples. Illustrating this point, William Shirer quotes Adolf Hitler on the swastika as a Nazi emblem: "In *red* we see the social idea of the movement, in *white* the nationalist idea, in the *swastika* the mission of the struggle for the victory of the Aryan man" (44). However, as Sylvia Söderlind argues, allegory also effects "a certain manipulation of the reader" by the author (38), indicating a similarity of intent between the text and the fascist allegorizing that it exposes.

One of *The Butterfly Plague*'s clearest allegorical meanings is the destructive potential in dreams, which become dangerous when their dreamers insist on their reality, a pattern that is repeated across the various chronicles of the narrative. Although Ruth is the only Damarosch to travel to Germany and experience the Nazi literalization of ideals, all the major characters are implicated in this process through their connections to the film industry and their own refusals to give up dreams damaging to themselves and to others. For example, Ruth's father, George Damarosch, is an alcoholic has-been who dreams of making his comeback directing the propaganda film/comeback of the Little Virgin, an ageing star from the silent screen;

he is excluded because he cannot raise the impossible sum she demands and is eventually driven to commit murder. The clichéd plot of Letitia Virden's film plays heavily on the "American dream" of founding a great nation, in this case against threats from hordes of Mexicans; it clearly has the profascist aim of keeping America out of the coming war by evoking sympathy for Germany's National Socialists and their racial agenda.[2] Naomi, Ruth's mother and a former movie star, was unable to relinquish her dream of children, even though she is a carrier of haemophilia; as a result, Ruth is a carrier who also dreams of having perfect babies, and her brother, another film director, is a haemophiliac, a condition that has ruled Dolly's entire life. Dolly is also a homosexual, and his creation of fantasy images for public consumption, in movies such as *Hell's Babies*, covers his private fantasies over erotic photographs of men, kept hidden in books of fairy tales and children's stories (325–26). Furthermore, as Donna Palmateer Pennee has pointed out, Dolly's name, Adolphus, suggests Hitler's first name in still another example of the novel's disturbing blurring of boundaries between German, American, Jew, and homosexual (30).

Having been away for years, Ruth attempts to interpret her surroundings, duplicating the reader's own activity, but her ability to negotiate between dreams and reality in Hollywood is compromised because of her fascist indoctrination in Germany. The reader is drawn into Ruth's confusion, having to decipher the text's blurring of reality and fantasy as well as connect the many plot lines: "Readers of allegory, . . . like allegorical protagonists, read an allegory by learning how to read it," learning partly by watching the protagonist "misread" (Quilligan 227, 229). As Lorraine M. York has shown, Ruth's Californian nightmare of Race is matched with the dates of actual events in Nazi Germany during 1938–39, producing a fiction that must be read in the light of historical intertexts (66–67). Ruth reads Hollywood in the context of the fascist ideas that she has learned and recognizes the similar, dangerous insistence on the reality of fantasy images in each setting. Her nightmarish experiences portray the destructive results of fascism as an expression of aggressive masculinity on one of its primary targets, women (Theweleit; York). The historical intertext underlies the horrors of Ruth's subjection to Bruno, first as an Olympic swimmer, then as a guinea pig in his experiments to prove her racial superiority, and later as the object of his demands for perfect children. Ruth's trainer, lover, and husband, Bruno is also an American who remakes himself into a German and a Nazi so that Ruth finds *Mein Kampf* a "mirror" for him (111). Bruno, like George, another abusive husband who demands a perfect family, exhibits the "little man" mentality that Wilhelm Reich identifies as fascist — "The fascist is the drill sergeant in the colossal army of our deeply sick, highly industrialized civilization" (xv) — illustrating a key connection between fascism and gender. Nazi Germany demanded the racial purity of its women and their cooperation in populating its empire through childbearing.[3]

Ruth has thematic connections to several of the other characters, such as Myra Jacobs. As a movie star, Myra is manipulated to produce an ideal of physical beauty, for which she then becomes an icon. However, the ideal is impossible, and Myra commits suicide after she is fired for being too old and fat for a film star. Ruth's response, that Myra was murdered, is troubling: "No one loved Myra enough to make her . . . *force* her to live for *their* sake" (296; ellipsis in original). From her own experiences, Ruth understands Myra's need to be praised for the one thing that Myra has been taught to value about herself, her body. When her audience ceases to love her, she is destroyed. Yet Ruth has learned from her marriage that love between men and women is expressed in male demands and female obedience. Her assertion that Myra should have been forced to live for another's sake is a sign of the degree to which Ruth has interpreted love as submission to masculine privilege, a lesson first grasped in childhood from her mother's careful concealment of Dolly's haemophilia from George and her subsequent obedience to his violent rejection of them when the secret was revealed at Ruth's fifteenth-birthday party (263).

The allegorical connections between gender and fascism continue with Dolly and Octavius. Dolly is a target for homophobic abuse such as his father's "hemo-homo" taunt (198), a pun that repeats Myra's earlier "homo-feely" joke (8). His haemophilia causes Dolly to fear both death and life, because any careless, spontaneous, or violent act could kill him. Both identities are marked as dangerous secrets, and the puns increase the textual associations between gender, sexuality, and disease. Yet Dolly is not just a potential victim; as a director, he controls Myra's image in a way that Myra cannot, and his obvious dismay at her weight gain after the studio fires her is part of what drives her to attempt suicide (215).

After living his whole life in fear of dying, Dolly is ironically killed in a spectacular accident — hit by a speeding car, he bleeds to death within minutes. His perennial attention to his physical safety is momen- tarily diverted by his first meeting with the beautiful, androgynous Octavius, with whom he has been tentatively flirting after offering him a ride to town. Octavius seems to be the embodiment of his dreams, and Dolly, struck, becomes careless. In effect, it is his dream that kills him, in a pattern consistent with the dangers of dreams in the novel. Frightened earlier by the sight of a man at the house next door killing butterflies with a baseball bat while yelling "Kill! Kill! Kill! You orange faggots!" (289), Dolly has escaped by driving his car for the first time, in an effort to take for once "what existed to be taken — which was life" (302). Stopped on the roadside after the brief madness of racing, he meets Octavius, who seems to be conjured up from his dreams at this intersection of reality and fiction (suggestively, Dolly gets part of the inspiration for his rebellion against his disease from reading a book). He is literally struck down: "Out there in the middle of the river of cement lay a man in pink trousers, drowning in blood" (314). Ruth thinks of the "wonderful" element in this tragedy: "The very last thing the dying man had heard had been his own name. On the lips of his dream" (320). Given Octavius's resemblance to his famous mother, Letitia Virden, the reader begins to suspect that a pun on starstruck is operating here, suggesting a connection through the emblem of the star between Dolly and the Jews whom Ruth calls dreamers.[4]

Furthermore, although it is never directly mentioned, the persecution of homosexuals in the Third Reich is a subtext for Dolly's death. Even though his death has always been a potential because of his disease, the seemingly gratuitous horror of his dying has significance in terms of his secret homosexuality. The Nazi government identified homosexuals as one of the group of "contragenics" that needed to be removed for the health of the German state. Richard Plant's *The Pink Triangle: The Nazi War against Homosexuals* documents how homosexuals were especially vilified and, after Jews, the most likely to die in the camps. Plant identifies Heinrich Himmler as the man chiefly responsible for the persecution of gays; in Himmler's homophobic version of the race theory, homosexuals were an evil that needed to be exterminated. He quotes Himmler as raging: "Just think how many children will never be born because of this, and how a people can be broken in nerve and spirit when such a plague gets hold of it" (99). The use of "plague" in this context is highly illuminating for the conflation of disease and sexuality in Dolly. Plant's title refers to the badges forced on homosexuals, the equivalent of the yellow felt star for Jews. Dolly's haemophilia, in this respect, metonymically identifies him as homosexual also, because the blood he fears shows up on his pale clothing like a badge: "Dolly's pale-blue suit," "his stockings and underclothes — even the handkerchief in his pocket — were all pale blue. He had chosen the colour himself. It showed up blood" (8).

Octavius is equally caught between illusion and reality. He is Letitia Virden's illegitimate son and best-kept secret, because acknowledging him would destroy her "virginal" screen image, the basis of her proposed comeback. Literally closeted behind the high walls around his home, he lives alone, waiting to hear from the mother whom he does not know. His cross-dressed impersonations of "Mother" — a parodic doubling of Letitia's own expertise in the use of makeup to fake youthfulness — finally enable him to take her place literally when he masquerades as the Little Virgin at the premiere of her movie. Even though there are two "Virgins" and Octavius is unmasked as male, the fans do not believe that the much older Letitia can be the real Virgin (364). Unlike Dolly, Octavius apparently survives the plague of dreams by entering the illusion created by his mother and usurping her place, although the last reference to him in the novel is followed by Ruth's premonitions of danger (366).[5] The success of his fiction over Letitia's demonstrates the novel's obsession with bodies as texts that are not only read and misread but also actively reconstructed and even deformed to produce ideal images. A superior "copy" that displaces the original destabilizes the naturalness of gender itself, Judith Butler argues: "Drag constitutes the mundane way in which genders are appropriated, theatricalized, worn, and done; it implies that all gendering is a kind of impersonation and approximation" (21). Drag exposes the codes used to establish the naturalness of gender, itself a form of drag in that it also imitates an ideal. Because this imitation only ever approximates the ideal, the performance of gender is a cumulative process of compulsory repetition (21). The context of Octavius's drag — Hollywood, where the movie industry plays a large role in reinforcing gender roles and codes for its audience — and the specific fiction of femininity Octavius imitates — his mother's — are especially well positioned to enable this subversion, and his successful cross-dressed performance links him to the failure of Myra to maintain her performance as a film star and to Ruth's failure for Bruno.

The focus on remaking the body produces another correspondence between the Nazi myth of racial perfection and the Hollywood dream industry. The essential element in this process is power; some characters refashion themselves (although this refashioning is actually more complicated, as, for example, Octavius's versions of "Mother" are all parodies of movie queens), exerting a degree of discursive power over their own bodies, whereas others are forcibly refashioned according to idealized images. Exploring the desire to rewrite the body, the text exposes the paradoxical notion of perfection itself. For Bruno to prove that Ruth is perfect, he must deform her: the stresses that he places on her body turn her hair prematurely white (111). Myra's ephemeral perfection rests less on who she is than on what makeup and lighting can make her seem to be, and she even contradicts her own image, as Dolly points out, when he asks her to stop chewing gum (7). Furthermore, the need for secrets — the hidden carrier gene for haemophilia and the hidden homosexuality — exposes the superficiality and normative function of aesthetic ideals of perfection.

The links between power and representations of the physical suggest Michel Foucault's analysis of the reciprocity of power and knowledge in discourse so that one can perceive "power relations inscribed on the body" (McNay 15). Repeatedly, Findley depicts the struggle for power and interpretative control as a contest for physical control played out at the level of the body. This struggle is largely represented by the power that men have over women's bodies, but the inclusion of Nazi Germany as a setting reminds the reader of the terrible power that the Nazis exercised over the bodies of their chosen enemies, particularly within the concentration camps. Through narrative parallels, Findley invites comparisons between characters such as Ruth, Myra, Dolly, and Octavius and the historical victims of fascism. Foucault's statement that the body "manifests the stigmata of past experience" ("Nietzsche" 83) argues that, rather than transcending history and culture, the body is discursively formed and known: "The body is the inscribed surface of events (traced by language and dissolved by ideas), the locus of a dissociated self (adopting the illusion of a substantial unity), and a volume in perpetual disintegration" (83). In this view, the body is the contested site of power relations that inscribe their physical traces on it.[6]

The ideals of perfection for which the various characters strive and the torture they undergo (voluntarily and not) to achieve their goals indicate a profound interpretative struggle in the novel, one that is not coherently resolved. Characters in both Nazi Germany and Hollywood attempt to control the generation of meanings by trying to make the surface of the body readable in terms of its depth; in other words, they try to make what is seen on the surface of the body reflect an inner essence. The struggle over outward appearances is actually an effort to force the surface of the body to be a transparent, motivated signifier for its essence. Ruth looks like a swimmer, so she becomes one. In the terms of Nazi ideology, if humanity is defined by Aryan looks, then those who look different cannot be humans.[7] The damage done to the various victims of such fascist readings reveals, in opposition to this desire for control over meaning, the resistance of an intractable essence. Even though the fixation of meaning explicitly denies any difference between surface and depth, Findley preserves a distinction between the surfaces that are manipulated and controlled and the deeper reality of identities that exceed the imposed meanings. The difficulties the characters have in conforming to the various demands made upon them arise in large part from the contradictions between image and identity, suggesting that externally based readings can destroy both the dream of perfection and, potentially, the body that is read.

Ruth's marriage exhibits this struggle. Ruth marries Bruno and wins gold medals at the Olympics for him as a result of his domineering and harsh training program. After the Olympic Games, at the height of her subjection, she allows him to shave her head and torture her in experiments to prove his theories of racial superiority: "He designed swimming paraphernalia, breathing devices, eye goggles, webbed feet. I even wore strange fins on my forearms and rubber things strapped to my legs. My breasts became deformed. I got ill. I was sick. I had headaches, nausea, rashes, and torn muscles" (100). The fact that Ruth is a carrier of haemophilia, thus genetically imperfect, stresses the insufficiency of appearance and ability as signs of perfection.[8] The fascist desire to make essence and surface fit is the desire to see a "natural" or motivated link between signifier and signified.[9] To allow the arbitrary relationship between the two is to renounce control over signification, which the Nazis were not prepared to do.

Ruth endures because, as she says, "I wanted to obey. . . . I wanted to love and be loved" (100). She loves Bruno largely because of his dominance over her, so that love to her means surrender. Yet Bruno needs her even more than she needs him, because she is necessary to the theories that have established his place in the Nazi party. This need and its corresponding fear perhaps explain his treatment of her. Their interdependence illuminates not only Findley's pessimistic view of gender relations but also the sadomasochism of fascism. The fascist obsession with allegorical readings reveals a dependence on and a fear of what it "others." As with the compulsory repetitions of gender, the jump between real and ideal must be performed continually in order to affirm the existence of perfection, a process requiring an absolute surrender of the object to the desired image. Ruth accepts Bruno's reading of her to the extent that, after her return home, she sighs, "How I hate my body" (36). Her self-loathing may indicate knowledge that her nearly perfect body has caused her suffering, or it may reveal her final internalization of Bruno's judgement of her imperfections: because she is a carrier, she cannot have his perfect babies. In the pursuit of perfection, any flaw is failure. Bruno has more success refashioning himself into a Nazi, although he cannot change his essence either, signalled by his brown eyes (69–70); the Aryan ideal, of course, is blue eyes. Ironically, it is not clear, either, if Bruno knows the reason for Ruth's refusal to have his children (107).

Ruth's unstable emotional and mental states throughout the novel are partly caused by her conflicting self-images. Her pursuit by the mysterious blond man whom she calls Race suggests a link between insanity and loss of discursive control over her body. After the long "Chronicle of Alvarez Canyon," which ends with a terrifying description of a fire that figures the Holocaust as it destroys thousands of trapped animals, Ruth is told: "No one was there. Or, so they all claimed" (143). Against the evidence of a reality denying her visions, Ruth insists on the validity of her perceptions: *"Alvarez Canyon Paradise did burn down. And someone was there. I was"* (143). Her exposure to Nazi propaganda appears to have made her able to see behind surfaces that others wish to remain impenetrable. Ruth has learned the importance of witnessing as a form of protest. The reader shares in her disorientation — the opposing interpretation comes only at the end of this narrative sequence, which has focused in turn on the various characters' wanderings through the woods. Put simply, if no one was there, then her insistence that she was is a denial of the real in favour of an allegorical reading; if they were there, then she is right, and the others are being fascist readers. The narration undermines the reality of the sequence, identifying the events as a dream without specifying whose (136–37), which invites the reader to read allegorically, like Ruth. Like a movie set, Alvarez itself refuses the split between real and unreal, combining plastic plants and stuffed animals with living things in a gaudy, confusing maze. The canyon is emblematic of Hollywood itself, just as Hollywood is emblematic of America. It is also emblematic of a concentration camp (prefiguring the comparison of the Maine setting in *The Telling of Lies: A Mystery* to a camp). Not only are the animals prisoners, but also, in a disturbing sequence in which Myra and Dolly — two of the novel's victims — become lost, they begin shedding their clothing in a parody of Hansel and Gretel that also evokes the compulsory stripping of prisoners on their way to the gas chambers. Not surprisingly, the fire begins almost immediately (136–38). Within this setting, it is not surprising either that Ruth encounters Race and that he forces on her the Nazi emblem, his swastika (134–46). Race is for Ruth (no other main character appears to see him) the personification of fascist propaganda as well as, like her, a victim of it (237).

Although Ruth's refusal to accept the easier version of the fire at Alvarez — none of her group was there, rather than that they were and did nothing to save its victims — is morally correct, it is also a sign that her mind has been affected by the fascist refusal of reality, compromising her interpretations. When Ruth encounters a situation with which she cannot deal rationally, she stands against a wall and practises swimming, counting mindlessly in the drill that Bruno taught her, which was designed to keep her from thinking and to make her submit to his decisions regarding her body (82–83). The image of Ruth against a wall suggests her continuing mental entrapment and her connection to those who were literally backed against walls by the Nazis. Her dream of pregnancy springs from her fascist desire to negate her body's imperfections for the purity of Race. In a telling exchange, she admits to her mother, "in spite of reading and listening and watching; in spite of overhearing and secretly seeing; in spite of *knowing* . . ." she still wants Race (155; ellipsis in original). She has convinced herself that she will have his perfect child despite her genetic flaws, and later her womb actually swells. Naomi, dying from cancer, has discarded illusions such as hope and thus claims access to a reality superior to Ruth's fantasies:

> But each human being is flawed. . . . But the greatest flaw of all, the very worst, the most destructive and the seat of all our woes and pain, is this dream — this damnable quest for perfection. . . . [W]hen I think of the misery and despair caused by people like you who will not accept — and will not cope with reality as it is, I find it small wonder that humanity is condemned to suffering. (156)

The authority of Naomi's appeal comes partly from her position on her deathbed and partly from the way in which her words sum up the central ideas of the novel. But, through the ambiguities in the chronicles of Alvarez and Race, the narrative does not completely invalidate the reality of Ruth's visions and their message: *"The Nightmare no one understands is more real than this reality"* (155). Outside the text, Findley confirms to Gibson Ruth's allegorical translation of Race, acknowledging the historical success of fascist regimes in the 1930s: "An 'idea' *was* going around killing things. The idea of Fascism" ("Timothy Findley" 146). Nevertheless, however sympathetic the reader is to Ruth's plight and her perception of the fascist elements in her surroundings, her interpretations are problematic and come to a crux in her false reading of herself as pregnant. Preserving the text's distinction between surface and essence, or mind and body, her "perfection" is foreign, an imposed reading, so her body finally rejects the "idea," bursting the bag of water in her womb (347–49), a metaphor for the mental purge necessary to read herself properly as imperfect.

The difficulties in interpretation are compounded by the connections between Ruth and Myra that further link them to the victims of the Holocaust. Late in the novel, Naomi reveals that Ruth's paternal grandmother was Jewish (154), increasing the irony of Ruth's (im)perfection. In the Nazi anti-Semitic race laws of 1933, one Jewish grandparent was enough to establish "non-Aryan descent" (Snyder 111). As a member of the Nazi elite, Bruno would be ruined if his wife were Jewish. This comparison is extended by Ruth's identification of the Jews trapped in the nightmare as "dreamers" (67). Myra acts out the dreams of others, whereas Ruth is repeatedly identified as a dreamer. Like Myra, Ruth decides at one point to kill herself. In a tank of water at the "lowest temperature" to demonstrate her endurance for the Jewish "specimens" in a concentration camp, she decides to die to save those who must submit to even more extreme experiments on their bodies (103). However, at the last minute, she panics and is rescued. Like Ruth, Myra calls for help at the last minute too, but in her case Dolly is too late in answering the phone, and she dies (220–21). The end of her film career comes when Dolly demands that she play a swimming scene in the nude, and her body is rejected as too fat by the sinister New York executives who are watching the shoot. The demonstration in the camp, in which Ruth is allowed only a bathing suit and is observed through a glass tank by Bruno and his researchers, ends her career as Bruno's guinea pig. Both women are thirty-two.

Ruth claims unity with Jewish prisoners — "I was one of them" (103) — and they do share a designation as bodies to be read through theories of race and perfection. The Nazi identification of Jews as diseased imperfections in the German body is a subtext in Ruth's identification with the Jews: her blood is also "poisoned" by the genetic disease she carries. However, the yellow felt star from Jakob Seuss that Ruth carries marks her contradictory place in such inscriptions. His clubfoot, in keeping with the Nazis' insistence on reading bodies, marks his Jewishness, seen as racial degeneration, as much as do his Semitic looks. Ruth admits, "People are afraid of deformity. I am afraid" (76). Seuss claims that he no longer needs his star now that he has escaped from Germany; however, he also does not need it anymore because his foot metonymically marks him as other. The star becomes a personal emblem for Ruth, who carries it back into Germany. At one point, she says to Lissl, a friend similarly trapped by her love for a Nazi husband, that "we" should all carry such stars (95). York reads this statement as meaning that women are victims of men and their destructive relationships with them (78), and, undoubtedly, the star strengthens the links between Myra and Ruth and Lissl, who has been similarly remade into an image of perfection: "She seemed cared for and turned out like a film star" (*Butterfly* 93). In the novel's metonymic syntax, the star conflates Jewishness, haemophilia, and a feminine ideal: whereas Myra is a star and Lissl looks like one, Ruth carries one identifying her as a carrier of all these meanings.

Yet this play on star is compromised by Ruth's fascist infection. Any easy identification with the Jews is tendentious because, unlike the dreamers caught in the concentration camps, Ruth can ultimately escape from the nightmare. Anne Geddes Bailey points out that Ruth is chosen for her near perfection, but the specimens are selected for their imperfection: "Whether she dies or not . . . they will be killed in any case" (65). Her identification with the yellow star is complicated by the second badge that she carries, the swastika forced on her by Race during the excursion to Alvarez. In this sequence, Ruth problematically reads herself as one of the "chosen," a word that evokes the term "chosen people" used to describe the Jews at the same time as it conveys the Nazi belief in Aryan racial superiority: "She had chosen — and been chosen. She would never be rid of it, ever. Bruno's damned perfection" (136). Furthermore, because Letitia Virden is inside Alvarez even before Ruth and her party arrive, the star and all that it signifies precede Ruth into "Paradise." Carrier of the star, Ruth also carries the Nazi taint, the swastika. If the whole episode is a dream, then it only reinforces the image of Ruth as a double carrier of disease: in the blood and in the mind. Because the narrative does not explicitly invalidate Ruth's versions of reality, it also demonstrates a susceptibility to an aesthetic summed up by Sontag, who discusses the Nazi propaganda films of Leni Riefenstahl in terms — "the dark themes of longing, purity, and death" (77) — that also fit the Virgin's movie: fascist aesthetics "flow from (and justify) a preoccupation with situations of control, submissive behavior, extravagant effort, and the endurance of pain. . . . Fascist art glorifies surrender, it exalts mindlessness, it glamorizes death" (91). As Ruth learns in Germany, reality is created by those who have the power to make their myths "true," not unlike the author.[10]

The conflation of fascism with the destructive preference for dream over reality expresses the central moral message of this book. This is what Ruth means when she commands the others to "Pay attention" while the animals die in Alvarez (141). Findley's version of this command, expressed to Bruce Meyer and Brian O'Riordan, shows an anxiety over the blurring of real and fictional extending beyond this novel: "Pay attention to real reality" ("Timothy Findley" 54). Choosing between competing interpretations thus becomes a morally charged activity, connecting Findley's use of allegory to the traditions of the genre: "Ultimately readers are forced to reflect on how they have read the action, but in reflecting on this operation they are forced to realize as well that the choices they have made about the text also reflect the kinds of choices they make in life" (Quilligan 253).

The unifying emblem throughout the novel is the plague of migrating butterflies; by the time the plague ends, "tens of millions of dead" remain behind (355). The beautiful insects, horrible and even deadly in their huge numbers, recall the locusts in Exodus 10, one of the plagues called down on the Egyptians by Moses as punishment for refusing to let the Hebrew slaves go. The last section's title, "The Chronicle of the Exodus," evokes both the Jewish victims of the Holocaust, treated as less than human and murdered, and God's punishment on the tormentors of his chosen people, implicating Germans and Americans — with their history of slavery and racism — together. The butterfly plague is also a punishment visited specifically on Hollywood. Ephemeral individually, in their masses they suffocate, a literalization of the "plague of dreams" stifling the main characters. The threat of plague includes the Little Virgin's plot to use her film as propaganda to gain the presidency for her backer, Cooper Carter (365). By extension, this plot device criticizes the naïveté of Americans who considered fascism to be a European phenomenon while they occupied themselves with celluloid fantasies. Such innocence is dangerous because it allows the dreamers to be manipulated by those who understand the seductive power of fantasy images. The end of the plague and the death of Letitia (but not her film) in the novel's final moments are to be read in the historical context of the impending war.

The overdetermined sign of the butterflies functions to unite the various narrative threads, but their many meanings make the allegory confusing. A more hopeful, if still compromised, image is contained in Noah Trelford, the sculptor who attempts to "capture" the butterflies in yet another dream.[11] Noah faces the nightmare and works with it, laying a claim for the artist as a witness of events in art, leaving them "interpreted and preserved" for the later comprehension of others (350). His artistic engagement with the butterflies enacts Ruth's early insight into the relationship between dreams and nightmares: "a dream may be more dangerous than a Nightmare. In a Nightmare you are pursued upright. In dreams you are helpless and float. However, you die only in Nightmares. In dreams you live forever. And that is marvellous and horrible" (69). Noah takes a plague of dreams, the butterflies, and turns it into art, engaging with it and making it, in Ruth's terms, a nightmare. As Ruth has already discovered, personal risk is involved in challenging the dream and turning it into a nightmare: "This is how a new nightmare begins. With an act. Sometimes an act of absolution. Sometimes an act of atonement. The act will inevitably involve your integrity" (67, 99).

With Ruth, *The Butterfly Plague* advocates awareness over passive dreaming. To enter the nightmare consciously is to try to affect the course of events, suggesting that the best defence against fascism is the assumption of moral responsibility. The mingling of reality and fantasy becomes the shaping of fact and history into fiction, and the artist as allegorist is consciously compromised and implicated in the lies that are also part of fascism. In their excess, the novel's multiple, conflicting allegories resist the fascist insistence on legibility at the same time as they reveal the attraction of fixing meaning. The power of Findley's portrayal of fascism lies precisely in his awareness of complicity with some of its ideas.

NOTES

[1] Using texts from *Piers Plowman* to *Gravity's Rainbow* as examples of allegory, Quilligan refutes critics who read allegory as a two-tier, hierarchical system of meaning, arguing instead for a horizontally arranged field of

multiple meanings generated by the wordplay. I have found both theories useful in understanding *The Butterfly Plague*'s allegories: the fascist system is closest to the vertical system defined by Benjamin, whereas the novel's many puns generate the multiple possible readings of Quilligan's theory, in which the reader must enter into the allegory and make choices that implicate him or her in the interpretation.

[2] The Little Virgin's film, *America — I Love You!*, is a crude invocation of race and national destiny. After slaughtering the "Dirty little Mexicans," the hero parts from his love, whom he cannot have as his just reward because she has been defiled by those Mexicans. She, played by Letitia (filmed through tinted gauze), founds a convent on the battlefield, and he goes off to "Kill the Indians and found America" (332). The plot suggests an intertextual reference to D.W. Griffith's 1915 epic *The Birth of a Nation*, about the Reconstruction after the American Civil War. It starred Lillian Gish and sympathetically depicted the establishment of the Ku Klux Klan (see Simmon for a discussion of this movie and its place in American film history).

[3] For example, Sontag describes the Third Reich as "a society in which women are merely breeders and helpers, excluded from all ceremonial functions, and represent a threat to the integrity and strength of men" (90).

[4] As Lorraine York points out in her essay in this volume, Dolly is explicitly compared more than once to Jakob Seuss, who gives Ruth his yellow star ("White Hand" 215).

[5] York's discussion in her essay collected in this volume of the connections between a racialized other, physical prominence, and nurturance, and of the eroticization of the racial other in Findley's writings, is very helpful in reading Octavius's escape at the end of the novel with his large, black chauffeur — "He's black and will protect me" (365).

[6] Nazi Germany, with its complex mechanisms for internal examination and control, such as the Gestapo, provides an excellent setting for the interdependence of power and knowledge analysed by Foucault: "We should admit rather that power produces knowledge . . . that power and knowledge directly imply one another; that there is no power relation without the correlative constitution of a field of knowledge, nor any knowledge that does not presuppose and constitute at the same time power relations" (*Discipline* 27).

[7] As Reich outlines it, Nazi race theory was based in the faulty extrapolation of supposed natural laws against species interbreeding among animals: "Their line of reasoning was something as follows: Historical experience teaches that the 'intermixing of Aryan blood' with 'inferior' peoples always results in the degeneration of the founders of civilization. The level of the superior race is lowered, followed by physical and mental retrogression; this marks the beginning of a progressive 'decline' " (76). Richard Plant argues

that this was the reasoning behind the fascist persecution of German gays, who were ruthlessly hunted down and killed, whereas homosexuals in undesired populations (e.g., Czechs) were left relatively alone to weaken further already inferior "races" (99–100).

[8] Genetically, Ruth has a fifty percent chance of being a carrier and if so of passing the gene for haemophilia to her children: "the transmission of this condition is characteristically sex-linked, being expressed mostly only in males, but transmitted solely by females; sons of a hemophilic male are normal, but daughters, although outwardly normal, may transmit the traits as an overt defect to half their sons and as a recessive or hidden trait to half their daughters" ("Hemophilia"). However, Ruth thinks that she is a carrier, and her mother's advice in the "Chronicle of the Wish" is predicated on the same opinion.

[9] I am drawing upon Kaja Silverman's discussion of the arbitrary or unmotivated nature of the linguistic sign in Saussure's theory of semiotics (6–8).

[10] The 1969 edition ends with Ruth's (apparently healthy) daughter meeting and falling in love with one of Noah Trelford's sons in the 1960s. By revising the ending, Findley removed a great amount of the hope that it gave the novel. The 1986 version ends as Ruth returns to her childhood home to scatter the mingled ashes of her dead family. Hope is now located in the end of the plague as she watches the last butterfly die in the rain that ends the drought and puts out the last fires, "Forever. Or awhile" (379). This ending places much greater stress on the irony of hoping, because the narrative ends on the eve of the war — the next cycle of the "plague" — rather than afterward with its survivors.

[11] Like the names of Ruth and Naomi, Noah's name has biblical connotations, and his house at the edge of the ocean, containing his fertile wife, eight children, and a dog, is a type of ark. The reference to Noah and the ark strengthens the image of survival and the life principle associated with the Trelfords. As a preserver of the imagination, this Noah contrasts Findley's later character Noah Noyes in *Not Wanted on the Voyage*.

WORKS CITED

Bailey, Anne Geddes. *Timothy Findley and the Aesthetics of Fascism: Intertextual Collaboration and Resistance.* Vancouver: Talonbooks, forthcoming 1998.

Benjamin, Walter. *The Origin of German Tragic Drama.* Trans. John Osborne. 1928. London: NLB, 1977.

Butler, Judith. "Imitation and Gender Insubordination." *Inside/Out: Lesbian Theories, Gay Theories.* Ed. Diana Fuss. New York: Routledge, 1991. 13–31.

Findley, Timothy. *The Butterfly Plague*. 1969. Markham, ON: Penguin, 1986.

——. "Timothy Findley." Interview with Graeme Gibson. *Eleven Canadian Novelists*. Toronto: Anansi, 1973. 115–49.

——. "Timothy Findley: Make Peace with Nature, Now." Interview with Donald Cameron. *Conversations with Canadian Novelists*. Toronto: Macmillan, 1973. 49–63.

——. "Timothy Findley: The Marvel of Reality." Interview with Bruce Meyer and Brian O'Riordan. *In Their Words: Interviews with Fourteen Canadian Writers*. Toronto: Anansi, 1984. 45–54.

Fletcher, Angus. *Allegory: The Theory of a Symbolic Mode*. Ithaca: Cornell UP, 1964.

Foucault, Michel. *Discipline and Punish: The Birth of the Prison*. Trans. Alan Sheridan. 1975. New York: Vintage, 1979.

——. "Nietzsche, Genealogy, History." *The Foucault Reader*. Ed. Paul Rabinow. New York: Pantheon, 1984. 76–100.

Gabriel, Barbara. "Performing the *Bent* Text: Fascism and the Regulation of Sexualities in Timothy Findley's *The Butterfly Plague*." *English Studies in Canada* 21 (1995): 227–50.

"Hemophilia." *Encyclopaedia Britannica: Micropaedia*. 15th ed. 1992.

Ingham, David. "Bashing the Fascists: The Moral Dimensions of Findley's Fiction." *Studies in Canadian Literature* 15.2 (1990): 33–54.

McNay, Lois. *Foucault and Feminism: Power, Gender and the Self*. London: Polity, 1992.

Pennee, Donna Palmateer. *Moral Metafiction: Counterdiscourse in the Novels of Timothy Findley*. Toronto: ECW, 1991.

Plant, Richard. *The Pink Triangle: The Nazi War against Homosexuals*. New York: Holt, 1986.

Quilligan, Maureen. *The Language of Allegory: Defining the Genre*. Ithaca: Cornell UP, 1979.

Reich, Wilhelm. *The Mass Psychology of Fascism*. Trans. Vincent R. Carfagno. 1933. New York: Touchstone, 1970.

Shirer, William. *The Rise and Fall of the Third Reich*. New York: Crest, 1964.

Silverman, Kaja. *The Subject of Semiotics*. New York: Oxford, 1983.

Simmon, Scott. *The Films of D.W. Griffith*. Cambridge: Cambridge UP, 1993.

Snyder, Louis L., ed. *Hitler's Third Reich: A Documentary History*. Chicago: Nelson-Hall, 1981.

Söderlind, Sylvia. *Margin/Alias: Language and Colonization in Canadian and Québécois Fiction*. Toronto: U of Toronto P, 1991.

Sontag, Susan. "Fascinating Fascism." *Under the Sign of Saturn*. 1980. New York: Anchor, 1991.

Theweleit, Klaus. *Women, Floods, Bodies, History*. Trans. Stephen Conway. 1977. Minneapolis: U of Minnesota P, 1987. Vol. 1 of *Male Fantasies*. 2 vols.

York, Lorraine M. *Front Lines: The Fiction of Timothy Findley*. Toronto: ECW, 1991.

——. " 'A White Hand Hovering over the Page': Timothy Findley and the Racialized/Ethnicized Other." *Paying Attention: Critical Essays on Timothy Findley*. Ed. Anne Geddes Bailey and Karen Grandy. Toronto: ECW, 1998. 201–20. Also published in the *Timothy Findley Issue*. Ed Bailey and Grandy. Spec. issue of *Essays on Canadian Writing* 64 (1998): 201–20.

"Running Wilde":
National Ambivalence
and Sexual Dissidence in
Not Wanted on the Voyage

PETER DICKINSON

Wilde proceeded to the Queen's Hotel for dinner, escorted by
Boyle and several other gentlemen. Little ragamuffins chased
his carriage down Yonge Street shouting, "Oscar, Oscar is
running Wilde." Wilde loved it. In Toronto he had the busiest
itinerary in Canada, and he fulfilled his social obligations with
vigour and unswerving graciousness. No one could accuse him
of laziness.
— Kevin O'Brien (97)

... I think, too, constantly of Oscar Wilde, who came here [to
Dieppe] after being released from gaol — and the Mayor
refused to let him stay because — *you will drive away all the
English tourists, Mister Wilde!*
— Timothy Findley, *Inside Memory* (207)

THIS ESSAY draws on recent discussions of nationalism and sexuality
by postcolonial and queer theorists to argue that Timothy Findley's
1986 novel *Not Wanted on the Voyage* occupies a chiasmatic space
within contemporary Canadian literature (and, indeed, within his
fictional oeuvre), rewriting the biblical flood myth as a narrative of
both national ambivalence and sexual dissidence. Adapting Homi
Bhabha's concept of the "iterative temporality" of the nation-space
and Jonathan Dollimore's notion of the "transgressive agency" of
sexual perversion, I attempt to develop an approach to (national)
ambivalence and (sexual) dissidence that takes into account not
only how the terms operate diacritically inside Findley's text but also
how they are experienced dialectically across a broad spectrum of
intertextual contingencies (the chance operations of language and
narrative) and extratextual exigencies (the historical and political
specificities of writing and reading). Posing the problem of ambivalence and dissidence in this way, to adapt Kobena Mercer, "not

only underlines the role of the reader, but also draws attention to the important, and equally undecidable, role of context in determining the range of different readings that can be produced from the same text" (170). Like Mercer, in his (re)reading of Robert Mapplethorpe via Jean Genet, I have thus chosen to situate my highly ambivalent (and increasingly dissident) reading of *Not Wanted on the Voyage* within a larger historical context, a supplementary "temporality of representation," to use a phrase from Bhabha ("DissemiNation" 293), embodied by the life and work of Oscar Wilde.

* * *

"[I]t is the mark of the ambivalence of the nation as narrative strategy," writes Bhabha in "DissemiNation: Time, Narrative, and the Margins of the Modern Nation," "that it produces a continual slippage into analogous, even metonymic, categories, like the people, minorities, or 'cultural difference' that continually overlap in the act of writing the nation" (292). Picking up where he left off in important essays such as "Of Mimicry and Man: The Ambivalence of Colonial Discourse" and "Signs Taken for Wonders: Questions of Ambivalence and Authority under a Tree outside Delhi, May 1817," Bhabha here applies the notion of ambivalence, which he had previously invoked to describe the colonial discourse of mimicry, to "the Janus-faced discourse of the nation" ("Introduction" 3). He uses the term, both linguistically and culturally, as a sign of doubleness, of indeterminacy, "a temporality of representation that moves between cultural formations and social processes without a 'centred' causal logic" ("DissemiNation" 293). Such an understanding of ambivalence, when applied to national narratives, forces a recognition that, despite the authority and conviction with which historians such as Benedict Anderson write of the origins of nationalism and the nation-state as the emblematic sign of cultural modernity, "the margins of the modern nation" — through the incorporation of new peoples, the generation of other meanings, and the formation of local sites of resistance in relation to the central body politic — have from the beginning been in the process of inscribing a much different national narrative, one whose temporal and spatial reconfiguration of boundaries is at once antinational, postnational, and transnational in dimension.

In "DissemiNation," Bhabha seeks to articulate a methodology for the writing of a national narrative that will accommodate the lived experiences of minority peoples, to theorize the basis for a hybridized, pluralistic politics of cultural difference. In so doing, he rejects the standard metaphoric temporality of representation — which erases difference in the horizontal movement of a "homogeneous empty time" — in favour of what he calls "a metonymic, iterative temporality" (306) — which allows for the nonsequential inscription of oppositional discourses and subjectivities within the often "ambivalent and chiasmatic intersections of time and place that constitute the problematic 'modern' experience of the western nation" (293). Bhabha, alluding to Anderson, labels this supplementary space of cultural signification "the meanwhile," a place "where cultural homogeneity and democratic anonymity make their claims on the national community," and where "there emerges a more instantaneous and subaltern voice of the people, a minority discourse that speaks betwixt and between times and places" (309).[1]

Bhabha's postcolonial concept of national ambivalence finds an interesting queer theory analogue, I would argue, in Dollimore's term "sexual dissidence." In attempting at least a partial answer to the question of "why in our time the negation of homosexuality has been in direct proportion to its symbolic centrality; its cultural marginality in direct proportion to its cultural significance; why, also, homosexuality is so strangely integral to the selfsame heterosexual cultures which obsessively denounce it" (28), Dollimore formulates a complex theory of "perverse dynamics" and "transgressive reinscriptions" whereby otherness is at once contained within and produced by its "proximate" relation to sameness (33). According to Dollimore, the "dissident dialectic" operating "betwixt and between" (to reinscribe Bhabha's phrase) dominant and subordinate cultures, groups, and identities — especially vis-à-vis desire — produces a series of "displacements which constitute certain repressive discriminations," but which also denote "certain instabilities and contradictions within dominant structures which exist by virtue of exactly what those structures contain and exclude" (33).

Needless to say, the "aesthetic of transgressive desire" performed throughout Wilde's oeuvre figures in Dollimore's eponymous book as a primary — if not *the* preeminent — example of sexual dissidence (11, passim). And as Eve Kosofsky Sedgwick has demonstrated in her analysis of *The Picture of Dorian Gray*, at least one key text by Wilde can also be read in terms of national ambivalence (see Sedgwick, *Epistemology* 171–76; and "Nationalisms" 241–43). Indeed, as she goes on to note, his "hyper-indicativeness as a figure of his age" made him uncannily susceptible (and responsive) to "mutual representations emerging national and sexual claims" ("Nationalisms" 243). Wilde's othered national identity (Irish) must have served as an index to — if not the precondition of — his sexual transgressions, especially because his literary apotheosis in Britain coincided with a public trial for "gross indecency." To put this another way, if the (always already) degenerate Irish Wilde could masquerade as English (in his comedies satirizing social manners no less than in his ventriloquized speech and deportment), then what was to prevent him from posing as a sodomite or, worse yet, a woman? This is precisely the scandal of Lucy's transvestism in *Not Wanted on the Voyage*. Lucy crosses not just sexual borderlines but also national ones, a point to which I shall return.

That Oscar Wilde remains for Timothy Findley an important literary-historical figure is clear from my second epigraph. Several critics have indicated that Wilde likewise occupies a privileged position within Findley's fictional universe. In a recent article on *The Last of the Crazy People*, for example, Barbara Gabriel has convincingly delineated "the Wildean traces" in Findley's first novel ("Staging" 188), demonstrating how the character of Gilbert Winslow in particular inhabits a stigmatized site of homosexual figuration and quasi-martyrdom. In her reading of *The Wars*, Lorraine York notes that Barbara d'Orsey's derision of her brother, Clive, and Jamie Villiers as "Oscar and Bosie" does not bode well for her relationship with the novel's Canadian protagonist, Robert Ross, "who shares the name of one of Wilde's closest and most constant lovers, one who stayed faithful to him throughout the trials" (*Frontlines* 39). What might not be so immediately apparent, however, is the connection between Wilde and *Not Wanted on the Voyage*. But if, as Gabriel has pointed out, *De Profundis* sits palimpsestically behind *The Last of the Crazy People*, and if, in *The Wars*, Juliet d'Orsey claims *The Picture of Dorian Gray* as one of her favourite novels (154–55), then it is, as I hope to illustrate by the end of this essay, *Salome* that provides the Wildean intertext for *Not Wanted on the Voyage*, in terms of both the play's textual status as an allegory of national ambivalence and the title character's contextual positioning within a camp genealogy of sexual dissidence.

*　*　*

As the prologue to Findley's fifth novel, *Not Wanted on the Voyage*, is set up typographically on the page, we first read the italicized quotation from chapter 7, verse 7, of the Book of Genesis:

128

And Noah went in, and his sons,
and his wife, and his sons' wives
with him into the ark, because
of the waters of the flood. . . . (3; ellipsis in original)

What follows is Findley's immediate deconstruction of this passage — "Everyone knows it wasn't like that" (3) — informing us that the traditional version of the biblical flood story will be radically rewritten and drawing our attention to his text as postmodern metafiction. Moreover, on the verso of this page, once again in italics, Findley (p)rewrites a portion of his text, reproducing the section in which Mrs. Noyes discovers the blazing funeral pyre that her husband has erected in their house prior to the ark's departure, a sacrifice that is nothing more than a senseless slaughter of defenceless animals, those deemed unworthy of boarding the ark (4, 123–24).[2]

It is this spatial and temporal disunity at the beginning of *Not Wanted on the Voyage*, located in the very act of writing (or rewriting) a new world/nation, and thus reminiscent of Bhabha's/Anderson's meanwhile, that points to the possibility of establishing a narrative of history (as opposed to a history of narrative) wherein cultural events can be recontextualized and reexamined both inside and outside the constraints of so-called marginality. Findley's use of such a narrative strategy points to his rejection of the mimetic tradition in literature, of the frequent "link between historicism and realism, between the plausibility of linear order and coherence in history and the immediate evidence of the real in Literature," which Bhabha sees as so characteristic of the representation of the colonial subject ("Representation" 95).

Not Wanted on the Voyage is, therefore, deliberately anachronistic and ahistorical, necessarily ambivalent with respect to iterative, or recursive, temporalities of representation (history may have a habit of repeating itself, to be sure, but never in the same way). Findley's awareness of history and fiction as contested markers of ideology makes it possible for him to reconfigure his social positioning — as a gay man, as a (post)national subject — in relation to critical moments in time and space (floods, wars, etc.), to reimagine *allegorically* the historical narratives of nations, for example, and the ways in which those narratives record minority experience. As such, *Not Wanted on the Voyage* reenters "the western episteme [not only] at one of its most fundamental points of origination" (Ashcroft, Griffiths, and Tiffin 104), that is, the *first* time the world ended, but also at a point in modern history known as the Holocaust, the *second time the world (almost) ended*. Diana Brydon is one prominent critic who argues convincingly for this kind of "post-Holocaust, post-colonial" allegorical reading of *Not Wanted on the Voyage*. According to Brydon, like *The Butterfly Plague* and *Famous Last Words* before it, "The novel may be read as a parable challenging the imperialist version of colonization as well as a warning against fascist eugenics and the impossible fascist quest for purity of any kind" ("Timothy Findley" 587).[3] Likewise, York claims that *Not Wanted on the Voyage* "is, in fact, every bit as much a retelling of the European Holocaust story as it is a nuclear-age revision of Biblical myth" (*Frontlines* 107).

Indeed, at the level of the text, the ark, with its seemingly endless depths of animals crowded together and starving in perpetual darkness, is easily equated with a concentration camp, Noah's blazing funeral pyre with Nazi ovens. Similarly, the barring of the fairies from the ark, and their consequent drowning, refigure allegorically the fate of many homosexuals during the Holocaust. Moreover, both Yaweh ("he-way") and Dr. Noyes ("no/yes"), with their categorical edicts and double-talk, serve as excellent studies in demagoguery. The former's references to "corruption," "contamination," and "monstrous perversions" in his impassioned speech on the "Great Experiment" (soon to turn into a kind of "Final Solution") when he first arrives at the Noyeses' house (89) echo similar anti-Semitic and homophobic pronouncements made by Nazi propagandists in the name of racial and sexual (i.e., national) purity.[4] In this regard, Noah's status as a putative member of the medical profession, along with his frequent "experiments" on Mottyl's kittens and his savage murder of the physically deformed Lotte-children, perhaps does more to establish him as a kind of Dr. Mengele figure. At any rate, his presence at the helm of the ark does not bode well for Lucy, who claims that she joined the human race "In order to survive the holocaust in heaven. In order to prevent the holocaust on earth" (110).

But if, at one level, Brydon sees Findley's rewriting of Genesis in *Not Wanted on the Voyage* functioning as an allegory of the cultural genocide enacted by Nazi Germany during World War II, at another level she interprets the text as a kind of *national* allegory, a postmodern fable — to transpose the title of one of her articles — about "inventing Canadian beginnings," a "dream of tory origins." Reading *Not Wanted on the Voyage* against the grain of George Grant's 1965

Lament for a Nation: The Defeat of Canadian Nationalism, Brydon
argues that

> Findley doesn't simply turn Biblical narrative on its head; he
> advocates change as a return to lost origins. . . . To what extent
> this technique works as a strategic claiming of formerly con-
> ceded ground and to what extent it undermines itself by
> excessive lamentation for what has been lost is an open
> question. ("Dream" 40)

The status of allegory as a contested narrative structure within
national literatures of the postcolonial diaspora (see JanMohamed)
took on added significance in academic circles when Fredric Jameson
boldly asserted in the pages of *Social Text* that "all third-world texts
are necessarily . . . allegorical, and in a very specific way: they are to
be read as what I will call *national allegories*" ("Third-World" 69).
Such a sweeping generalization necessarily raised the ire of several
prominent critics. Not only is Jameson's theory of textual production
"grounded in a binary opposition between a first and a third world,"
according to Aijaz Ahmad (5), but it also valorizes nationalism as
"the necessary, exclusively desirable ideology" (6). Likewise, Stephen
Slemon prefers to shift Jameson's "modality of critical access away
from the determining structure of the first-world/third-world binary
into the problematics of what might more accurately be called the
conditions of post-coloniality" (9–10), a move that also allows for
the identification of an "interventionary, anti-colonialist" allegorical
impulse within "those colonising/settler societies such as anglophone
Canada or white Australia and New Zealand" (11).

I recognize that the critical caveats made by Ahmad and Slemon
are integral to any reading of Findley's "second-world" text as
allegorical. But, like Sara Suleri in her analysis of the "necessary
misreadings" of Jameson and Ahmad, I am unwilling to dispense
completely with "the situatedness of nationalism in the colonial
encounter" (14). Echoing Bhabha's comments on national narratives,
Suleri calls for a "provisional" "collapsing of the idea of nation into
the structure of allegory" and a "reading of the narratives at hand
for their revision of the more precarious question of the complicities
of memory *between* a colonial and a postcolonial world" (14;
emphasis added). Add to this Christopher Lane's more recent assertion that, in the case of British colonialism at the turn of the century
at any rate, it was often homosexuality that performed the "figurative
and allegorical work" of the nation (7), dramatically "transforming"

and "encoding" British subjectivity (8), and we begin to see how coimplicated and cross-identified are these basic social formations and cultural rhetorics.

A provisional reading of the postcolonial/national allegories in *Not Wanted on the Voyage* reveals them to be profoundly ambivalent. Writing between two worlds, Findley is attuned to the one-step-forward-two-steps-backward march of time (in this regard, Lucy, herself caught between two worlds [heaven and Earth] can be seen as incarnating Benjamin's "Angel of History") and to what Bhabha, following from Ernest Renan, has called the nation's "syntax" of remembering and forgetting, or "forgetting to remember" ("Dissemi-Nation" 311; see also Anderson 204–06; and Renan). As Bhabha writes, "It is this forgetting — a minus in the origin — that constitutes the *beginning* of the nation's narrative" ("DissemiNation" 310). Yet Findley is conscious of another temporality of representation shaping his story. That is, he recognizes that a national narrative, in essence a "new world" narrative, "cannot be written evangelically" (Anderson 205); it cannot exist a priori, like the Bible. Rather, it can only be endlessly rewritten, making visible in the process all the discontinuities and cultural differences that compose it. As Brydon remarks, "Findley shows the narrative of origins as the site of a power struggle. He redefines Noah's new order, not as a divinely sanctioned origin for a new world but as a strategically grasped beginning" ("Dream" 39).

Unlike Grant, then, Findley does not "lament" what has been lost in this power struggle; however, neither does he speculate overly long on what might have been gained. Indeed, just as Marlene Goldman, in her contribution to this volume, notes "the absence of the topos of the New Jerusalem" (37) in *Headhunter*, an equally apocalyptic novel, so, I would argue, does Findley subvert in *Not Wanted on the Voyage* the notion of creating a new world in any way different from the old world by removing the central topos necessary for any utopian representation of cultural alterity, namely Mount Ararat, the symbol that Northrop Frye identifies as the new world type to the old world antitype figured in Mount Parnassus.[5] To the extent that postdiluvial diasporas and post-Holocaust nationalisms function in Findley's text as potential allegories for the processes of colonization and decolonization, their effect, as with most allegories, is thus principally rhetorical, identifying narrative closure or end time as something to be *resisted* rather than *consecrated*. With his temporally disjunctive rewriting of the traditional Genesis story, Findley offers an ironic postcolonial, postnational twist to an old myth — re-creation as simulacrum — at the same time as he exposes the potential beginnings of a new one — difference as sameness (e.g., as encapsulated in the national metaphors of Canadian pluralism and multiculturalism).

But if, to adapt Slemon, *Not Wanted on the Voyage* "inhabit[s] the site of allegorical figuration" in order to subvert "the social 'text' of [nationalism]" (11), then this process also involves a reclamation of certain disavowed subtexts of sexuality. And, again to adapt Slemon, "the ways in which [Findley's text] performs this counter-discursive activity are inherently differential and diverse" (11). By locating the novel's moral consciousness in Noah's long-suffering wife, Mrs. Noyes, and her blind female cat, Mottyl, Findley offers us an alternatively gendered worldview to the dominant patriarchal discourse espoused by Yaweh and Noah. Moreover, at the level of individual speech acts, or utterances, Findley imbues these characters with dissident/dissonant modes of discourse (Mrs. Noyes's semiotic communication with the fairies, Mottyl's whispers), private vernaculars that are positioned in defiant opposition to the hegemony of Noah's oracular pronouncements. However, it is the "dissident vernacular"[6] disseminated by the cross-dressing angel, Lucy, that provides the most serious challenge to Noah's authority. And it is my contention that this particular counterdiscourse is articulated in Findley's text through camp stylistics.

In her recent article on *The Butterfly Plague*, Barbara Gabriel argues that, "Though an over-determined *allegory of a plague of dreams of perfection* governs the narrative strands of the novel dealing with both Hollywood and Nazi Germany, transgressive meanings around gender and sexuality repeatedly break up this frame, providing a textual underground of *dissident meanings*" ("Performing" 228–29; emphasis added). According to Gabriel, "The most pervasive of these [dissident meanings] operates in the performative register of camp, providing a subversive reading of the dominant narrative cinema of Hollywood that operates within the codes and conventions of gay spectatorship" (229). So too with *Not Wanted on the Voyage*, I would argue. In his sexually dissident rereading of the biblical flood myth, Findley uses camp simultaneously to operate and destabilize his (post)national allegory of origins. Through this supplementary temporality of representation, he is able to record a minority (counter)discourse, or vernacular, inscribed "betwixt and between" the unwritten and the endlessly rewritten spaces of cultural difference.[7]

Camp, for many decades regarded, along with drag, as one of the worst identificatory manifestations of internally homophobic and misogynistic gay men, has been repoliticized by contemporary queer criticism.[8] To this end, Carole-Anne Tyler has noted in a recent article that not only "femininity" but even "macho masculinity" is starting to come under the purview of camp and, as such, of the potentially subversive (33). Tyler cautions that it is important to read camp as an interpretative discourse that participates in the production of meaning and, therefore, "the re-production of subjectivity," con-textually and "symptomatically" (33): "In whose eyes is what chic radical? This is the difficult question theorists need to ask themselves when considering the function of camp, which is not . . . the same thing to everybody" (33–34). Echoing Bhabha on colonial mimicry, Tyler concludes that "Camp (like mimicry) functions complexly by dragging in many differences articulated with phallic narcissism in a symbolic which is really a white, bourgeois, and masculine fetishistic imaginary" (62).

Dollimore, who likewise associates the (counter)discourse with mimicry, prefers to drag camp's differences out, situating them "in relation to other strategies of survival and subversion, especially the masquerade of femininity, and the mimicry of the colonial subject" (312). In so doing, he emphasizes not only camp's inherent dissidence but also its peculiar ambivalence:

> What it [camp] might be found to share with the first [mas-querade] is a simultaneous avoidance and acting out of the *ambivalence* which constitutes subordination, and a pushing of that *ambivalence* to the point of transgressive insight and possibly reinscribed escape. As for the colonial context, Homi Bhabha argues that here mimicry is both a strategy of colonial subjection — an appropriation, regulation, and reform of the other — and, potentially, a way of menacing colonial discourse in and through an inappropriate imitation by the native, one which reveals the normative structure of colonial control. (312–13; emphasis added)

Dollimore's invocation of the concept of "strategy" here is, I believe, important and is consistent with a number of other recent queer reevaluations of the discourse (see Bergman, "Strategic Camp"; and Denisoff). In examining how camp functions in Findley's text, I likewise want to make a distinction between camp as parodic, imitative excess and camp as a kind of tactically deployed, politically resistant self-styling. Like Dollimore, I see the former definition of camp as corresponding with psychoanalytic theories of masquerade and with Bhabha's notion of colonial mimicry, both of which are enacted through an appropriation of the symbolic imaginary of the other.[9] By contrast, I am suggesting that camp, when conceived of as resistant self-styling, functions analogously not only with Foucault's discussion of sexual aesthetics/ascetics/ethics in the later volumes of *The History of Sexuality*, but also with postcolonial theories of national hybridity, practices, or "technologies," of self-discipline and self-invention both actualized and resisted through the body.[10]

To the extent that bodies are also texts, camp thus legitimates not simply a way of *being* in the world but also a way of *reading* the world, one that admits the aesthete, the sexual nonconformist, the decadent liar "into [its] charmed circle," one that deems truth "entirely and absolutely a matter of style" (Wilde 301, 305). For Sedgwick, camp, when viewed as a kind of hermeneutics of reader response, "involve[s] a gayer and more spacious angle of view": "the sensibility of camp-*recognition* always sees that it is dealing in reader relations and in projective fantasy (projective though not infrequently true) about the spaces and practices of cultural production" (*Epis temology* 156).

In such a realm of projective fantasy, at least as it is constructed in Findley's text, it thus becomes possible to recognize a camp sensibility not only within Lucy but also within her/his seeming antithesis, Japeth. Indeed, it appears that Japeth and Lucy — in their respective self-stylings as hypermasculine and hyperfeminine — occupy opposite poles on the camp continuum. According to Martin Humphries, "exaggeratedly masculine men are 'camp,'" if for no other reason than that "The shift to machismo has redirected our attention to ourselves as objects of desire and this results in a radical reversal of the self-image of many gay men" (79, 72).

It is just such a radical reversal of self-image that Japeth — the "sexual ignoramus and a virgin to boot," the person who "did not even know what 'perverted' meant" (77) — is looking for at the beginning of *Not Wanted on the Voyage*:

About two weeks ago — driven to distraction by Emma's refusal to sleep with him and by his own inability to force the issue — Japeth had taken off along the road, heading for the Cities. His leaving was not unlike the stories told in fairy

tales of lads who, unhappy at home, set off to conquer the great
world as dragon slayers and giant killers. Japeth's quest was to
find his manhood once and for all — and, returning, to slay
the dragon of Emma's virginity and kill the giant of his shame.
    But things had not worked out that way. Japeth had crept
home, naked and blue and almost silent. (23)

Implicit in Japeth's encounter with the Ruffian King on the road to
Baal and Mammon (read: Sodom and Gomorrah) is an allegory (or
fairy tale) of homosexual — and, what's more, sadomasochistic —
awakening and denial: "Even so — in spite of having made the
necessary reconciliation between the horror he could not imagine and
the horror he had known — he was still unable to confront the central
event without feeling ill" (79). Moreover, Japeth's resultant discolour-
ing works counterdiscursively to turn this scene into a specific
instance of camp recognition, for Japeth, as "Blue Boy," not only
evokes recollections of Thomas Gainsborough's "femmey" 1770
painting but also alludes to one of the oldest magazines of gay male
pornography, which goes by the same name and which is renowned
for its pictorials of "innocent" boys.[11] York, in her contribution to
this volume, astutely reminds us that "this bizarre episode also
burlesques colour-associated racial labelling" ("White Hand" 210),
rendering Japeth not only sexually but also racially other.
    Japeth's anxiety about his masculinity translates into an extreme
fascination with that of another dragon slayer in the text, Michael
Archangelis, who is camped by Findley as a specific gay fantasy type:
"Japeth had his mind on Michael Archangelis — a figure of glory
unlike any he had ever dreamed could exist. The great angel's height
— his strength — his golden hair — and his armour presented the
most dazzling images of manhood that Japeth had ever encountered"
(75). Of course, these descriptions of homosocial desire at the outset
of *Not Wanted on the Voyage* are part of a larger discursive continuum that includes a specific instance of homosexual panic toward
the end of the text: in cutting off the Unicorn's horn (the instrument
used by Noah to rape Emma), Japeth is able to displace symbolically
the "castration" enacted upon him by the Ruffian King and thereby
reaffirm his masculinity and virility.
    Yet, whereas Japeth sees a great warrior worthy of emulation in
the "Supreme Commander of All the Angels" (86), Lucy sees her
brother as nothing more than "a bore" (108). Notwithstanding the
fact that angels have long been associated with a particular homo-

sexual iconography (from Caravaggio to Kushner), the confrontation between Michael, the "golden boy," and Lucy, the "rogue" whose "star has fallen" (108), reads like pure camp spectacle, a "*Wonderful* scene" as Lucy describes it to her brother, whom she refers to as "ducky" (106):

> "What do you hope to accomplish by all this?" Michael asked.
> "All what?" Lucy shook out her frail skirts and lifted her hand to her hair.
> "Well — dressing as a woman to begin with. *And* a foreigner."
> "Nothing wrong with dressing as a woman. Might as well be a woman as anything else. And what, may one ask, do you mean by 'a foreigner'?"
> "Someone not of these parts," said Michael, as if he was quoting from a book of rules for border guards.
> "The slanted eyes, et cetera? The black, black hair — the white, white face? You don't like it? I *love*." (107)

Although it is possible to identify in this passage several stylistic or syntactical elements of what we might call a particular camp rhetoric — the exaggerated emphasis of certain words ("*Wonderful* scene," "I *love*"), the linguistic repetition ("black, black hair," "white, white face"), the use of epicene epithets and pronouns ("ducky," "may one ask?") — what I find most significant here is that Michael (the "border guard") sees Lucy as transvesting not just across genders ("dressing as a woman to begin with") but also across cultures ("*And* a foreigner").

According to Marjorie Garber, "a transvestite figure in a text . . . indicates a *category crisis* elsewhere, an irresolvable conflict or epistemological crux that destabilizes comfortable binarity" (17). Garber defines "category crisis" as "a failure of definitional distinction, a *borderline* that becomes permeable, that permits of *border crossings* from one (apparently distinct) category to another: black/white, Jew/Christian, noble/bourgeois, master/servant, master/slave" (16; emphasis added).[12] In the case of Findley, we might add to this list of crisscrossed categories human/angel as well as Occidental/Oriental. Indeed, Findley's deliberate orientalizing of the transvestite figure in his text — his use of makeup, costume, gesture, symbol, and stylization traditionally associated (at least in the minds of Western readers) with Chinese opera and Japanese kabuki theatre — adds another element of national ambivalence to Lucy's already evident sexual dissidence.[13] As in David Henry Hwang's M. *Butterfly*, "crises of nationalism and sexuality [are] troped on the transvestite figure" (Garber 239). Hwang's similar deployment of a "transvestite figure borrowed from *both* Chinese and Japanese stage traditions," according to Garber, "functions simultaneously as a mark of gender undecidability and as an indication of category crisis"; as she goes on to point out, in M. *Butterfly* Hwang seems to be preoccupied "with the transvestite as a figure not only for the conundrum of gender and erotic style, but also for other kinds of border-crossing, like *acting* and *spying*, both of which are appropriations of alternative and socially constructed subject positions for cultural and political ends" (238–39).

Of course, the "gay-affirming and gay-occluding orientalism" — to borrow a phrase from Sedgwick ("Nationalisms" 242) — inherent in Findley's depiction of Lucy's "foreignness" also returns us intertextually to Wilde's protofeminist reinscription of another biblical story in *Salome*, not to mention the Japonesque drawings by Aubrey Beardsley that accompanied the original 1894 English translation of the play. Garber reads the Dance of the Seven Veils at the centre of the Salome myth, and Wilde's play, as "a transvestite dance," another instance of "border-crossing" (342). As she puts it, "gender undecidability," rather than mere exoticized sensuality, "is the taboo against which Occidental eyes are veiled. The cultural Imaginary of the Salome story is the veiled phallus and the masquerade" (342). (So too, I would argue, with Lucy's last-minute stand-in as Eve in Noah's production of "The Masque of Creation": "Lucy . . . made her appearance — clothed in a long, transparent gown and wearing a crown of golden hair that fell to the ground all around her, gracefully hiding every bit of sexual evidence" [*Not Wanted* 98].) However, in noting that Wilde, an Irishman, originally wrote his play in French — responding in part to earlier versions by Huysmans and Flaubert — Garber points out that "the veils drawn aside have been national as well" (342).

Garber supplements her reading of *Salome* by alluding to "an amusing and disconcerting photograph" (343) contained in Richard Ellmann's biography of Wilde, a photograph that Ellmann identifies with the cutline "Wilde in costume as Salome" (428). Having no apparent reason to dispute Ellmann's assertion, Garber ruminates on what she assumes to be the "transvestite masquerade" operating in the photograph, offering a final catalogue of Wildean personae:

138

"Wilde the author, Wilde the libertine, Wilde the homosexual, as Salome" (343). In fact, recent archival evidence suggests that the Salome depicted in the photo is *not* Wilde but a real woman, "an opera singer named Alice Guszalewicz" (Macdonald).[14] Not that this evidence at all changes the category crisis implicit in the image. The iconographic readings of Ellmann and Garber among others have so shifted the focus of our gaze — at least with respect to Wilde in this context — that it is now possible to read this Salome only as a kind of Victor/Victoria, that is, as a woman masquerading as a man masquerading as a woman — a form of gender undecidability and cultural espionage with which the border-crossing Wilde and his successors — among them Findley and Hwang — would undoubtedly approve.

Of course, as Lucy well knows, and as Mrs. Noyes and Hannah intuit, dominant culture will continue to see only what it wants to see, to interpret only what it wants to interpret: a volcanic ash storm in the middle of August it will call a "blizzard" (*Not Wanted* 21); friendly dolphins marauding "pirates" (235); a paper rainbow a "symbol of the Covenant" (351); "Lotte-like-children" a shameful "secret" (160); and "[a] seven-foot woman" "dressed for a foreign court" a "rogue," a spy, a freak (60). Which is why the semiology of camp, troping as it does on the arbitrary divisions between inside and outside, surface and depth, artifice and reality is such an effective counterdiscursive strategy. And which is why it is Lucy, with her ambiguous sexuality, her hybrid human-angel status, and her camp vernacular, who most obviously disrupts the familiar binary oppositions of this world (male versus female, human versus animal, upper orders versus lower orders, old world versus new world) and who launches the most formidable challenge against Noah's "apparently axiomatic significatory system which has *invested* itself with absolute authority over those it has constructed as 'Other'" (Ashcroft, Griffiths, and Tiffin 103; emphasis added). For it is Lucy whose magic is as powerful as Noah's, who leads the rebellion of the lower orders, who befriends the demons and the bees and brings them topside, and who, after removing her white face makeup (a sign in Japanese theatre, according to Garber, "of the ideal white complexion of the noble, who can afford to keep out of the sun" [243]), wig, and kimono toward the end of the novel, starts a "rumour" of "another world," where "darkness and light are reconciled." "I don't know when it will present itself," she tells those assembled around her on the deck, her face streaked with running mascara and rain, "I don't know where it will be. But — as with all those other worlds now past — when it is ready, I intend to go there" (284).

The irony is that, within the aporetic space of Findley's text, Lucy's rumour remains just that and thus, as mere gossip or speculation, a further example of camp vernacular. For, to reconfigure once again Slemon's phrase, *Not Wanted on the Voyage* "inhabit[s] the site of allegorical figuration" in order to articulate the relation between the unrepresented and the unrepresentable, between dominant discourse and the marginalized subjects inscribed with/in it. As such, Mrs. Noyes seems to offer the only possible answer to Lucy's que(e)ry about "another world." In "pray[ing] for rain" (352), she is enunciating (from a minority position) both an act of resistance and a gesture of despair.

Findley's revisioning of the biblical flood myth, like Wilde's retelling of the Salome myth, is thus decidedly antimythic. Indeed, both writers — as ambivalent national allegorists *and* dissident gay genealogists — seem to suggest that myth (national, sexual, or otherwise) can only be exposed as myth, as a process that all too easily allows dominant culture to forget to remember (and to remember to forget), when it becomes culturally removed, defamiliarized, alienated. In other words, myth itself must be demythologized, its discursive scaffolding assailed, and its cultural baggage unpacked through still more creative ways of knowing and fantastical modes of storytelling. In *Not Wanted on the Voyage* (more so than in any of his other novels, I would argue), by positioning himself and his story aslant of history rather than directly parallel to it, at an angle to the dominant narratives of nationalism and sexuality recorded therein (a "gayer and more spacious angle," to be sure) — that is, by writing neither at the end of one world nor at the beginning of another but in the projective fantasy of spectacle and camp recognition — Findley effectively employs just such a Wildean methodology.

ACKNOWLEDGEMENT

This essay is excerpted and adapted from a chapter in my book *Here Is Queer: Nationalisms, Sexualities, and the Literatures of Canada*, forthcoming in 1999 from University of Toronto Press.

NOTES

[1] Anderson uses the term "meanwhile" to describe the "simultaneity" of the process of nationalism, a "transverse, cross-time, marked not by prefiguring and fulfilment, but by temporal coincidence, and measured by

clock and calendar" (24). Anderson in turn bases his assertions on Walter Benjamin's notion of "Messianic time," as outlined in his "Theses on the Philosophy of History." According to Bhabha, however, "In embedding the *meanwhile* of the national narrative, where the people live their plural and autonomous lives within homogeneous empty time, Anderson misses the alienating and iterative time of the sign" and thus "fails to read that profound ambivalence that Benjamin places deep within the utterance of the narrative of modernity" ("DissemiNation" 309, 311).

2 Findley employs a similar narrative technique in *The Wars* (see 9–10, 181–83).

3 Cf. Barbara Gabriel on *The Butterfly Plague*: "If the eugenics discourses of *The Butterfly Plague* have been either marginalized or elided altogether in readings of the novel, that is partly due to Findley's own straining for allegory in a fiction in which the unrepresentable of the Holocaust confronts the historical subject who is *already* outside of the frame of representation" ("Performing" 243).

4 George Mosse's *Nationalism and Sexuality: Middle Class Morality and Sexual Norms in Modern Europe* is particularly illuminating on this subject (see, especially, 153–80).

5 See, especially, 31–52 for Frye's discussion of how classical myth functions in relation to the Bible. It is interesting to note the extent to which the symbol of Mount Ararat (or a derivation thereof, most often in the form of a tower or ziggurat) figures in modern Canadian poetry. See, for example, Lee; Page; Scott; and Webb. The last three lines of Webb's poem "Leaning" serve as the epigraph to *Not Wanted on the Voyage*.

6 The term, although it nicely recalls Dollimore, is actually Cindy Patton's. In *Inventing AIDS*, Patton uses "[t]he idea of dissident vernaculars" to suggest "that meanings created by and in communities are upsetting to the dominant culture precisely because speaking in one's own fashion is a means of resistance, a strengthening of the subculture that has created the new meaning" (148 n12). On how (homo)sexual vernaculars resist the seductive rhetoric of endtime implicit in oracular pronouncements on AIDS, see Dickinson. On the moral dimensions of counterdiscourse in Findley's meta-fictions, see Ingham; and Pennee.

7 In a recent article on *Not Wanted on the Voyage*, Cecilia Martell has demonstrated how, "Through a radical infusion of 'Camp' elements, Findley not only ironizes social practices, but also criticizes the kinds of binary ideologies that function as filters for exclusivity and inclusion on various coded levels of a social text — and readers unwilling or unable to move beyond the parameters of the 'norms' that construct their readings are forcibly excluded from having access to the encoded criticisms inherent in Findley's text" (97). Although Martell and I are more or less in agreement in this regard, we differ markedly in our critical "unpacking" of the camped

codes at work in *Not Wanted on the Voyage*, in large part, I would argue, because of her overreliance on Susan Sontag "as a guide on [her] voyage" through the text (103). For example, Martell notes in passing how *Not Wanted on the Voyage* "pays tribute to the influences of . . . Oscar Wilde" (110 n1), but she fails to explicate in any concrete manner where these influences manifest themselves in the text. See my discussion of *Salome* below.

[8] See, for example, Bergman, ed.; and Meyer. Of course, contemporary discussions of camp owe much to two classic studies: Esther Newton's *Mother Camp: Female Impersonators in America* (1972) and Susan Sontag's "Notes on Camp" (1966). Although I take issue with Sontag's assertion that "Camp sensibility is disengaged, depoliticized" (277), and with her remarks on the "peculiar relation between Camp and homosexuality" (290), I am in general agreement with her definition of camp as "a certain mode of aestheticism," "*one* way of seeing the world," "not in terms of beauty, but in terms of artifice, of stylization" (277).

[9] The link between femininity and masquerade in psychoanalysis was first made by Joan Rivière in her 1929 essay "Womanliness as a Masquerade." More recently, lesbian-feminist theorists such as Sue Ellen Case (in "Toward a Butch-Femme Aesthetic") and Judith Butler (in *Gender Trouble: Feminism and the Subversion of Identity*) have used Rivière's essay to subvert traditional categories of identity, so that gender, for instance, is read ironically or parodically and is thus displaced into a series of performing signifiers. For his part, Bhabha claims that "colonial mimicry is the desire for a reformed, recognizable Other, *as a subject of a difference that is almost the same, but not quite. . . .* Mimicry is, thus, the sign of a double articulation; a complex strategy of reform, and discipline, which 'appropriates' the Other as it visualizes power" ("Of Mimicry" 126).

[10] In *The Use of Pleasure*, the second volume of *The History of Sexuality*, Foucault focuses on sexual practices in classical Greece as they are elaborated and "problematized" through technologies of the self, "bringing into play the criteria of an 'aesthetics of existence' " (12). Similarly, what Foucault calls "a history of 'ethics' and 'ascetics,' " encapsulated in the phrase "care of the self" (the title of the third volume of *The History of Sexuality*), is "concerned with the models proposed for setting up and developing relationships with the self, for self-reflection, self-knowledge, self-examination, for the decipherment of the self by oneself" (29).

[11] Blue as a signifier has further scopophilic and erotic associations: the gaze solicited and undermined by a "blue movie," for example, or the looks exchanged between model and viewer as the viewer flips through the artistically decadent pages of *L'Amour bleu*.

[12] For her part, Sontag claims that "Camp taste turns its back on the good-bad axis of ordinary aesthetic judgment. Camp doesn't reverse things.

It doesn't argue that the good is bad, or the bad is good. What it does is to offer for art (and life) a different — a supplementary — set of standards" (286).

[13] Gabriel has perceptively pointed out how Octavius Rivi's "coding as oriental ephebe" in *The Butterfly Plague* "anticipates the Lucy figure of Findley's *Not Wanted on the Voyage*, who is even more explicitly drawn as the *Onna gata* of the Japanese Kabuki theatre, that ideal stylization of the feminine, which is always performed by a man" ("Performing" 233).

[14] My thanks to Marni Stanley for drawing my attention to this article.

WORKS CITED

Ahmad, Aijaz. "Jameson's Rhetoric of Otherness and the 'National Allegory.'" *Social Text* 17 (1987): 3–25.

Anderson, Benedict. *Imagined Communities: Reflections on the Origin and Spread of Nationalism*. London: Verso, 1991.

Ashcroft, Bill, Gareth Griffiths, and Helen Tiffin. *The Empire Writes Back: Theory and Practice in Post-Colonial Literatures*. New Accents. London: Routledge, 1989.

Benjamin, Walter. "Theses on the Philosophy of History." *Illuminations: Essays and Reflections*. Ed. Hannah Arendt. Trans. Harry Zohn. New York: Schocken, 1968. 253–64.

Bergman, David, ed. *Camp Grounds: Style and Homosexuality*. Amherst: U of Massachusetts P, 1993.

——. "Strategic Camp: The Art of Gay Rhetoric." Bergman, ed. 92–109.

Bhabha, Homi. "DissemiNation: Time, Narrative, and the Margins of the Modern Nation." Bhabha, ed. 291–322.

——. "Introduction: Narrating the Nation." Bhabha, ed. 1–7.

——, ed. *Nation and Narration*. New York: Routledge, 1990.

——. "Of Mimicry and Man: The Ambivalence of Colonial Discourse." *October* 28 (1984): 125–33.

——. "Representation and the Colonial Text: A Critical Exploration of Some Forms of Mimeticism." *The Theory of Reading*. Ed. Frank Gloversmith. Brighton: Harvester, 1984. 93–122.

Brydon, Diana. "The Dream of Tory Origins: Inventing Canadian Beginnings." *Australian-Canadian Studies* 6.2 (1989): 35–46.

——. "Timothy Findley: A Post-Holocaust, Post-Colonial Vision." *International Literature in English: Essays on the Major Writers*. Ed. Robert L. Ross. New York: Garland, 1991. 583–92.

Butler, Judith. *Gender Trouble: Feminism and the Subversion of Identity*. New York: Routledge, 1990.

Case, Sue Ellen. "Toward a Butch-Femme Aesthetic." *Making a Spectacle: Feminist Essays on Contemporary Women's Theatre*. Ed. Lynda Hart. Ann Arbor: U of Michigan P, 1989. 282–99.

Denisoff, Dennis. "(Re)Dressing One's Self: Artifice and Identity Construction in John Glassco." Theorizing Fashion/Fashioning Theory Panel. ACCUTE Conference. U of Calgary, 6 June 1994.

Dickinson, Peter. " 'Go-Go Dancing on the Brink of the Apocalypse': Representing AIDS: An Essay in Seven Epigraphs." *Postmodern Apocalypse: Theory and Cultural Practice at the End.* Ed. Richard Dellamora. Philadelphia: U of Pennsylvania P, 1995. 219–40.

Dollimore, Jonathan. *Sexual Dissidence: Augustine to Wilde, Freud to Foucault.* Oxford: Clarendon, 1991.

Ellmann, Richard. *Oscar Wilde.* New York: Vintage, 1988.

Findley, Timothy. *Inside Memory: Pages from a Writer's Workbook.* Toronto: HarperCollins, 1990.

——. *Not Wanted on the Voyage.* Markham, ON: Penguin, 1984.

——. *The Wars.* Markham, ON: Penguin, 1978.

Foucault, Michel. *The Use of Pleasure.* Trans. Robert Hurley. New York: Pantheon, 1985. Vol. 2 of *The History of Sexuality.* 3 vols. 1978–86.

Frye, Northrop. *The Great Code: The Bible and Literature.* New York: Harcourt, 1982.

Gabriel, Barbara. "Performing the *Bent* Text: Fascism and the Regulation of Sexualities in Timothy Findley's *The Butterfly Plague." English Studies in Canada* 21 (1995): 227–50.

——. "Staging Monstrosity: Genre, Life-Writing, and Timothy Findley's *The Last of the Crazy People." The Gender Issue.* Ed. Gabriel and Lorraine M. York. Spec. issue of *Essays on Canadian Writing* 54 (1994): 168–97.

Garber, Marjorie. *Vested Interests: Cross-Dressing and Cultural Anxiety.* New York: Routledge, 1991.

Goldman, Marlene. "The End[s] of Myth: Apocalyptic and Prophetic Fictions in *Headhunter." Paying Attention: Critical Essays on Timothy Findley.* Ed. Anne Geddes Bailey and Karen Grandy. Toronto: ECW, 1998. 32–55. Also published in the *Timothy Findley Issue.* Ed Bailey and Grandy. Spec. issue of *Essays on Canadian Writing* 64 (1998): 32–55.

Humphries, Martin. "Gay Machismo." *The Sexuality of Men.* Ed. Andy Metcalf and Humphries. London: Pluto, 1985. 70–85.

Ingham, David. "Bashing the Fascists: The Moral Dimensions of Findley's Fiction." *Studies in Canadian Literature* 15.2 (1990): 33–54.

Jameson, Fredric. "Third-World Literature in the Era of Multinational Capital." *Social Text* 15 (1986): 65–88.

JanMohamed, Abdul R. "The Economy of Manichean Allegory: The Function of Racial Difference in Colonialist Literature." *Critical Inquiry* 12 (1985): 59–87.

Lane, Christopher. *The Ruling Passion: British Colonial Allegory and the Paradox of Homosexual Desire.* Durham: Duke UP, 1995.

Lee, Dennis. *Civil Elegies and Other Poems.* Toronto: Anansi, 1972.

Macdonald, Marianne. "Oscar's Grandson Recalls a Century of Pain." *Independent on Sunday* 12 Feb. 1995: 6.

Martell, Cecilia. "Unpacking the Baggage: 'Camp' Humour in Timothy Findley's *Not Wanted on the Voyage*." *Canadian Literature* 148 (1996): 96–111.

Mercer, Kobena. "Skin Head Sex Thing: Racial Difference and the Homoerotic Imaginary." *How Do I Look? Queer Film and Video*. Ed. Bad Object-Choices. Seattle: Bay, 1991. 169–222.

Meyer, Moe, ed. *The Politics and Poetics of Camp*. New York: Routledge, 1994.

Mosse, George. *Nationalism and Sexuality: Middle Class Morality and Sexual Norms in Modern Europe*. Madison: U of Wisconsin P, 1985.

Newton, Esther. *Mother Camp: Female Impersonators in America*. Chicago: U of Chicago P, 1972.

O'Brien, Kevin. *Oscar Wilde in Canada: An Apostle for the Arts*. Toronto: Personal Library, 1982.

Page, P.K. "Cry Ararat!" *Cry Ararat! Poems New and Selected*. Toronto: McClelland, 1967. 102–07.

Patton, Cindy. *Inventing AIDS*. New York: Routledge, 1990.

Pennee, Donna Palmateer. *Moral Metafiction: Counterdiscourse in the Novels of Timothy Findley*. Toronto: ECW, 1991.

Renan, Ernest. "Qu'est-ce qu'une nation?" *Oeuvres complètes*. Vol. 1 Paris: Calmann-Levy, 1947. 887–906. 10 vols.

Rivière, Joan. "Womanliness as a Masquerade." *International Journal of Psycho-Analysis* 10 (1929): 303–13.

Scott, F.R. "Lakeshore." *Selected Poems*. Toronto: Oxford UP, 1966. 12–13.

Sedgwick, Eve Kosofsky. *Epistemology of the Closet*. Berkeley: U of California P, 1990.

——. "Nationalisms and Sexualities in the Age of Wilde." *Nationalisms and Sexualities*. Ed. Andrew Parker et al. New York: Routledge, 1992. 235–45.

Slemon, Stephen. "Monuments of Empire: Allegory/Counter-Discourse/Post-Colonial Writing." *Kunapipi* 9.3 (1987): 1–16.

Sontag, Susan. "Notes on Camp." *Against Interpretation*. New York: Farrar, 1966. 275–92.

Suleri, Sara. *The Rhetoric of English India*. Chicago: U of Chicago P, 1992.

Tyler, Carole-Anne. "Boys Will Be Girls: The Politics of Gay Drag." *Inside/Out: Lesbian Theories, Gay Theories*. Ed. Diana Fuss. New York: Routledge, 1991. 32–70.

Webb, Phyllis. "Leaning." *Literary Half-Yearly* 24.2 (1983): 91–92.

Wilde, Oscar. "The Decay of Lying." *The Artist as Critic: Critical Writings of Oscar Wilde*. Ed. Richard Ellmann. Chicago: U of Chicago P, 1969. 290–320.

York, Lorraine M. *Frontlines: The Fiction of Timothy Findley.* Toronto: ECW, 1991.

———. " 'A White Hand Hovering over the Page': Timothy Findley and the Racialized/Ethnicized Other." *Paying Attention: Critical Essays on Timothy Findley.* Ed. Anne Geddes Bailey and Karen Grandy. Toronto: ECW, 1998. 201–20. Also published in the *Timothy Findley Issue.* Ed Bailey and Grandy. Spec. issue of *Essays on Canadian Writing* 64 (1998): 201–20.

PART III: PERFORMANCE

"The Repose of an Icon" in Timothy Findley's Theatre of Fascism: From "Alligator Shoes" to *Famous Last Words*

BARBARA GABRIEL

I had never seen a figure of such compelling menace. . . .
[D]ressed as he was in a teeming leather coat, hatless, no
umbrella, with rainy hair curled against a skull like Roman
marble, and a skin Italianate in colour . . . not quite six feet
tall, I should say. . . . Shiny shoes; glossy shoes; sensual shoes,
if such a thing exists — but appropriate, I suppose, for walking
in the mud.

> — Timothy Findley, *Famous Last Words*
> (120–21; second ellipsis in original)

It is the repose of an icon that interests me.

> — Timothy Findley, "Masks and Icons" (36)

WHEN MAUBERLEY FIRST ENCOUNTERS the sadistic Nazi Harry
Reinhardt at Allenby's funeral in *Famous Last Words*, he is obsessed
with a singular *detail* of his appearance: the alligator shoes that
register his simultaneous attraction and repulsion. In fact, his specular
gaze has fastened on one of the classic metonymic substitutions in
the lexicon of desire: the shoe as fetish object. Historically linked to
codes of the perverse, the fetish is always a stand-in for something
else, a partial object of longing whose reification is caught up in what
Walter Benjamin read early on as "the sexuality of things" (Apter 2).
Mauberley cannot take his eyes off Reinhardt's shoes in an intensity
of response that flagrantly displays the nature of his fatal attraction.
But what happens when the projected look is returned, as it is in the
mirror of Reinhardt's "alligator eyes" (121)? This is the moment
when desire turns into death, and it comes to Mauberley with all the
inevitability of Greek tragedy played backward, in a violent and
grotesque scene acted out high in the Tyrol. Its "messenger" is
Reinhardt himself, and it is delivered with an icepick to his eye that
recalls the blinding of Oedipus (361).

The novel's textual performance of the "detail" that inscribes Mauberley's desire belongs to a rhetoric of the fetish that spans key cultural discourses of our century.[1] Born in the magical properties ascribed to objects in "primitive" societies by European ethnographers, the economy of the fetish was a theme taken up by both Marx and Freud to describe structures of transvaluation. For Marx, a commodity fetishism replaced the loss of an earlier religious fetishism; for Freud, the fetish was the fraudulent stand-in for the phallus in a scene of castration simultaneously disavowed by and displaced onto woman. Mauberley's own secret drama is inseparable from the masochistic structure of desire that is also his moral undoing. But how integral could such a reading be to the historical moment of European Fascism? And how, in turn, might this "detail" be recovered as central to the novel that we have come to know as *Famous Last Words*?

The ironic title of *Famous Last Words* now seems entirely inseparable from the way in which we talk about the novel: as a narrative embedding of Mauberley's writing on the wall, a tale that unfolds in a Chinese box structure that refuses the transparency of the realist text. Words are stubborn things in this novel, which is staged as a hermeneutic struggle from the start, one summed up in the philosopher's paradox scratched out in a room in the Grand Elysium Hotel. "'All I have written here,' Quinn reads, 'is true; except the lies'" (59). The familiar themes and formal issues with which this fiction has been read have been inevitably coaxed into shape by the "rightness" of its title — one that has enabled its status as a model text for what Linda Hutcheon first called "historiographic metafiction."

For the most part, then, it is outside the framework of these epistemological lessons that readers have engaged other clusters of meaning: Mauberley as modernist aesthete, Mauberley as Fascist sympathizer, Mauberley as homosexual. Yet this splitting off of issues around meaning production and structure of desire covers darker and more radical insights in the novel, repeating the normalizing strategy effected by the curious history of its title. For, at the time of completion of his manuscript, Findley still called his novel "Alligator Shoes," foregrounding Mauberley's dialectic of disgust and desire for the "damned beauty" (360) of Reinhardt in the very structure of the fetish (see Findley, "Long Live" 79; and York 84).

To reframe the novel in terms of its earlier title is to recover a very different constellation of issues, one in which Findley's metonym for dangerous desire leads us straight to the heart of Susan Sontag's

"Fascinating Fascism." Yet Findley's interrogation of the erotic allure of the Fascist hero does not stop there. It opens up to a much wider analysis of the way in which power operates in the social field: mediated by iconic figures who focus cultural discourses and desires in discrete historical moments — and in ways that mimic the production of the Hollywood star. When read at this level, *Famous Last Words* fictionalizes the widespread interest in the postwar period in reading the Fascist moment on the world stage as a problematic of *power* and *consent*. As a totalitarian regime that elicited widespread popular support, National Socialism, like Italy under Mussolini, exposed the inadequacy of both liberal humanist and Marxist economist explanatory models to raise new questions about the subject and desire. Georges Bataille's notion that "the unity of Fascism lies in its actual psychological structure and not in the economic conditions that serve as its base" is exemplary here (157), as is the work of the Frankfurt School of Sociology in the immediate postwar period (see Benjamin, "Work"). Moreover, both National Socialism and Italian Fascism made conscious use of theatre and the new technologies of photography and film to mobilize mass support, reworking an existing semiotic field to produce new gendered meanings and power relations centred on a charismatic figure (see Macciochi).

In the outer narrative of *Famous Last Words*, Mauberley's last will and testament is read and debated by Quinn and Freyberg, the defendant and prosecuting attorney who become the reader's moral interlocuters in what is effectively a staged trial.[2] Figures of theatre and cinema are central markers of this debate, operating, on the face of it, within the second term of a fact/fiction antinomy that has been seen as central to the novel's metafictional status. Quinn's defence of Mauberley as an artist who hated Nazis is answered by Freyberg's insistence on the facticity of history:

> And the war never happened. And Hitler was just an actor with a moustache made up to look like Charlie Chaplin. . . . But I'd also like this movie to include the scenes at Dachau . . . so you could walk back through the gates and tell me nothing happened there. . . . Playtime. Movie time. (53–54)

What Freyberg's account leaves out is any attention to the *why* and *how* of history, to the way in which power relations are themselves inseparably bound up with productions of signs. Hitler studiously mimed the gestures of the silent cinema and proudly called himself "the greatest actor in Europe" (Lindholm 104). He was also an avid student of early-twentieth-century treatises on the crowd influenced by theories of mesmerism. The emphasis on the new medium of film as well as on theatrical spectacle and staging was critical to evoking mass enthusiasm in both Nazi Germany and Fascist Italy. Yet, for Findley, this Theatre of Fascism is, above all, a performative arena in which mass obedience and enthusiasm are elicited by iconic figures who echo Jean Genet's call for the actor as highly charged sign out of Greek tragedy. As *Famous Last Words* evolved, Findley gradually came to understand that

> This wasn't just the story of men and women — but *of men and women and the gods to whom they are obedient*; of the fates that rule their lives and of the fact that history is created through the enactment of symbolic gesture — and told best through the evocation of icons. So what I must do is transpose this story, which is history, into another key — which is mythology. (*Inside Memory* 191; emphasis added)

Findley's myth-history in *Famous Last Words* is an intensely theatrical space, a performance of the way in which power and obedience are elicited through a sign system that circulates through a desiring subject. There is no *outside* to this historical subject made in a symbolic order of language and culture. Even Mauberley's own oedipal drama is traced over a patriarchal logic that was both a scene of crisis and hypostatized within the *Männerstaat* of Nazi Germany (Mosse 167). In the Fascist discourse of the hero, it unites a number of elements in the text. Just as the very logic of the fetish is mapped onto the charismatic figures of the Hollywood star and the dictator, so Mauberley's masochistic structure of desire, foregrounded in that earlier title, is closely bound up with modalities of power. These meaning clusters come together in a discourse on iconicity that provides the central organizing theme of *Famous Last Words*, extended in a formal triptych of rhyming scenes in the text whose integral relationship to each other has largely gone unexplored.

Like Foucault, Findley reads Fascism in the structures of domination and subordination that inform all of history, in the *"amour pour le pouvoir"* played out in postwar French cinema's stylizations of National Socialism but largely left out of the official record.[3] If Foucault's reading of the coordinates of power and desire has particular resonance for Findley's second novel of Fascism, then that is, in part, because of the shared gay positioning of the two writers, which is traced over the subjugated knowledge of erotic structures no longer naturalized within dominant codes of representation (Gabriel, "Performing" 234 ff.). In spite of the normalizing gesture of his change of title, Findley's penchant for domesticating transgressive insights, for turning danger into safety, cannot be fully sustained here. Part of the reason for this lies in the very relevance of Mauberley's sexuality for the story that Findley is telling, in a reading of the degree zero of power relations that is fully as radical as Foucault's own. Yet how did Findley arrive at a working through of the relations of power and desire that seems so close to the French philosopher's in its outlines — staged in an erotic choreography that seems to anticipate Foucault's life as much as his work? A clue lies in the central influence on *Famous Last Words* of another French writer of the "limit" (Miller 35–36).

Findley's radical insights into power relations in *Famous Last Words*, fusing questions of the sign and the subject, were directly influenced and enabled, I suggest, by one of the most important and original dramatic texts of the twentieth century: Jean Genet's *The Balcony*. As a professional actor in the theatre for over fifteen years, Findley has frequently acknowledged that play texts were a formative influence in his earliest novels and that they are traced over all his fiction. But the context for the centrality of Genet's influence here is even more concrete. Findley himself performed the pivotal role of Roger, the revolutionary, in a March 1962 production of *The Balcony*, staged by The Red Barn Theatre at the Central Library in Toronto.[4] Genet's play moves back and forth between a revolution against the palace and erotic scenographies in a brothel that act out relations of power in the real world. The drama's masked hieratic style, along with its reading of the relationship between power, desire, and the sign, would come to influence centrally Findley's own reading of the repose of an icon. In what follows, I suggest some of the ways in which these connections are both articulated and obscured in the novel that we have come to know as *Famous Last Words*, opening out onto one of the most charged scenes of twentieth-century history.

* * *

Why do we listen? . . . Why do we obey?
    — Timothy Findley, *Can You See Me Yet?* (121)

Findley's provocative wearing of a scarf like Mauberley's own and
"initialed 'H.S.M.' for Hugh Selwyn Mauberley" extends the novel's
reading of Fascism as something incipient in all of us (Findley,
"Marvel" 45). The characteristics that pave the way for Mauberley's
"fall" into the vortex of Fascism, in a figure repeated throughout the
text, are deliberately displaced along a continuum of characters in
the novel. Findley would have been aware of the same central
leitmotif in Arthur Miller's play *After the Fall*, a scarcely veiled
autobiographical account of the dramatist's marriage to Marilyn
Monroe, which first appeared on Broadway in 1964.[5] But its theological resonances also echo ironies that he had invoked in *The
Butterfly Plague* between the Fascist ideal of perfection and the place
called Paradise Canyon. Its analogue in *Famous Last Words* is the
Grand Elysium Hotel, a compendium of both the title of Greta
Garbo's most famous film and Tennessee Williams's Elysian Fields in
A Streetcar Named Desire.

Mauberley's final descent into darkness comes with his instruction
to Reinhardt to murder Harry Oakes at the implicit behest of Wallis
Simpson. Having done so, Mauberley recognizes that "My fall was
over. All the way down" (365). There is not merely blood on his hands
in the Macbeth-like sequence of images that follow but also, more
appropriately for this novel, "smears on the wall" (377). Yet how did
he fall so far so fast?

Stephen Scobie charges that Mauberley's story "skirts very conveniently around the issue of how and why he became involved with
Fascism in the first place" (90). In fact, Findley's text offers a *surplus*
of reasons, which cumulatively trace a genealogy of Fascism. It is this
very overdetermination of Mauberley's motives that has helped to
obscure the most searching aspects of Findley's analysis. At one level,
Mauberley repeats the central strands of Pound's character in *Hugh
Selwyn Mauberley* (1920), in which Mauberley is drawn as the
artist-poet whose formal values spiral back to fin de siècle aestheticism. Framed within a modernist poetics, he is the inheritor of an
autotelic ideal in which the work of art seeks no external referent.
Yet this thematics also poses a problem for the Pound-Mauberley
palimpsest at the heart of the novel, for the American poet and
wartime traitor could hardly be accused of retreat from the world.
Indeed, engagement with historical, economic, and political issues

makes his masterpiece, *The Pisan Cantos*, an aesthetically revolutionary text that is also scurrilously anti-Semitic and Fascist.[6] How, then, can this novel problematize both the artist as Fascist exemplified by Pound and his poetic protagonist? Although the question of the moral responsibility of the artist remains central to the novel, Mauberley's attraction to Fascism extends far beyond the critique of aestheticism at the heart of Pound's analysis. In Findley's text, Mauberley's moral abdication has darker taproots.

At one level, the search for beauty aligns Mauberley with the dreamers of *The Butterfly Plague* in their dangerous yearning for perfection. He also shares this trait with the two characters — Lieutenant Quinn and Captain Freyberg — who both read and frame his core narrative. Although their positions in the novel appear to be dialectically opposite, they are also, in a sense, secret sharers, caught up in their own respective hankering after the ideal. Both characters evince the traumatic nature of the events revealed to the world in the immediate postwar period, the heart of darkness crystallized for Findley in his dazed response to the first photographs of the concentration camps of Dachau (*Inside Memory* 310). Demolitions expert Quinn finds Freyberg a "fanatic when it came to Nazis" (44). Supported by his official status as intelligence officer, Freyberg spends his days compiling dossiers and developing an exhaustive filing system. But, although his rage is silent, "he pursued his obsession like a man collecting butterflies" (44). The deliberate echo of the imagery in *The Butterfly Plague* marks him with the incipient trace of the Fascist himself, seeking a perfection in human species harnessed to the deadly model of National Socialist Eugenics Theory.[7] Yet, although he is patently "traumatized" by the events recently uncovered to the world (44), he is also rendered suspicious by his equivocal response to being named a Jew. Quinn, too, suffers "the trauma of being confronted by the horror of what the Nazis had done in Europe. . . . But Quinn's sense of shock had not left him. Quinn could still look around him and wonder how these things had been accomplished *by the race of which he was a part*" (47; emphasis added). It is the dream of perfection that is damned in this novel, as in Findley's first novel of Fascism: "*Elysium, though it were in the halls of hell . . . ,*" in the words of the epigraph from Pound (37). But, though Quinn himself stands accused of aestheticism without moral responsibility in his worship of Mauberley, he is — *pace* Findley's comments on the moral shortcomings of both his interlocutors — closer to the novel's point of view: one that insists on the Fascist germ in each and every one of us. Quinn's own fetishistic taking up of Mauberley's scarf replicates the search for the father that characterizes Mauberley's relationship to Pound. Yet, although this structure is drawn in terms of Quinn's personal history, it has much greater resonance in both a patriarchal and a Fascist thematics of fathers and sons. *The Odyssey* provides the very type of the patriarchal journey of the son in search of the father: a quest that begins in the first two books of the novel as an explicit overthrowing of the mother and continues as an arduous journey by Telemachus toward the long-absent Odysseus. But a narrative of fathers and sons has also been widely read as relevant to twentieth-century Fascism.[8]

Both Italian Fascism under Mussolini and German National Socialism were characterized by a radical recuperation of a nineteenth-century ideology of separate spheres, which sought to stabilize earlier fractures in the gender system (see Fout). In turn, both responded to the wounding of an earlier generation of men in World War I with a newly forged hypermasculine ideal, what recent cultural critics of Fascism have read as an "armoured" masculinity, protected against both boundary loss and memory of the trenches (see Huyssen; and Theweleit). Hence, what appears to be Mauberley's personal family romance reconstructs the drama of patriarchy that is the hinge of much of Findley's fiction. In *Famous Last Words*, as in *Not Wanted on the Voyage*, this thematics is traced over a psychic and social structure that is part of the larger historical narrative of twentieth-century Fascism.

National Socialism as a dream of beauty in the aesthetic sphere, whose grotesque mirror image is an ideal of perfection in the human species; Fascism as a historical agon between fathers and sons: these are two of the markers of Fascism in Findley's fiction, and they constitute part of the narrative drama of Hugh Selwyn Mauberley, echoed and displaced along the continuum of minor characters. But Findley is also asking darker questions here that speak to what Milan Kundera has called the terrible "anthropological question": *"What is man capable of?"* (qtd. in Lindholm 116). If the postwar revelation of the concentration camps operated as a scene of ontological crisis in the West, then it also cancelled forever the conception of "man" in rational Cartesian terms, even where it sought to perform a salvage operation in the ruins of Enlightenment ethics.

At the close of the novel, Quinn returns to the Grand Elysium Hotel to read Mauberley's epilogue one more time. The final scene conjures up a mysterious spectre rising to the surface of the sea. In *The Telling of Lies: A Mystery*, the same figure is invoked to suggest the Freudian metaphor for the unconscious as iceberg, the spatializing trope at the heart of depth psychology (see Gabriel, "Sex"). But, as in the later murder mystery, it also operates as a figure for reading the darkness in searingly moral terms. It reminds us that no understanding of the horror of the Fascist moment can avoid confronting the *"shadow"* that proceeds *"from the other side of reason"* (396). Readers of the novel who have interpreted Mauberley's sexuality as a moral lapse, in which the novel itself is complicit, may have missed the radical nature of the questions that Findley is asking here. They are posed in even more explicit terms in Findley's play text *Can You See Me Yet?* when the female protagonist, Cassandra, listens to the sounds of Hitler delivering a speech on the radio. The scene concludes with the rapturous sound of the crowd chanting *Sieg Heil!* followed by a series of urgent interrogatives: "Why do we listen? Why do we pay attention? Why do we obey? I cannot say, except to say there's something eager and malignant in us all that yearns to cringe, wants to be obedient. That is the secret of their power. Our willing weakness" (121).[9] *Famous Last Words* sets out to explore "the degree of darkness" (361) inherent in this impulse in ways that move outward to the logic of domination and submission throughout history: to the structure of masochism that is complicit in Fascism's stylized choreography, but also to the function of the icon as a catalyst in organizing meanings and desires in the wider cultural field. Findley notes:

> I'm interested in icons. It is the repose of an icon that interests me. Somewhere in *Famous Last Words* there is a moment where a character says that if this were the Trojan War you would choose your icon this way. And that's what Mauberley is doing. He is saying . . . , "Who is Helen?" Okay, it's Wallis Simpson. Now, a lot of people no longer recognize Wallis Simpson as being as powerful as she actually was. They think, "What a silly creature to have chosen!" But, ironically, Wallis Simpson was one of the great icons of that age, without any question, and there is no question she pulled together the focus of what was going on in Britain. . . . ("Masks" 36)

In *Famous Last Words*, Simpson's status as empty sign provides a complex lesson in both the charismatic figure and the institution. What interests Findley is the way in which the historical icon functions like the celluloid star, a screen image and projection for the masses' own structure of longing. In the more concrete historical terms of its Fascist problematic, this text asks us to consider how it was that heroes-dictators such as Hitler and Mussolini mobilized cultural technologies, the studied art of the actor, and familiarity with early-twentieth-century treatises on the psychology of the crowd in order to secure not merely consent but also enthusiasm.

Major twentieth-century sociologists such as Weber and Durkheim have agreed that the charismatic relation "implies a loss of personal will and identity in the subject" (qtd. in Lindholm 34). In turn, Charles Lindholm argues in his study *Charisma* that "the impulse to self-loss" can be diffused and tamed at alternative sites in modern society, such as "identification with the nation, hero worship, religion, and especially through intimate personal relationships" (8). This panoply of social spaces, indifferently marked out as public and private, returns us to *Famous Last Words*, in which structures of desire that belong to the subject mediate power relations in the social field.

If Hitler stands as the quintessential charismatic figure of the twentieth century, he was also alert to power as a scene of theatre, a thematics as well as a style central to *Famous Last Words*. Hitler's biographer Joachim Fest reminds us how the German leader studiously constructed his performances and their mise en scènes. As he saw it, the "chief concerns of the politician were matters of staging" (qtd. in Lindholm 104). Hitler actively developed his speeches as grand-scale performances calculated to move the crowd to mass ecstasy, a phenomenon not lost on David Bowie, who has proclaimed that "Hitler was the first Rock Star" (qtd. in Adam 90). The key to his success, like that of Mussolini, was his power to elicit in his followers a desire to *obey*.[10] Hitler boasted frequently about the huge base of his support, regularly achieving ninety-eight percent of the vote in plebiscites held throughout his reign. Nor did his hypnotic power die with the fall of the Third Reich. Historian Martin Gilbert provides a lesson in the response of von Ribbentrop to a film of Hitler during the Nuremberg Trials. Reduced to tears by what he saw, the once-powerful arm of the führer tried to explain the Hitler effect to interlocuters whom he likely thought had no ability to understand: "Can't you see how he swept people off their feet? . . . [D]o you know, even with all I know, if Hitler should come to me in this cell now and say *Do this!* — I would still do it" (qtd. in Lindholm 202).

What, then, is the relationship of Mauberley's sexuality to this moment when state power joins forces with moral darkness? If this is, after all, a scene of "Fascinating Fascism" (Sontag), then is the gay enunciation of the novel caught up in what it sets out to read? At one level, the novel insists on the complicity of us all in potential or realized form, setting up internal echoes in which Annie Oakley's and Little Nell's worship of Lana Turner or Quinn's hero worship of Mauberley repeats the protagonist's own call for a Fascist hero in another register. In turn, Findley's description of Quinn as resembling Tyrone Power deliberately *performs* this structure of displacement and desire at the level of the erotic gaze.

Yet the construction of the male body as erotic spectacle also belongs to codes that haunted Fascism historically (Gabriel, "Performing" 227). It is his own scene of crisis within a dominant sign system that makes Findley an astute *reader* of these codes — as well as of the ways in which erotic structures map relations of power in the social field. Although these choreographies are naturalized within a patriarchal representational regime, they repeat the nexus of power and desire foregrounded within same-sex relations. In fact, the heterosexual relationship between Ruth and her Nazi trainer-husband Bruno in *The Butterfly Plague* directly anticipates Mauberley's dangerous desire for Reinhardt as well as the lesson in Fascism that it dramatizes. But, just as the importance of this connection is muted by Findley's change of title in *Famous Last Words*, the scene that dramatized it explicitly in *The Butterfly Plague* was edited out in the radically revised 1986 edition.

What remains, however, is a directly parallel description of Findley's protagonists, with a striking repetition of the very metaphor intended to code their respective structures of masochism. When Mauberley takes leave of Simpson in Nassau, he recognizes that he has "seen the last of the woman I had loved — *as a dog loves its mistress* — for the past two decades" (376; emphasis added). In *The Butterfly Plague*, Ruth describes how she became the willing automaton of Bruno, her eroticism inseparable from her descent into the Nazi nightmare that he has come to embody: "I wanted to obey. I wanted to be obedient. I wanted to function without thought, to respond to his voice *like a dog*" (79).[11] Here is the excised scene from the first edition of *The Butterfly Plague*:

> Ruth locked herself in her room, took off her clothes, stood with her back hard up against the wall and began secretly, with a growing, widening silence, to raise her right arm rhythmically, over and over, in a strangely angular salute. Her expression

slowly changed from one of exhaustion and despair to one of willful obedience. . . . [S]he seemed to have joined a throng. (48)

As so often in Findley, this dramatic tableau makes important connections across the text at the level of highly distilled gestures. No theatrical or cinematic rendering of this scene could avoid the fusion of her nakedness with the scripted indication of the Nazi salute to signal the *wilful obedience* in which *she seemed to have joined a throng*. It is an almost kitsch visual effect belonging to the period in question, in which Ruth is frozen in relief as a 1930s Art Deco sculpture. Likely, it is the graphic and plastic quality of the scene that Findley later found troublesome and over the top. Yet similar stylizations, more formally integrated in a novel whose entire surface is theatricalized, abound in *Famous Last Words*. As in *The Butterfly Plague*, moreover, a mirrored or rhyming structure of scenes is central to reading the text. I want to return to a key sequence of such scenes, which situate Mauberley's own eroticism in relation to the historical problematic of Fascism and consent, this time around in a more fully evolved as well as radical analysis of relations between power and iconicity.

But first it is important to look more closely at the meanings foregrounded in Findley's original title of "Alligator Shoes," which, had it stood, would have led the reader straight to the "damned beauty" of Reinhardt in charting Mauberley's fall into Fascism (360). Yet these meanings also unfold scenically in an often montage structure of deliberate juxtapositions. Mauberley's encounters with Reinhardt can be seen in this light as integrally related to choices in history. The scene in which Mauberley first meets Reinhardt, at the funeral of Allenby, directly follows the dramatic tableau in which Allenby is morally tested by an invitation to join the worldwide cabal of Fascists by opposing war with Germany in his capacity as parliamentary undersecretary of state for foreign affairs. A menacing connection is drawn between his refusal, von Ribbentrop's coded message to Rudolf Hess (". . . ALLENBY DECLINES" [119]), and his subsequent death with his son in a car accident. It is directly against Allenby's refusal of moral abdication (occurring at the precise moment of the news that Edward VIII has abdicated the throne in England) that Mauberley's fatal attraction to Reinhardt is announced. This structural juxtaposition of scenes paves the way for our reading the whole trajectory of Mauberley's decline and fall.

Like the character Race, who stalks Ruth in *The Butterfly Plague*, Reinhardt operates in an almost allegorical mode, focusing the meaning cluster of Fascism=desire=death that is integral to *Famous Last Words*. It is a triad dramatized at an even earlier moment in the text, one that is also chronologically the end of Mauberley's journey. In his hiding place high up in the Tyrol, the concièrge of the Grand Elysium Hotel, Herr Kachelmayer, offers Mauberley the services of a boy of twelve or thirteen years who, in turn, is sent to fetch Mauberley a gun for his safety. Mauberley has already made a mental notation of him as a "well-made boy," so pale and albino-like that the youth, whose real name is Hugo, is christened by him as *die weisse Ratte* (28). The scene that follows is overtly coded as gay s/m pornography:

> And then the boy undid the button of his shirt, exposing for an instant one pale nipple and a flaunting exhibition of his skin so raw that Mauberley wondered what might be going to happen next and how this gesture would end. But when the boy withdrew his hand, it held a small, bright nickel-plated gun. . . . All this seduction was silent. . . . (34)

The conflation of sexuality, danger, and a homoerotic gaze will become central to the meaning of Reinhardt in the novel. Mauberley's description of his "rainy hair curled against a skull like a Roman marble" (121) places him iconographically within a neoclassical Italian Fascist aesthetics. But it is his *shoes* that fetishistically focus the simultaneous attraction and repulsion that he generates for Mauberley, who is both frightened and riveted by Reinhardt's "beauty" at this point (121). But what directly follows is another scene that connects this desire with a lesson in history. In a newspaper editorial, journalist Julia Franklin accuses Mauberley of being a man "out of key with his time," caught up in the vortex of "the morally bankrupt crew that mans the élite but sinking lifeboat of a Fascist-dominated Europe . . ." (128; ellipsis in original).

When Mauberley later spots the man with alligator eyes once more in Charles Bedaux's office, he can only ask his secretary: *"One of us?"* (141). What follows is a brief excursus on his inchoate sexuality, staged in autobiographical terms that only serve to heighten his

> fear of being powerless in the presence of desire. Such as the desire that rose against my will when I saw Harry Reinhardt's

inhuman eyes. Inhuman and, therefore, without the impediment of moral choice. There was nothing — nothing one could not imagine him doing. But this was dangerous. *This was appallingly dangerous.* (142; emphasis added)

He subsequently discovers that Reinhardt has been sent to track him through Diana Allenby's stable boy, and, just when Mauberley thinks he is finally rid of him, he turns up as the "messenger" of the cabal in the Bahamas, his shoes still "the sick lime-brown of alligator skins" (361, 360). For the first time, Mauberley understands the nature of Reinhardt's "message" here as "the ultimate rendezvous" "in the dark," in a cluster of images that joins eroticism and death (361). In the end, this death will be both the murder of Harry Oakes, which he requests of Reinhardt in his final descent into evil, and his own brutal end at Reinhardt's hand.

Reinhardt's "damned beauty" repeats the formal stylizations of National Socialism in postwar cinema, the cultural reading of both Weimar and Nazism as a peculiar sexual fascination or "divine decadence" (Misejewski). In turn, Findley's gay iconography marks Reinhardt as erotic "rough trade" in a sadomasochistic structure whose dangerous implications are even more explicit in Findley's short story "Losers, Finders, Strangers at the Door."[12] Yet the meanings invoked here also draw a conscious moral. Reinhardt's shoes are not just leather but also alligator skin, their reptilian origins simultaneously attractive and repulsive. Their beginnings are in the primeval swamp, and they continue to connote menace.

Almost certainly, Findley took his title image from the fetishized snakeskin jacket of the gigolo character Val in Tennessee Williams's *Orpheus Descending*, in which the jacket operates as a central metaphor for both the character's erotic spell and his moral corruption.[13] In *Famous Last Words*, this structure of displaced desire is mapped onto the screen projection of the figure who attains the status of icon in history. This is the terrain that the charismatic Fascist hero shares with the Hollywood star. The diminutive and seedy gossip columnist, whose reading of graffiti in public toilet stalls provides a grotesque mirror image of Quinn's and Freyberg's — as well as our own — reading of Mauberley's writing on the wall, yields another variation on the pervasive search for the god-hero in the text. His quest for God's shoes, echoing Mauberley's own dark obsession, recalls "the *eternal twilight* of the world's latrines and the rows of feet beneath the cabinet doors" (275; emphasis added). His own

Götterdämmerung comes in a scene of conflagration in which, still lusting after the breasts of Lana Turner, he has a final apocalyptic vision: "God's shoes were size Twelve" (287). The scene provides a parodic send-up of both Wilde's own rewriting of the death of Little Nell and Pound's epigraph, which opens the third chapter of the novel: "*O bright Apollo . . . / What god, man or hero / Shall I place a tin wreath upon!*" (59).

The lesson for the reader is about the fickleness of the crowd in attaching heroic status to seemingly arbitrary figures in history. Like the commodity-fetish, "the object that had been an *accidental* means to achieving some desired end becomes a fixed necessity, the very embodiment of desire, and the effective exclusive means for gratifying it" (Pietz 147; emphasis added). But Findley's interest in drawing connections between Hollywood and Fascism, the star and the dictator, also raises questions about the altered conditions for constructing charismatic figures in modernity and postmodernity, periods marked by dramatically new and changing cultural technologies as well as a heightened alertness to the status of the sign. For if, as Baudrillard argues, our own historical moment is one of intensified "passion for the code" (92), then what are the shifts and displacements in relation to iconic figures newly put into play?

* * *

Diana, Princess of Wales, became skillful at constructing the image of herself that she wanted people to see. . . . Diana was not given to using words like "semiotic," but she was a capable semiotician of herself. With increasing confidence, she gave us the signs by which we might know her as she wished to be known.

— Salman Rushdie (68)

The central thread of *Famous Last Words* is the interrogation of the icon in history in a structure of reification that extends the fetish foregrounded in the original title of "Alligator Shoes." In his attempt to explore the mystical foundation of state authority, Michael Taussig draws on a range of anthropological as well as political theories to consider "the peculiar sacred and erotic attraction, even thralldom, combined with disgust, which the State holds for its subjects" (218). It is what he calls the modern fetishized state with a big *S* that provokes this structure to its point of crisis, enlarged and even parodied in the official state Fascisms of the twentieth century presided over by charismatic dictators. What various political structures share in this historical moment is the capacity of technology to enlarge on the older impulse toward an impure sacred in ways understood by Bataille (Taussig 224). For the father of modern sociology, Émile Durkheim, this penchant for "imageric seduction" is manifest even in the rock face of caves (Taussig 235), an example that has special relevance for readers of *Famous Last Words*.

In our era of "The Work of Art in the Age of Mechanical Reproduction" (Benjamin), it is the images of Andy Warhol, in their play on the aura, that exemplify the star-making capacity of the new technologies of photography and film. But Benjamin himself understood early on the implications of the shift from theatre to cinema, creating conditions in which the actor is separated from his or her "reflected image," a phrase that has particular resonance in the mirrored universe of *Famous Last Words*:

> But now the reflected image has become separable, transportable. And where is it transported? Before the public. Never for a moment does the screen actor cease to be conscious of this fact. While facing the camera he knows that ultimately he will face the public, the consumers who constitute the market. . . . The film responds to the shriveling of the aura with an artificial build-up of the "personality" outside the studio. The cult of the movie star, fostered by the money of the film industry, preserves not the unique aura of the person but the "spell of the personality," *the phony spell of a commodity.* (231; emphasis added)

Findley draws much the same lesson in his wry description of the visit of the Duke and Duchess of Windsor to Yugoslavia as a "Dalmation Camelot" (64), conscious of the cultural construction of the idealized Kennedy era. Warhol's screen prints of Jackie Kennedy in the moments following the assassination of the president mingle side by side in the museum with the grainy images of Marilyn Monroe. But these ironies of history also hold lessons for us on the relations between power and desire, their enlarged status in Warhol's blowups a variation on Findley's own rewriting of the death of Little Nell.

Most of the characters in *Famous Last Words* are starstruck in one form or another. The soldier named Annie Oakley, like the transvestite Octavius in *The Butterfly Plague*, lives in a fantasy universe almost entirely dominated by movies. Faced with the moral obscenity of the Holocaust, he can only draw on Humphrey Bogart in *Casablanca*; in turn, Rudecki only values Mauberley as a writer when he learns that Mauberley has scripted the movie *Stone Dogs* as star vehicle for Bette Davis. It is a world in which the power of the star is inseparable from her erotic charge: "Movie queens. Sometimes they could really get you down. Some, of course, could get you up. He smiled" (299). Whereas Quinn worships the aesthetic ideal represented by Mauberley, the artist-poet is seduced by the glamour of the Grand Elysium Hotel in its heyday:

> Isadora Duncan, Greta Garbo, Somerset Maugham and Richard Strauss had all come up the famous tiers of marble stairs, crossing the lobbies to sign the registry and collect their keys. Edward VIII and Mrs Simpson had danced incognito in the Winter Garden. It had been in those days that Mauberley had known the hotel first. (22)

Findley's concern in this novel is not just to make the connection between the charisma of the star and that of the dictator or monarch but also to show that both are contingent on the desire of a subject who constructs them as screen projections, fetish objects wrought large. In his *Daily Mail* article of 1936, Mauberley calls for the very type of the charismatic hero: "Not a Mussolini of whom we are afraid. Not a Hitler, who drives us to our feet. But an emblem whose magnetism pulls us upward" (180). With the same penchant for hero worship, he reads Edward VIII as "tanned and golden.... He literally shone from head to toe, so you could pick him out a mile away in any crowd and this *shining* was so pronounced and unique that I ultimately found myself believing in the magic 'inner lights' of which one hears superior beings are possessed" (95). In the novel, it is Mauberley himself who provides Wallis Simpson with a central lesson in the theatrical icon. In terms that anticipate von Ribbentrop's advice to her that "there are other crowns . . ." (181), Mauberley reminds Wallis that *"anyone could hold the stage who had the power"* (144; emphasis added). Yet Wallis is also caught up in the passion for the code in her very desire to be queen.[14] This "fetishism of the signifier" (Baudrillard 92) is what Edward and Wallis share in divergent ways in their respective sadomasochistic positionings. Accordingly, they can only engage in erotic rituals overseen by the stern photographic gaze of the queen. As Mauberley watches Wallis applying her makeup in Shanghai, she confesses to being a virgin, a masquerade of innocence that links her to silent-screen actress Letitia Virden ("The Little Virgin") in *The Butterfly Plague*. Consummate actress as well as rumoured courtesan, Wallis is drawn as the Rita Hayworth femme fatale in Orson Welles's *Lady from Shanghai*, frozen in "ruthless stillness" (75). Moreover, as in the chiaroscuro of film noir, moral and epistemological instability are inseparable. It is a thematics brilliantly formalized in Welles's film in an elaborate play with mirrors. In turn, when Mauberley first meets up with Wallis in Shanghai, she is sitting in her lacquered chair with a mirror directly behind her: "Intermittently, I could see myself in the mirror, floating on and off like a nervous white light . . ." (68). For Mauberley, her silver-screen glamour is integral to her allure. Even at the close of his account, she retains her magic for him, descending the staircase "like an actress in a film. She used the stairs quite consciously and made a scene of dignified bereavement. The 'star' upstairs had died, and here came the widow, walking into the future, music swelling up with every measured step she took" (348).

But truth and lies trade places in Wallis Simpson in ways that confirm her status as the central icon of the novel, a function underlined by the British cover of the paperback edition of *Famous Last Words*, which featured a theatrical mask of the Duchess of Windsor. Yet it is only in retrospect that Mauberley realizes that her whole appearance is one of masquerade:

> It is only now — after twenty years — that I see her face as lacquered; only now that I realize she has never lived without the application of a mask. There is a mole you would never see, for instance, down by the corner of her mouth, which I saw that day for the first and last time. As she worked — she was an expert: her mouth, her eyes, her hair were masterpieces of illusion — she went on speaking through her teeth; her voice as sibilant as *something from behind a screen*. (73; emphasis added)

Although the novel mutes Mauberley's erotic structure, suggesting that it is both bisexual and dormant, this scene repeats the triangular relationship of Wallis and Mauberley with Dmitri Karaskavin ("He played Charlie Chaplin for Wallis, Mary Pickford for me") (71). Wallis speaks to Mauberley of Edward VIII: "That boy we loved is dead. You wanted him; I wanted him; Now what we have is each other" (73–74). This is their secret pact, one that will be sealed by Mauberley's infatuation with Wallis's own iconic status. In contrast to her elaborately staged femininity as masquerade, the duke's feeble performance ends in the bathos of the drag queen's running mascara. In the end, he replaces the "woollen mask in which he had begun to suffocate" (212) for a face of bandages, exchanging, as Diana Brydon notes, "his suffocating mask of royalty for the mask of bandages that more truly reflects his state as a wounded, outcast king" (68).

It is fitting that the two characters who hold the fate of the Duke and Duchess of Windsor in their hands are drawn in the same idiom. The thematics of power as theatre is played out in the internecine rivalry between Schellenberg, chief of the Reich Central Security, and von Ribbentrop, head of the Foreign Office, who is party to the kidnapping plot. Although it is the former who wins out in the end, both characters are drawn in a theatrical register. Schellenberg has an alter ego named "Fritzi Schaemmel" (198), in a sexual playing of changes that connects dissident desire with the taking up of roles: "He had slept with men and women, boys and girls and made them all believe he loved them" (222). Unlike the real-life Hitler, who took his stylized gestures from the melodrama of the silent screen, Schellenberg "became the characters he played, much as an actor trained by Stanislavsky might do. He had played the character of Schaemmel entirely from the inside" (222). In turn, "von Ribbentrop had his own mask to wear — though not so elaborate a mask as Schellenberg-Schaemmel" (228). As a diplomat, he operates as a craftsman rather than an artist: "There is too much at stake from moment to moment to sit back and give a mere 'performance' " (235).

*   *   *

There is a place in the world where theatricality does not conceal any power, and that's the theatre.
— Jean Genet, interview with Hubert Fichte (79)

What could Findley have taken from those lines he memorized as Roger, the plumber-revolutionary, the character who enters into the fantasy role-playing of the brothel only to destroy the power of the sign? *The Balcony* is one of the most daring and imaginative dramatic texts of twentieth-century European theatre. As a masked drama in which the actors are larger than life, wearing the elevating *cothurni* of classic Greek tragedy, it fulfils Genet's ideal in the preface to *The Maids* of the actor as "highly-charged sign." Findley learned more than one lesson from his close familiarity with Genet, but no insight is closer to the thinking of the French writer than his statement that "A myth is not a lie, as such, but only *the truth in larger shoes.* Its gestures are wider. Its voice is projected to cover distance. . . . It is the ultimate theatre of human intrigue" (*Inside Memory* 191; emphasis added).

In its dramaturgy of power and iconicity, *Famous Last Words* is more intent than any other novel by Findley on drawing a "theatre of human intrigue" — and in ways that strikingly mirror both the radical insights and the formal strategies of *The Balcony*, which itself grew out of an older plan by Genet for a play on Franco's Fascist Spain (White 414). Like *Famous Last Words*, the "Grand Balcony" of Genet's play unfolds in a scenic structure — one set in Madame Irma's bordello or House of Illusions. It is an establishment of many rooms in which clients act out phantasmatic desires: "Each individual who rings the bell and enters brings his own scenario" (36). But these erotic fantasies are inseparable from choreographies of power in the "real" world, just as the identities that unfold are contingent phenomenologically on a mirroring by an other in a motif that becomes central to *Famous Last Words*. "Look here; You've got to be a model thief if I'm to be a model judge," the client who engages in the "secret theatre" tells the prostitute crawling toward him abjectly on her stomach. "My being a judge is an emanation of your being a thief — you need only refuse . . . for me to cease to be" (19). In another room, a timid-looking gentleman assumes the costume of a general in which he takes on gigantic proportions by means of the broadened shoulders, mask, and *cothurni* of the ancient Greek actor. Next door, an old man dressed as a tramp and whipped by a beautiful girl cries out, "What about the lice?" (20). Like Mauberley's own structure of masochism, his desire for self-abasement is played out on a social field shot through with power relations.

In fact, far from being hermetically sealed off from the outside world, Madame Irma's Grand Balcony is caught up in the revolution taking place outside, in which the Andromeda network plans to capture the royal palace to set up its own power base. Like the Fascist cabal of *Famous Last Words* in search of the puppet regime of the Duke and Duchess of Windsor, it is in search of a figurehead to focus desire, the singer Chantal. Frozen into a hieratic image of the revolution, "she doesn't belong to herself any more. She's ours, she's our own sign" (57). Genet's inspiration for the Chantal figure was almost certainly both the Spanish *La Passionera* and Evita Perón, a well-known radio and film actress surrounded by rumours of a secret sexual history before marrying the Argentinian director and emerging as a charismatic figure who focused the support of the masses.

The regime's understanding of Evita as an iconic figure who could be used to rally support was something that Genet fully realized in his balcony scenes in a play written in the years immediately following her death. What he could not have anticipated was the way in which his analysis prefigured the turn of events in Juan Perón's real-life Fascist regime, in which his second wife, Isabel, would be unsuccessfully mobilized to perform the same function. The language of *The Balcony* directly anticipates Findley's concept of the repose of the icon, a central figuration in understanding his reading of power and desire in *Famous Last Words*. In order to fight against an image of power generated by the monarchy, Chantal — as iconic figure for the rebels — has herself "frozen into image. . . *It's the combat of allegories*" (157; emphasis added).

The role that most centrally embodies the passage between the brothel and the revolution, between desire and power, is the chief of police, the role that Findley's Roger character goes on to impersonate. The lesson of this character hungering after power through the inscription of his image in the liturgies of the brothel was not lost on Findley when he came to discuss *Famous Last Words* in an interview over a decade later in relation to "the seeds of fascism" (qtd. in Ingham 37):

What power-hungry people do . . . can be embraced very generally by my use of the term "fascist," because I think that's what fascism is: all power-hungry people can touch the rest of the people where they are hungry to be powerful too, but no, *they can never be powerful without the powerful iconic people doing things for them, and in their name.* (qtd. in Ingham 38; emphasis added)

No statement by Findley comes closer to his reading of both the Fascist cult of the charismatic hero and *the cultural icon* (Evita *or* Madonna) who mediates desire in the wider social field. Richard Dyer has theorized the ways in which film stars operate as screen projections for representations and discourses that circulate in the wider historical field: "Stars matter," Dyer concludes, "because they act out aspects of life that matter to us; and performers get to be stars when what they act out matters to enough people" (197). Findley's point is that dictators *matter* in much the same way.

It is a lesson dramatically staged in *The Balcony*. With the royal palace surrounded and the queen in hiding, Roger asks if, having murdered with abandon, he has at last entered the ranks of the dramatis personae requested by clients. Madame Irma tells him: "your image does not yet conform to the liturgies of the brothel" (47). The radical lesson here is that power can only be consolidated at the site of desire. In terms that mimic the Hegelian dialectic of master and slave, the chief of police understands that he is nothing until he has achieved the desire of the other. Like all the characters in *The Balcony*, in short, he is "haunted by the quest of immobility. By what we call the hieratic" (64).

In *The Balcony*, as in *Famous Last Words*, the connection between immobility and the sign is figured in a Bataille-like connection between Fascism and death. The Fascist thug Harry Reinhardt is not only Mauberley's object of desire but also his murderer in a grotesque scene of death.[15] In fact, the most elaborate room in Madame Irma's House of Illusions is the Mausoleum of Death, the place where the chief of police hopes to be enshrined as "a gigantic phallus, a prick of great stature" (78). In the end, it is Roger, the role played by Findley in the 1964 Toronto production, who marks the chief of police's entry into the pantheon of iconic figures. Yet no sooner does he inscribe his power in the transcendental figure of the phallus, dressed in the signifying garments of the chief of police, than he proceeds to castrate himself. It is the most climactic moment in the text, enacting a radical critique of the sign of the phallus itself as transcendental signifier.[16]

Given that Genet's play provides a central twentieth-century cultural site for drawing the connections between power, desire, and iconicity, it is little wonder that it informed *Famous Last Words* in such dramatic ways. In the penultimate scene of *The Balcony*, a familiar cast of characters emerges on the balcony — one that confounds the distinction between the "real" and the "fiction" — in a metatheatre that anticipates Findley's own strategies but that also dramatizes a radical lesson in *power*. The figures include the bishop, general, and judge, familiar from earlier erotic scenarios, but also the queen — this time around played by the brothel keeper herself. Unlike the historical Wallis Simpson, who aspired to the throne but was surrounded by rumours of secret sexual knowledge derived from the brothels of China, this impostor queen only half-understands her function as transmuted sign. "If the Queen is dead . . . ," she begins.

To which the envoy responds: "Long live the Queen, madam" (65).

Readers of Findley will recall the elaborate play on queens and the queenship in *Famous Last Words*, alternately linked to Queen Mary herself in an oedipal drama with her son, the would-be queen Wallis Simpson, and the dressmaker's dummy of the queen. It is extended in scenes alternately comic (the misrecognition of the "queen" by Elsa Maxwell) and bathetic (Edward's maudlin and childlike clinging to the life-sized doll that is both the queen and his mother). But the most important scene — and the one most certainly traced over Genet's play — is that in which Queen Mary herself explains the meaning of royalty as sign system.

She takes her son into a narrow, ill-lit room with a dressmaker's dummy, whose kid-leather head and human hair construct a surreal human likeness. "Is it you?" asks Edward; "It is the Queen," answers his mother (103), in terms that directly replicate Genet's play. But, as in *The Balcony*, the reading of the icon as both charismatic figure and institution is inseparable from a structure of submission and desire. This is the relationship that has almost entirely gone unread in *Famous Last Words*, although it is embedded in a dramatic triptych of scenes that repeat the motif of *kneeling*. Although they culminate in the official ritual of obeisance to the institution of monarchy, bodied forth in the figure of the monarch herself, this scene spirals back to two equally important moments in the text that share its formal character of heightened gesture in frozen exemplary tableau: the death of Lord Wyndham and Mauberley's desire to prostrate himself before the eroticized figure of the Blackshirt.

In a suggestive essay on *Famous Last Words*, Richard Dellamora has rightly read the earliest of these scenes in terms of its gay coding as fellatio. Yet, despite Findley's penchant for covering over his darker and more radical insights in a textual game of hide-and-seek, manifest here in the change of title of *Famous Last Words*, this sequence, I would argue, is not a moment of "ethical/political failure" after all (Dellamora 181; see Brydon 76 ff.). Rather, it is the *scenic structure* of *Famous Last Words* — conceived along theatrical rather than traditional narrative lines — that has helped to obscure central connections in the text. Not only do these scenes accumulate meaning in a conscious and deliberate relation to each other, but they also operate within the grammar of a particular kind of antinaturalistic tradition: a theatre of heightened gesture and tableau.[17]

Mauberley's encounter with the Fascist Blackshirts, celebrating their recent victory in Addis Ababa, takes place in a bar in Venice on

5 May 1936, just after his old friends Ned and Diana Allenby have berated him for his pro-Fascist articles in the *Daily Mail*. Caught up in Mauberley's erotic gaze, the Blackshirts exude "an *aura* of masculinity that caused an imbalance in the atmosphere as if something quite invisible, but huge was taking up more and more space between the tables" (90–91; emphasis added):

> At one point one of them stood up — very tall — not more than twenty-two years old and wearing boots and a wide brown belt. . . . I wanted so desperately to follow him, but I could only think of what Allenby had said; "you are some kind of pilgrim looking for a faith . . . under rocks."
> And yet I turned in my chair and watched that young man going away. And I went away with him — in my mind. *And knelt before his strength. And his victory.* (91; second ellipsis in original; emphasis added)

The description activates in code ("wearing boots and a wide brown belt") the same scene of sadomasochistic desire played out at the narrative level of the novel, one in which Mauberley's fatal attraction to Reinhardt focuses his twin descent into Fascism and death: a story frame sufficiently central to have provided the novel's original title. Yet it is this shorter scene that has been seen to perform the very scandal of "Fascinating Fascism" for readers, almost certainly because of its theatrical quality of frozen tableau, which inscribes the semiotic register of the index: the finger that points (Krauss 216). Yet its larger meaning resides in its place as only the first of three such scenes. What directly follows is the elaborate, staged death of Lord Wyndham. His mistress, Baronessa Isabella Loverso, marks with approval Mauberley's call for "a new kind of leader" (93), and Mauberley sees in her a fellow traveller in Fascism. But this encounter has already been framed by a theatrical mise en scène that should be read as a rhyming sequence to the eroticized encounter with Mussolini's Blackshirts:

> The room filled up with the sound of rustling clothes, like wings, as *everyone fell to their knees*. Falling down myself, I realized I was *kneeling* more in awe of history than of death. For the old man dying on the bed *had knelt himself*, as a child, to kiss the hand of Wellington. There we all were in the midst of the twentieth century, but now his daughter and his mistress

kissed his hands, through which time flew to Waterloo and Bonaparte. Somewhere a clock was striking. The reigns of Victoria, Edward, George rose up and fell away in seconds. (92–93; emphasis added)

The ubiquitous gesture of kneeling in the room connects the scene to the one that precedes it in a thematics of obedience, power, and iconicity. In turn, this scene of institutional charisma, one that transcends particular historical figures, is mapped onto central discourses of kingship and queenship, in a third and final variation of the leit motif.

Immediately after her central enactment to Edward VIII on power as bound up with the aura that belongs to the very institution of monarchy, the queen opens the doors and steps "*out onto the balcony*"; "The *balcony* was very small and only large enough for three or four to stand there comfortably" (104; emphasis added), and it is there that she instructs him to break up the sandwich that he guiltily pilfered and throw it down to the eager birds on the grass. Restored to her position of power as both mother and queen, she leaves him "alone *on the balcony*" for a time, to contemplate the meaning of her lesson, before he returns inside:

the Queen was still in her place, nailed down forever. Her eyeless gaze was like a pressure on his back as he went through the door and left her there in the dark. But this was more than he could bear, so he turned again and opened the door again so the light from the gallery fell on the hem of her long pale gown and the oval of her white kid face could just be seen. It was easy enough, he thought as he watched, to understand the power of the mystery that had *drawn his mother to her knees* before this image all those years ago. *He would kneel himself, if he was not her King. But he was her King and he must not kneel.* (105; emphasis added)

As these three scenes unfold in quick succession, miming the central meanings around iconicity in the text in highly stylized theatrical tableaus, it becomes clear that discourses of desire and the sign are inextricably bound up with each other in *Famous Last Words*. But this triptych also serves as a lesson in reading Findley theatrically, alert to performance values of mise en scène, genre, and acting style that tap important meanings side by side with a diegetic or narrative level of the text. In the case of *Famous Last Words*, these submerged codes mimic the novel's central thematics, just as elsewhere cinematic codes and conventions introduce still other registers into the fiction, alerting us to power as a cultural production, *a staged arena of signs*.

In *The Butterfly Plague*, the Hollywood sex goddess Myra is first fetishized and then killed by her fans in a characterization that Findley modelled directly on Marilyn Monroe. In *Famous Last Words*, it is Edward VIII who is destroyed by his elevation to the status of icon. As with most of the characters in *Famous Last Words*, his ontological instability is figured in the Genetesque image of the mirror. Wallis Simpson reads her own masquerade in the mirror of her compact, and even Hitler, in a cameo appearance with von Ribbentrop, accidentally drops his own mask for a moment: ". . . Hitler looked in the mirror and smoothed his hair. 'Ruin! Ruin!' he muttered" (302).

But the Duke of Windsor's confrontation with the triple mirror becomes a split screen of past, present, and future, which explicitly references both *Through the Looking Glass* and *A Christmas Carol*. Haunted by the spectre of his former majesty, unable to contemplate the "hunched old man" that he will become, the Duke of Windsor experiences his historical dilemma in this second "triptych" in the register of fantasy (247). But, once again, this scene demands to be read in terms of performance as well as novelistic values. In fact, it repeats the stage directions that Genet provides for the fourth tableau in the bordello: the very scene of the masochist's longing for a staged ritual of abasement. These directions read: "a room, the three visible panels of which are three mirrors in which is reflected a little old man, dressed as a tramp though neatly combed. . . . Three actors are needed to play the role of the reflections" (*Balcony* 28). This, then, is the formal theatrical genesis of the scene that enacts the shifting identities of Edward VIII in the triple play of the looking glass — in a ritually staged scene of abjection that links his own structure of masochistic desire to that of Mauberley himself.

Yet Findley's mirror tableau, unlike that of Genet, culminates in a shattering of both identity and mimesis that recalls the famous mirror scene that closes Welles's *Lady from Shanghai*. Crossed with a foiled kidnapping plot of which he is unaware, the duke panics and goes "*Straight through the mirror*" (252; emphasis added). But in *Famous Last Words* this shattering of the mirror converges once more with a Genetesque thematics of iconicity. Like Roger's castration of the chief of police as hieratic function, the duke's self-wounding in the mirror stands in for a *breaking of the sign*. In *The Balcony*, the transcendental signifier is the phallus itself, in a radical deconstruction of Fascism's erotics of power that also provides an underground text in *Famous Last Words*, one traced over Mauberley's own scene of ruined masculinity. In the end, though, Findley's staging of the repose of the icon takes us beyond both Mauberley's secret drama and the moment on the world's stage known as Fascism — to that ongoing struggle for the sign that is the arena of history itself.

Epilogue

After Diana, the Princess of Wales, was killed in a car crash while speeding through the Seine tunnel in Paris, the woman who would never be queen was declared by Prime Minister Tony Blair to be Queen of Hearts, amid a crowd in mass mourning. The car's destination, it was rumoured, was the French estate where the Duke and Duchess of Windsor had spent their last years and on which the father of Diana's companion, Dodi Fayed, had taken out a lease. Longing for their own version of myth-history, the European tabloids speculated that, after their marriage, the two lovers would install themselves there permanently.

NOTES

¹ I am indebted to Apter and Pietz for my discussion of the cultural discourse of the fetish here.

² The "surplus" in this thematics of the Fascist artist on trial would, of course, become Findley's play text *The Trials of Ezra Pound*.

³ The interview with Foucault published in *Cahiers du cinema* in 1974 frames Fascism within the same historical problematic of power and consent that informs Findley's novel — in a discourse on Fascism and subjectivity first pioneered by the Frankfurt School of Sociology. Given her intellectual traffic with France, it is likely that Sontag read this interview before publishing "Fascinating Fascism" the following year. Both texts address the question of s/m stylizations of National Socialism, but, whereas Sontag draws a lesson in moral complicity from this erotic theatre, Foucault, like Findley and Genet, is more concerned to understand the nexus of power and desire that made Fascism possible. The postwar cinematic texts under discussion include *Night Porter, Lucien Lacombe, The Chinese in Paris,* and *The Infernal Trio.* Whereas Foucault focuses on the openings for power paradoxically multiplied within the Nazi dictatorship, Findley is more interested in the space afforded masochistic investments. Historically, they

included the fealty to a mass führer or *Duce* in the structure of the crowd and a feminine dramatically recuperated to the domestic sphere.

⁴ I am grateful to William Whitehead, who coproduced this staging, for confirming these details. I first raised the issue of *The Balcony*'s relationship to *Famous Last Words* in my 1986 interview with Findley (see "Masks"). Details of this exchange were edited out for the published version.

⁵ Not only was Miller one of the leading American playwrights in the period of Findley's professional involvement in the theatre, but Miller's moral integrity in the McCarthy anticommunist trials remained exemplary for Findley. See his discussion of Marilyn Monroe in my 1986 interview with him: "glamour is very sinister. What it's hiding, masking, is so many other things. Think about what it's masking in *a cultural icon like Marilyn Monroe*. Which is what vulnerability is really about — death" ("Masks" 36; emphasis added).

⁶ Only recently has the Pound criticism treated these issues in an unflinching way. Important recent studies include McGann; and Perloff.

⁷ In a useful essay on Fascist themes in Findley's fiction, David Ingham notes how Findley frequently aligns Fascism with a desire for perfection. I would add that this discourse only has meaning — both in Findley and in the historical framework of National Socialism — when it is linked with Nazi eugenics theory. See Gabriel, "Performing," for a fuller discussion of this thematics, central to *Not Wanted on the Voyage* as well as Findley's first novel of Fascism, *The Butterfly Plague*.

⁸ For a reading of Fascism as a crisis of the father in the postwar German painting of Gerhard Richter, see Buchloh.

⁹ The "voices" heard in *Can You See Me Yet?* include "Hitler, Mussolini, Roosevelt, Ma Perkins. Yes: and Aimee Semple McPherson" (121), a list confirming my argument that the Fascist dictator shares the same structure of projected desire as the Hollywood star and the icon in history. The passage in the play continues: "We are the horses they ride, the beasts they hunt, the cattle in their abattoirs" (121). Compare *Famous Last Words*: "What they were responding to were the whispers of chaos, fire and anger in themselves" (77).

¹⁰ Here is the advice that Hitler found in the classic turn-of-the-century treatise on the crowd by Gustave Le Bon: "It is a faculty independent of all titles, of all authority, and possessed by a small number of persons whom it enables to exercise a veritably magnetic fascination on those around them, although they are socially their equal, and lack *all ordinary means of domination*. They force the acceptance of their ideas and sentiments on those around them, and they are *obeyed* as is the tamer of wild beasts by the animal that could easily devour him" (qtd. in Lindholm 42; emphasis added).

¹¹ It is the identical trope employed in the locus classicus of masochistic narratives, Sacher-Masoch's *Venus in Furs*. His very name was taken up by

sexologist Kraff-Ebing to describe the "sexual anomaly" in which the "individual affected is controlled in his sexual feeling and thought by the idea of being completely and unconditionally subject to the will of a person of the opposite sex; of being treated by this person as a master, humiliated and abused" (qtd. in Lenzer 277). The narrativization of Sacher-Masoch's desire in *Venus in Furs* includes not only the central fetish of his title and the recurring fantasy of submitting to the female foot under which the masochist is trampled in a structure of submission but also the very figure repeated in both of Findley's masochistic protagonists. Sacher-Masoch's Severin wants to be humiliated and tortured by his beloved; he has the *"nature of a dog"* and not a man (qtd. in Lenzer 301; emphasis added). Mauberley's grotesque licking of the blood from Reinhardt after the murder of Oakes repeats a persistent motif of abasement in *The Balcony* in which the dominatrix prostitute holds out her shoes and commands the masochist to "Lick it! Lick it . . ." (see 14, 20).

[12] Findley's simultaneous fascination with and horror of sadomasochistic scenarios recur in his work. The story "Losers, Finders, Strangers at the Door" is exemplary. Daisy McCabe seeks an erotic companion for her husband, who desires to be beaten "half to death." Caught up in the hysteria of her situation, she recounts to her interlocutor how one friend asked dryly, "which half?" (200).

[13] The central influence of Tennessee Williams on Findley's early work has been confirmed repeatedly by Findley (see "Masks").

[14] Absent in my essay are the inevitable camp associations around the "queen" in any gay discourse. See Gabriel, "Performing" 231 ff., for an extended discussion of camp in *The Butterfly Plague*. Simpson's longing to be queen cannot be separated out from this extended play with the sign. In *The Balcony*, Irma as queen asks plaintively, in words that might well echo those of Simpson: *"Will I never therefore be who I am?"* (94; emphasis added).

[15] Bataille's work takes up the Hegelian thematics that the master is dependent upon the slave for recognition, an insight traced in *The Balcony* over Sartre. Bataille's emphasis, however, is on expanding a Marxist economic theory of exchange to include the domain of sexuality, one in which "eroticism is the ultimate *dépense*" (qtd. in Richman 75).

[16] For Jacques Lacan, the phallus is the transcendental signifier in a patriarchal symbolic order. In a fascinating confluence in French intellectual history, Lacan's classic essay on "The Signification of the Phallus" was first delivered as a lecture the same year that *The Balcony* appeared (1958). Both read the reified sign of the phallus as fraudulent, another version of masquerade. Given Lacan's interest in Genet's play, this connection needs revisiting (see White 422 for Lacan's response to the Paris production of *The Balcony* directed by Peter Brookes).

17 Genet's theatre, like that of Bertolt Brecht, who influenced his later work, disrupts both a naturalist theatre of mimesis and an Aristotelian theatre of rising and falling interest. In their emphasis on plastic values of gesture (what Brecht called *gestich*) and scenic construction, both are indebted to the traditions of non-Western theatre. Findley shares their interest in the traditions of Oriental theatre, the source of almost all his iconography of the Japanese, including the Lucy/Lucifer figure in *Not Wanted on the Voyage*, who is an *onnagata* of the kabuki theatre.

WORKS CITED

Adam, Peter. *Art of the Third Reich*. New York: Abrams, 1992.

Apter, Emily. Introduction. Apter and Pietz 1–9.

Apter, Emily, and William Pietz, eds. *Fetishism as Cultural Discourse*. Ithaca: Cornell UP, 1993.

Bataille, Georges. "The Psychological Structure of Fascism." *Visions of Excess: Selected Writings, 1927–1939*. Ed. Allan Stoekl. Trans. Stoekl, with Carl R. Louitts and Donald M. Leslie, Jr. Minneapolis: U of Minnesota P, 1985. 137–60.

Baudrillard, Jean. *For a Critique of the Political Economy of the Sign*. Trans. Charles Levin. St. Louis: Telos, 1981.

Benjamin, Walter. "Theories of German Fascism." Trans. Jerolf Wikoff. *New German Critique* 17 (1979): 120–28.

———. "The Work of Art in the Age of Mechanical Reproduction." *Illuminations*. New York: Schocken, 1969. 217–51.

Benson, Eugene. "Whispers of Chaos: *Famous Last Words*." *World Literature Written in English* 21 (1982): 599–606.

Brydon, Diana. *Writing on Trial: Timothy Findley's* Famous Last Words. Toronto: ECW, 1995.

Buchloh, H.D. "Divided Memory and Post-Traditional Identity: Gerhard Richter's Work of Mourning." *October* 75 (1996): 61–82.

Dellamora, Richard. "Becoming-Homosexual/Becoming-Canadian: Ironic Voice and the Politics of Location in Timothy Findley's *Famous Last Words*." *Double Talking: Essays on Verbal and Visual Ironies in Canadian Contemporary Art and Literature*. Ed. Linda Hutcheon. Toronto: ECW, 1992. 172–200.

Dyer, Richard. *Heavenly Bodies: Film Stars and Society*. London: Macmillan, 1987.

Findley, Timothy. *The Butterfly Plague*. New York: Viking, 1969.

———. *The Butterfly Plague*. Rev. ed. Markham, ON: Penguin, 1986.

———. *Can You See Me Yet?* 1977. Vancouver: Talon, 1986.

———. *Famous Last Words*. Toronto: Clark, 1981.

———. *Inside Memory: Pages from a Writer's Workbook*. Toronto: Harper-Collins, 1990.

———. " 'Long Live the Dead': An Interview with Timothy Findley." With Johan Aitken. *Journal of Canadian Fiction* 33 (1982): 79–93.

———. "Losers, Finders, Strangers at the Door." *Dinner along the Amazon*. Harmondsworth, Eng.: Penguin, 1984. 189–203.

———. "The Marvel of Reality." Interview with Bruce Meyer and Brian O'Riordan. *In Their Words: Interviews with Fourteen Canadian Writers*. Toronto: Anansi, 1984. 45–54.

———. "Masks and Icons: An Interview with Timothy Findley." With Barbara Gabriel. *Canadian Forum* Feb. 1986: 31–36.

———. *The Trials of Ezra Pound*. Winnipeg: Blizzard, 1994.

Foucault, Michel. "Anti-retro: Entretien avec Michel Foucault." With Pascal Bonitzer and Serge Toubiana. *Cahiers du cinema* 251–52 (1974): 5–18.

Fout, John C. "Sexual Politics in Wilhelmine Germany: The Male Gender Crisis, Moral Purity, and Homophobia." *Journal of the History of Sexuality* 2.3 (1992): 388–421.

Gabriel, Barbara. "Performing the *Bent* Text: Fascism and the Regulation of Sexualities in Timothy Findley's *The Butterfly Plague*." *English Studies in Canada* 21 (1996): 226–50.

———. "Sex, Lies and Photography: Reading Detective Fiction as Psycho-analysis in Timothy Findley's *The Telling of Lies*." *Gender and Narrativity*. Ed. Barry Rutland. Ottawa: Carleton UP, 1997. 87–113.

Genet, Jean. *The Balcony*. Trans. Bernard Frechtman. New York: Grove, 1958.

———. *Les Bonnes et comment jouer les bonnes*. Paris: Barbezat, 1963.

———. Interview with Hubert Fichte. *Gay Sunshine Interviews*. Vol. 1. Ed. Winston Leyland. San Francisco: Gay Sunshine, 1978. 67–94.

Hutcheon, Linda. "Canadian Historiographic Metafiction." *Essays on Canadian Writing* 30 (1984–85): 228–38.

Huyssen, Andreas. "Fortifying the Heart — Totally: Ernst Junger's Ar-moured Texts." *New German Critique* 59 (1993): 3–32.

Ingham, David. "Bashing the Fascists: The Moral Dimensions of Findley's Fiction." *Studies in Canadian Literature* 15.2 (1990): 33–54.

Krauss, Rosalind. *The Originality of the Avant-Garde and Other Modernist Myths*. Cambridge: MIT, 1985.

Lenzer, Gertrud. "On Masochism: A Contribution to the History of a Phantasy and Its Theory." *Signs* 1.2 (1975): 277–325.

Lindholm, Charles. *Charisma*. Oxford: Blackwell, 1993.

Macciochi, Maria-Antonietta. "Female Sexuality in Fascist Ideology." *Feminist Review* 2 (1979): 67–82.

McGann, Jerome J. "The Cantos of Ezra Pound: The Truth in Contradiction." *Critical Inquiry* 15 (1988): 1–25.

Miller, James. *The Passion of Michel Foucault*. New York: Simon, 1993.

Misejewski, Linda. *Divine Decadence: Fascism, Female Spectacle, and the Making of Sally Bowles*. Princeton: Princeton UP, 1992.

Mosse, George L. *Nationalism and Sexuality: Respectability and Abnormal Sexuality in Modern Europe*. New York: Fertig, 1985.

Perloff, Marjorie. "Fascism, Anti-Semitism, Isolationism: Contextualizing the *A Case of EP*." *Paideuma* 16 (1987): 7–21.

Pietz, William. "Fetishism and Materialism: The Limits of Theory in Marx." Apter and Pietz 119–52.

Pound, Ezra. "Hugh Selwyn Mauberley." *Selected Poems*. New Directions Paper Book 66. New York: New Directions, 1957. 61–77.

Richman, Michele H. *Reading Georges Bataille: Beyond the Gift*. Baltimore: Johns Hopkins UP, 1982.

Rushdie, Salman. "Crash." *New Yorker* 15 Sept. 1997: 68–69.

Scobie, Stephen. "'Eye-Deep in Hell: Ezra Pound, Timothy Findley, and Hugh Selwyn Mauberley." *Essays on Canadian Writing* 30 (1984–85): 206–27.

Silverman, Kaja. *Male Subjectivity at the Margins*. London: Routledge, 1992.

Sontag, Susan. "Fascinating Fascism." *A Susan Sontag Reader*. New York: Farrar, 1982. 305–25.

Taussig, Michael. "*Maleficium*: State Fetishism." Apter and Pietz 217–47.

Theweleit, Klaus. *Male Fantasies*. Minneapolis: U of Minnesota P, 1987.

White, Edmund. *Genet*. New York: Knopf, 1993.

Williams, Tennessee. *Orpheus Descending. The Theatre of Tennessee Williams*. Vol. 3. New York: New Directions, 1971.

——. *A Streetcar Named Desire*. New York: New Directions, 1947.

York, Lorraine M. *Front Lines: The Fiction of Timothy Findley*. Toronto: ECW, 1991.

Performed and Performing Selves in Findley's Drama

KAREN GRANDY

THERE IS AN INTRIGUING DISCREPANCY between the recent burst of scholarly interest in the performative aspects of Timothy Findley's fiction and the chronic lack of scholarly interest in the works that Findley wrote to be performed.[1] Indeed, the fact that Findley is a playwright, or that he was an actor, is generally invoked as a lead into a discussion of the dramatic qualities of his nondramatic works. Nevertheless, all three of Findley's published plays highlight the issues of performance that currently garner such critical attention. In his most recently published dramas, *The Stillborn Lover* and *The Trials of Ezra Pound*, sexuality and sanity are presented as social and political acts. A look back to *Can You See Me Yet?* (a play published two decades earlier) reveals the perhaps more radical proposition that memory and subsequently identity are also performative acts. This essay will examine the evolution of Findley's dramatic and metadramatic treatment of social and personal performance, as seen in these three texts. As a body of work, these plays address two central and controversial issues in performance theory. First, is there an essential, coherent self independent of all the enacted roles? Second, is such a foundation necessary for political and social critique?

In *The Man Who Mistook His Wife for a Hat and Other Clinical Tales*, neurologist Oliver Sacks describes Mr. Thompson, a patient whose short-term memory was severely impaired by Korsakov's syndrome: "He remembered nothing for more than a few seconds. He was continually disoriented. Abysses of amnesia continually opened beneath him, but he would bridge them, nimbly, by fluent confabulations and fictions of all kinds. For him they were not fictions, but how he suddenly saw, or interpreted, the world" (109). Mr. Thompson would identify Sacks "as a dozen different people in the course of five minutes" (109). The encounters with this comically tragic patient lead Sacks to the following contemplations: "We have, each of us, a life-story, an inner narrative — whose continuity, whose sense, is our lives. It might be said that each of us constructs and lives, a 'narrative', and that this narrative is us, our identities" (110). Mr. Thompson lost his life story and was consequently forced to continually reinvent one for himself.

Mr. Thompson's case, and Sacks's thoughtful commentary on it, raise a number of the same issues addressed, in a fictional context, in Findley's first published play, Can You See Me Yet? Sacks's patient was a raconteur, desperately trying to construct and maintain an identity with a constant stream of words. By contrast, Cassandra Wakelin, the protagonist of Findley's play, is a dramatist: she stages, rather than relates, her memories. Early in the play, she refers to her photograph album, her bridge to the past, as "all I have that tells me who I am" (42).[2] Cassandra is by no means a passive audience of that past. With the album as script, she sets the background, casts her fellow asylum patients, observes, directs, participates in, and interprets the performance of her past. We watch her mount a production of her memories. Furthermore, the work's metadramatic markers draw attention to the creative activities of its other playwright. It is not just her remembered past, but her present reality as well, that is clearly shown to be a dramatic enactment. Can You See Me Yet? investigates what we make of the past — and what the past makes of us.

One of Cassandra's first duties, as memory dramatist, is to set the backdrop. The primary setting of Can You See Me Yet? is the garden of the asylum at Britton. The play's secondary setting is another garden, that of the Wakelin family home in Laurel. The asylum scenes take place on a day in late summer 1938, the Laurel scenes on the day of Cassandra's homecoming from missionary work. The same scenery is used to represent both gardens and thus reminds us that, in one sense, we never leave the asylum. There are, however, notable differences between the two places. Cassandra recalls "Grass that was cool . . . bricks that were hot beneath my feet . . . holes in the yard we used to fill with water. . . . Doesn't anyone remember?" (41; first two ellipses in original). Her fellow asylum patients, of course, do not remember, but Findley's audience will remember — and be reminded of — these features in the Laurel scenes.

In her introduction to the play, Margaret Laurence states that the memory scenes occur "on the stage of Cassandra's mind" (9); they also occur on the stage of Findley's play. The memories affect not only what Cassandra sees but also what the audience of Can You See

Me Yet? sees. Her power to control what happens on stage is evident from her first appearance. Following her entrance at the beginning of scene 2, the stage directions specify that the patients arrange themselves in groupings appropriate to the characters that they will become on the secondary dramatic level. She immediately sees and casts the others in the roles that they will play in the Laurel scenes. It is not surprising that Cassandra, as casting director, meets with some resistance from her fellow asylum patients. When she first asks one of them "Are you my brother?" he replies, "No, Ma'am" (40). However, in the very next scene, the actor who plays this patient takes on his second role: Cassandra's brother Franklin. The actors move in and out of their secondary roles, and Cassandra, understandably, has trouble keeping up with them. She can conjure up the past, but she cannot maintain it to the exclusion of the present. Of course, it is important to keep in mind that it is not the patients but the actors who take part in the Laurel scenes. Cassandra's inability to distinguish her present companions from those of her past is underscored by the audience's own confusion about which role an actor is playing (although there are clothing and lighting cues). The effect of dual roles is at times that of an optical illusion: we, like Cassandra, look at the actor and see both the patient and the father.

Cassandra's relationship with the Laurel characters, and with her past, is most intriguingly explored in scene 9, entitled "Father and Daughter." Here Cassandra reveals herself as director, in control of this episode and critical of another's performance. Midway through this scene, Cassandra shouts, "You've lied! You're not the father I recognize. You make him like a man of pity: someone I could *love*!" (97). It is not clear whom Cassandra is accusing of lying. Edward's reply, "But . . . I'm only who I am" (98; ellipsis in original), raises questions of identity: is he just a product of her mind? If so, then perhaps she suspects her own memory, tainted with nostalgia, of misrepresenting the past. Laurence suggests in the introduction that Cassandra's memory of the Laurel characters might be affected by her current circumstances — that is, by their asylum alter egos (10). The patient-Edward is a gentle man, still mourning the death of his children. Perhaps some of his mildness has seeped into Cassandra's recollection of her father, Edward Wakelin. It is notable, however, that the stage directions specify that, after Cassandra criticizes him, he "assumes the second role ascribed to him . . . i.e. the Bastard" (98). Findley's directions point up the scenic quality of her memories. She is presented as an active director of these scenes. Her unusual assumption — intradramatically insane, but metadramatically valid — is that others are viewing her past with her.

As well as director, Cassandra is both participant in and spectator of the memory scenes. There are scenes in which she is back in Laurel. Elsewhere, however, the stage directions specify that she stand at the side of the stage and observe. She tries to communicate with the Laurel characters, but she cannot make herself seen or heard. Instead, she provides a commentary on the characters from the primary dramatic level. Cassandra is positioned as the most important spectator of this performance. In scene 6, she is both participant, acknowledged by the Laurel characters, and spectator/commentator, explaining what follows to her fellow patients: she never loses consciousness of the asylum; she appears to be in both places and times simultaneously. The scene dramatizes the moment of remembering, described by philosopher Mary Warnock as "experiencing two fragments of time together, the present with the past" (100).

As I have already noted, the script for the memory scenes is Cassandra's photograph album. A photograph album is the perfect script for a presentation of the past that combines mimesis with diegesis, showing with telling. In his essay "Uses of Photography," John Berger argues that, "unlike memory, photographs do not in themselves preserve meaning. They offer appearances — with all the credibility and gravity we normally lend to appearances — prised away from their meaning" (51). Susan Sontag, in *On Photography*, states that "understanding is based on how [something] functions. And functioning takes place in time, and must be explained in time. Only that which narrates can make us understand" (21). In *Can You See Me Yet?* Cassandra recognizes that the other patients, and the play's audience, need to be told what the photographs show. She supplies the interpretation; in effect, in addition to her roles as playwright, actor, and spectator, she is a drama critic.

As an asylum patient, Cassandra is marked as a potentially unreliable rememberer. Furthermore, Berger reminds us that it is because photographs "carry no certain meaning in themselves, because they are like images in the memory of a total stranger, that they lend themselves to any use" (53). It is the patient-Annie who remarks to Cassandra, "There aren't any pictures of you in there." She then asks, "Did you steal it?" (145). Despite Cassandra's denial, Annie concludes, "You don't even know their names. You made them all up. Liar!" (145). To suggest that Cassandra is not remembering the Laurel scenes but inventing them is to broach a subject that has caused

184

much controversy among those interested in the function of human memory, from philosophers to psychologists. The debate turns on the question of whether remembering is the retrieval of stored information, an act of creative construction, or both. *Can You See Me Yet?* portrays Cassandra's attempt to reconstruct her past. We see Cassandra make it, but does she make it up?

Her memories are certainly affected by her present circumstances. When she remembers her father, she sees the patient-Edward (assuming that we see what she sees in the memory scenes). Does the death of the asylum dog, hit by a fire truck, remind Cassandra of the dog massacre, on the day of the hotel fire, in Laurel? Or does she incorporate the asylum episode into her memory? Her Aunt Doretta tells Cassandra to "Join the real world" (80), an extraordinary request from a character whom we know to be a product of Cassandra's mind. Cassandra herself also expresses doubt about the reality of the Laurel scenes. When her sister, Rosemary, begs her for help, she replies, "There's nothing I can do. I . . . *don't exist?*" (159; ellipsis in original).

Findley deliberately leaves our questions about his protagonist's past unanswered. The Laurel scenes are significant not for what they tell about Cassandra's past but for what they reveal about the importance of that past, remembered or invented, to her sense of self. Sacks proposes that "To be ourselves we must have ourselves — possess, if need be repossess, our life-stories" (111). Findley's character Doretta concurs: "If she says the book's the story of her life, then it's the story of her life" (148). *Can You See Me Yet?* presents Cassandra's attempted repossession of her life story, and hence of herself, through the dramatic reenactment of that story.

Cassandra returns to the past in search of identity and sanctuary. In the sixth scene, she "gazes at the pictures in her book" and recalls that "it was so lovely here. So safe. So *safe*" (81). When she discovers that she can no longer invoke Laurel, she throws the photograph album away and calls out for help (164). She is about to kill herself when an unexpected voice forces her to begin reinventing herself. Doberman sacrifices the protective identity that he has taken on, a dog (which he plays on both levels), to save her. He calls out, speaking for the first time, and leads her back from the precipice. Cassandra finds safety — and identity — in relationships, not those of the performed past but those of the present.

Doretta suggests that Cassandra join the real world. Near the end of the play, the curtain falls on the Laurel scenes, and Cassandra joins the others in the present. There are metadramatic reminders throughout, however, that this primary world is as much a dramatic construction as the secondary world that we watch Cassandra create. In the first scene, Enid's hysterical announcement, "THE SKY IS FALLING," is undercut by Edward, who pronounces, "Piffle. The sky is all in your imagination. Everybody knows the sky is just a lot of blue gas" (22) — or in this case blue paint. Cassandra's suicide attempt is dramatized by her "plung[ing] blindly towards the brink of the stage" (164). Their world ends at the brink of the stage, although Cassandra elsewhere defies that boundary by speaking directly to the audience.

The setting of the play's primary dramatic level also has metadramatic implications. This asylum has a lot in common with a theatrical performance.[3] Its boundaries are well defined. The setting is contrived to be both controlling and aesthetically pleasing (for example, the sunlit garden, enclosed by a fence). The uniforms of patients, different for each ward, and nurses can be seen as a type of costume. As well, patients may improvise their own roles, such as that of Doberman's dog. Their day is neatly divided into scenes — quarters as Edward names them — that are marked by food breaks. Most significantly, both insane asylums and theatres make us think about our notions of perceived reality. The play's final speech, in which nurse Alma announces Cassandra's death, is a direct address to the audience: "Ladies and gentlemen . . . 'brothers and sisters' . . ." (166; first ellipsis in original). Alma joins the world of the audience, a technique that Findley favours in all his writing: dissolving the boundary between real and unreal, so that we see the work in the contexts of our own lives. In the asylum scenes, a radio belonging to one of the guards is always playing in the background. We can hear, faintly, voices from the extradramatic world: songs, commercials, radio programs, Hitler. The intrusion of our reality into Findley's surreality, and vice versa, is disturbing, because it implies that our own pasts and presents may be as constructed as Cassandra's.

"What is the final form, the natural form, of our life's repertoire?" Sacks asks (146). He suggests that "Personal patterns, patterns for the individual, would have to take the form of scripts or scores . . ." (148). Can You See Me Yet? presents the construction of one's past — memory — and hence of oneself — identity — as a dramatic performance. How can one's present, then, be other than likewise constructed and performed?[4] And what better vehicle could there be for exploring those necessarily imaginative and performative strategies than a metadramatic memory play?

Findley's earliest published play takes an unequivocal stand on a contested issue at the crux of performance theory: the relationship between self and performance. A strong spokesperson for one side of this debate is phenomenologist Bruce Wilshire, who insists on a transcendent self and argues that "all theatrical *and* paratheatrical performance is inherently limited, circumscribed within a larger domain of human action and experience" (177). Findley's protagonist, however, dramatically demonstrates the opposing argument, put forward by sociologist Erving Goffman, who himself uses a sustained theatrical analogy throughout *The Presentation of Self in Everyday Life*:

> The self, then, as a performed character, is not an organic thing that has a specific location, whose fundamental fate is to be born, to mature, and to die; it is a dramatic effect arising diffusely from a scene that is presented, and the characteristic issue, the critical concern, is whether it will be credited or discredited. (252–53)

Cassandra's identity, her sense of self, is shown to be both thematically and literally (because this is a play) "a dramatic effect arising diffusely from a scene."[5] The play's metadramatic markers indicate that here Wilshire's "larger domain," Cassandra's present, is also a dramatic performance.

Cassandra, a private citizen and an asylum patient, leads a very secluded life. In two plays published more than fifteen years later, Findley returns to the question of performed and performing selves, but with protagonists whose lives are much more public: a Canadian ambassador, and Ezra Pound. These plays go on to consider the performing self within society and the conflicts and crises that arise within this self.

Elizabeth Burns, in *Theatricality: A Study of the Convention in the Theatre and in Social Life*, observes that "The social system is in fact a system of roles which are defined by the negative and positive sanctions of law, custom and norms of behaviour" (128). Hayden White describes such systems in terms of narration:

> a society narrativizes itself, constructing a cast of social "characters" or "roles" for its members to play, if they are to play its game; a "plot" or ideal course of development for the relations presumed to exist among its recognized character

types; and appropriate sanctions for those who deviate from the norms of social being and comportment adequate to the reinforcement of the values the society takes to be its own. (158)

The Stillborn Lover examines its protagonist's deviation from his appointed social role and the sanctions that follow.

An earlier version of the opening scenes of *The Stillborn Lover* was published in *Books in Canada* in 1989 under the title "Inquest." *Inquest* is also the title of a play published two decades earlier, by American dramatist Donald Freed, about Julius and Ethel Rosenberg. In addition to the working title, Freed's and Findley's plays have in common protagonists whose lives are destroyed by Cold War ideology and poignant portrayals of individuals struggling against and overwhelmed by self-serving bureaucracies. Freed's play, however, belongs to a dramatic subgenre that emerged in the mid-1960s, theatre of fact. As Freed explains in his introduction, he employs "the vocabulary of the myth of the twentieth century: film, tape, trials, technology, confessions" (4), and "every word is taken from primary sources" (7). *The Stillborn Lover*, although based — like much of Findley's work — on historical personages and incidents, is clearly not theatre of fact. Nevertheless, like *The Trials of Ezra Pound*, *The Stillborn Lover* shares with theatre of fact certain thematic and structural elements: most significantly, the situation of the individual on trial and the investigation and interrogation of political power structures.

As *The Stillborn Lover* opens, Canadian diplomat Harry Raymond faces deportation to Moscow to answer charges for the murder of his lover, a Russian spy. Significantly, the murder trial that awaits Raymond in Moscow is a show trial. The victim was actually killed by his Russian employers to create a potentially damaging international scandal, a situation particularly undesirable for Raymond's friend Michael Riordan, who appointed Raymond to Moscow and who is now poised to become the next prime minister of Canada. The Russian government constructed the situation to leverage power over Riordan by offering to trade silence for influence. Riordan is willing to accept this offer, but Raymond, required to admit to betraying his oath of office, balks. He is coerced into a repugnant choice: "A murder trial — or the confession of a misdemeanour — and retirement, abroad" (86). To Riordan, "the choice is obvious," but Raymond disagrees: "To be loyal, I must appear to be disloyal

— to the end of my days. Throw over everything I've stood for, all my life" (86).

Sociology defines "role," most basically, as "the primary mechanism through which human beings interact with one another" (Fein 2). Sociological approaches to this complex mechanism follow two major traditions: the structural and the interactionist (Nye 4). The former, Melvyn L. Fein explains in *Role Change: A Resocialization Perspective*, "sees roles as imposed upon individuals from the outside. . . . It defines roles in terms of 'expectations' people have of one another" (13). By contrast, the interactionist view is that "a person's own norms and values, that is, her own way of understanding what she is doing, define her role. It is her intentions and understandings which make the role what it is" (13). Fein, whose book is a study of the causes and treatments of dysfunctional roles, presents social roles as "a joint construction of people and their role partners" (4). Therefore, he argues, "If they cooperate, they may succeed in developing role patterns that are mutually satisfying. If not, one or both will be frustrated" (4). *The Stillborn Lover* dramatizes the latter crisis.

Harry Raymond speaks with anguish of the personal cost of past social performances: "I'm telling you I killed my self," he tells his daughter, Diana, because that self "stood in my way" (57). More explicitly, his homosexuality stood in the way of his career — his vocation — in the diplomatic service. To Diana he responds, "You say 'who gives a damn' if I'm homosexual. I *do*. My work does. My government does. *Do not be a homosexual. Do not be a homosexual. Do not be that. Be anything — but do not be a homosexual*" (56).

"We all know they [the Russians] entrap the gay boys, drop of a hat," RCMP sergeant Jackman bluntly observes (68). Sex and politics are indeed shown to be inextricably linked in *The Stillborn Lover*. The investigating detectives attempt to connect Raymond's membership in the communist party while at university with his romantic relationship at that time with Francis Oliver. Marian and Harry Raymond, as a political statement, choose to honeymoon in Nagasaki and arrange that Diana be born there, as "their gesture of atonement" (37). That the RCMP has a unit whose mandate includes "rooting out homosexuals" (69) demonstrates the conflation of public and personal — the intimate and the explicit — highlighted throughout this play.

Marian Raymond confirms her husband's terminal self-diagnosis: "I was living with a man who was dying — of denial. Do you know what that does? It kills. And I had to save his life" (76). She relates how her chance discovery of a sexual encounter between two employees leads her to Harry's salvation:

> One of the messenger boys — a runner — was standing in the shadows. His back was to the wall. His eyes — I can still see his eyes. He was in some kind of ecstasy. And . . . the blond young man — the secretary — was kneeling in front of him . . . down on his knees in his white linen suit. I didn't understand, at first. And then I did. . . . And it was then — because I had seen his eyes — that I knew how I could save your father. (76; first two ellipses in original)

On this occasion, she arranges a sexual liaison with the Egyptian messenger. Years later in Russia, she sends another lover to Harry. Both Marian and Harry declaim a true, knowable self, distinct from, yet potentially endangered by, the public roles that we are compelled to enact. And both suggest the affirmation of self through sexuality. Harry recalls his initial encounter with Mischa in the baths at Yalta: "When I saw him first, it was like those meetings you have in dreams, when a stranger greets you and you recognize him instantly. You, is it? I've been waiting for you. I was his Lazarus, he was my miracle worker. Rise up and walk. Rejoin the living . . ." (57; ellipsis in original). We also learn, however, that this reawakening of what Harry sees as his true self was occasioned by a skilful, politically motivated, sexual performance:

> JACKMAN: He [Mischa] was an actor. And a good one.
> MAHAVOLITCH: You mean — he wasn't a homosexual? He was a plant, pretending to be queer? (65)

Mischa, in fact, is the play's most explicit symbol of sexuality as political performance.

Mischa Andreevitch Bugarin's name does not appear in the character list of *The Stillborn Lover*. Although Mischa is central to the complication and unfolding of the play's plot, his notable absence from the dramatis personae is appropriate. He is dead when the play opens. His death, in fact, precipitates the congregation of the characters at the beginning of the play. The Raymonds and the Riordans have not come together, however, to commiserate with Harry. As the play opens, it is only Michael Riordan who knows that Mischa is dead, and it is he who has convened this meeting and invited two

RCMP officers to join them. Riordan's purpose is not to mourn but to control this potential diplomatic scandal: the violent death of a young Russian, now known to be an employee of the KGB and the lover of the Canadian ambassador.

The Stillborn Lover focuses on Harry: his daughter's response to the revelation of his homosexuality; his long, rich relationship with his wife; the personal sacrifices and subterfuges required of him to continue in public service; and his interrogation by the RCMP officers as a suspect in Mischa's murder. Harry's past and future grip our attention; Harry, not Mischa, is the stillborn lover referred to in the play's title. Yet Mischa, absent and dead, is central to the main plot and themes of the play. His body — sold, brutalized, photographed, manipulated, absent — is a central symbol in this work.

As Heather Sanderson observes in her discussion of *The Butterfly Plague* elsewhere in this volume, Findley's work repeatedly "depicts the struggle for power and interpretative control as a contest for physical control played out at the level of the body" (113). Mischa's body, like Ruth's in *The Butterfly Plague*, becomes a dramatic manifestation of a theory put forward by Foucault in *Discipline and Punish*: "But the body is also directly involved in a political field; power relations have an immediate hold upon it; they invest it, mark it, train it, torture it, force it to carry out tasks, to perform ceremonies, to emit signs" (25). Initially, the KGB tries to blackmail Raymond with sexually explicit photographs of him and Mischa together. These pornographic photographs are an important prop in the play. Riordan hands them in the second scene to Jackman, who later passes them to Mahavolitch with the observation, "Potent stuff, this" (41). Jackman, like the Russians, attempts to use them to put pressure on Raymond; he warns, "I could show them to your wife" (48). The potency of the photographs, however, is determined by the viewer. The blackmail attempts fail when these photos are found to be politically impotent; Raymond refuses — then and now — to be manipulated in this way.

Mischa's body is once more pressed into political service. Mischa is murdered, seemingly brutally, if we can gauge by the characters' responses to the postmortem photographs. His photographed body is again invested with political power relations. Jackman interprets the photographed murder victim as an ideological icon. He instructs an "obviously sickened" Mahavolitch to study the picture: "Look at *him*. A portrait of commitment" (64, 65). Moreover, the political is here again shown to be imbued with the sexual. The setting is a —

perhaps the same? — "hotel room in Moscow" (48), and Mischa's death is intended to be used to influence, via his former lover, the Canadian government. The conflation of the two incidents, sexual entrapment and murder, is suggested by Raymond's own confusion about the photographs:

> HARRY: I'm sorry. I can't . . . I cannot look at him dead.
> . . .
> JACKMAN: Well — these may show a hotel room in Moscow, Ambassador, but . . . *(He looks at the pictures.)* the boy in here sure ain't dead. (48; ellipses in original)

Mischa is present on stage only in these two sets of photographs, the desired, reviled, and manipulated object of the gaze of others. He is completely subsumed by a political bureaucracy that first casts him in a role and then degrades him to a prop. Even Raymond refers to him as "the body" before calling him by name (33).

Mischa's Canadian counterpart is RCMP corporal Mahavolitch, whose role as sexual bait is commented on by both Marian and Harry; the former calls him "a rather splendid specimen" (78), and the latter labels him a prostitute (83). Their suspicions are confirmed by Jackman, who elsewhere explains, "That's why I brought in Corporal Mahavolitch, sir. It's part of his unit's mandate — rooting out homosexuals" (69). The potential power of Mahavolitch's body, and its symbolic function in this homicide/espionage investigation, are impressed upon the play's spectators in two scenes in which Mahavolitch undresses. In both scenes, the audience's main focus is on Harry, who is talking about Mischa. Mahavolitch's pleased awareness of the power of his body is made clear at the end of the first nude scene: "Then he [Mahavolitch] stands up and straps it [his revolver] on with a shoulder holster. He crosses to an imaginary mirror, his back to the audience. Watching himself, he removes his shorts and stands there — contented" (34). His physicality is emphasized by his actions on stage: jogging, exercising, towelling himself dry, dressing, and undressing. The sexually suggestive nature of his appearance, actions, and comments is blatantly obvious to all the characters. At one point, Raymond wryly observes, "I'm not interested in young men wearing purple running shorts" (83). Mahavolitch overplays his role.

Does this overt demonstration of politicized sexuality undermine Harry and Marian's profession of a transcendent self, affirmed through sexuality? Raymond articulates his own dismayed discovery of Mischa's betrayal: "The shock — the shock was that he was one of them. One of theirs. Not his own person, but someone else's person all along" (81). These statements indicate, however, a persistent belief in the existence of one's "own person." Raymond presents himself thus to Diana: "I am not in hiding. I am here. Right here — standing in front of you. *Me*" (56). His words echo those of Wilshire in "The Concept of the Paratheatrical": "And even when my activities *are* performances in one sense or other, I as a person cannot be reduced to them . . ." (177). The play's conclusion, Raymond's refusal to adopt the role proffered by Riordan, dramatizes his newfound resistance to the bureaucratic imposition of roles upon him, his movement from the structural to the interactionist stance. Raymond now intends to direct his public and personal performances in roles that he (Wilshire's irreducible "I") casts for himself.

The Stillborn Lover takes a more ambivalent stance on the controversy of the performing self than we saw in *Can You See Me Yet?* It is akin to other Findley works that, Catherine Hunter argues in the first essay of this collection, "display an ambivalence toward self and story — both a nostalgic desire for stable absolutes and a desire for fragmentation, or even destruction, of them" (17). The play demonstrates the politically manipulated role enactment and scenic construction that permeate all levels of public and private life, yet the protagonist continues to profess and act on a belief in an essential self. Perhaps such ambivalence is necessary to accommodate the play's own private/public concerns: its sympathetic portrayal of an individual in crisis and its critical examination of the social systems that precipitate the crisis. Like Freed's *Inquest*, *The Stillborn Lover* clearly condemns Cold War society's treatment of what it considered to be dangerously deviant, whether politically or sexually or both.[6] All theatre of fact is activist, dramatizing "the victimization of the individual by the State" and intended to "bring passive lookers-on — for that is what an audience is — to a point of action" (Isaac 132, 131). Reviewer Harry Lane identifies a similar effect at the end of *The Stillborn Lover*: "But recognition of contradictions creates opportunity to act. As Marian says, in her final line to Harry, 'It's your move.' Given Findley's determination to make his readers 'pay attention!' Marian's line may also apply to the reader or spectator" (453).

The seeming contradictions within *The Stillborn Lover*'s presentation of the performing self highlight what Marvin Carlson identifies as a "critical challenge" within performance theory:

the frequent associations of the postmodern . . . with a loss of origins, a free play of signification, and an instability of truth claims seem to suggest that to the extent that performance is a significantly postmodern form it is very ill-suited to the grounding of subjectivity or identity, either for the purposes of defining or exploring the self or for providing a position for political or social commentary or action. (8)

Wilshire sternly warns against allowing paratheatricality — performance — to extend into what he labels "the ethical domain" (178); Carlson here points to potential ramifications within the political domain. If agency depends on a stable agent, then is it necessary for Findley to modify his portrayal of self as dramatic enactment if he also wants his plays to work as social criticism? *The Stillborn Lover* appears to suggest so, but an alternative solution might be found in his most recent published play, *The Trials of Ezra Pound*. This play also has a trial looming in its background — a trial for treason. "The trial situation has provided a favourite dramatic motif since Aeschylus," Gregory Mason observes in his article "Documentary Drama from the Revue to the Tribunal" (268).[7] *The Trials of Ezra Pound* is a variation of the tribunal play; it presents the preliminary hearings held, at the end of World War II, to determine Pound's mental fitness to stand trial for treason.[8]

Trials are dramatic in both subject — human conflict — and structure, with witnesses, spectators, "the stand,"[9] and an anticipated outcome. Overt exploitation of the theatricality of the courtroom may be seen in such diverse instances as the Stalinist show trials or the American media's melodramatic presentation of sensational trials, complete with theme music, souvenirs, and critiques of the participants' performance, clothing, and hairstyles. Furthermore, even obscure trials may be seen as performances with well-defined roles, lines, places, and costumes. These performative aspects are highlighted in tribunal plays and serve as metadramatic markers by drawing attention to the drama as (another) performance.

To say that trials have theatrical components may be to state the obvious; less obvious is anthropologist Victor Turner's suggestion that theatre has judicial components. In *From Ritual to Theatre: The Human Seriousness of Play*, Turner proposes: "the performative genres of complex, industrial societies, as well as many of their forensic and judicial institutions, the stage and the law court, have their deep roots in the enduring human social drama, particularly in its redressive phase, the drama that has its *direct* source in social structural conflict" (110). Theatre and trials both occupy, Turner argues, "a liminal time, set apart from the ongoing business of quotidian life, when an interpretation . . . is constructed to give the appearance of sense and order to the events leading up to and constituting [a] crisis" (75). His thesis is concisely summarized by performance critics Carol Simpson Stern and Bruce Henderson: "theater investigates, interrogates, and involves judgment and punishment; in short, it enacts a kind of law-in-action . . ." (9). We may go on to surmise that the trial play, a dramatized drama, should provide an excellent vehicle for the investigation of performance itself. The judicial situation enacted in *The Trials of Ezra Pound* investigates and interrogates sanity and identity as performance and the political and personal implications thereof.

Pound delineates the choice before him: "They're trying to make me say I'm crazy, Bill. Stand up in public and say I'm crazy — otherwise they'll hang me" (14). Pound is resistant to this defence, which he sees as a misrepresentation and a dangerous threat to his identity. The situation is a peculiar twist of the elements in *The Stillborn Lover*; Raymond is asked to present himself as traitorous in order to avoid a trial for murder; Pound is presented as insane in order to avoid a trial for treason and the death penalty. The hearing scenes focus on the testimony of two psychiatrists. Dr. Muncie claims that Pound's "fixed ideas are either clearly delusional or verging on the delusional" and that Pound "shows a remarkable grandiosity" (25). He also describes him as "vague, distraught — relying almost exclusively on confrontation" (27). Delusional, grandiose, and confrontational: Muncie ascribes to Pound the characteristics that we associate with theatrical performance. In other words, he is insane because he acts like an actor. But Muncie himself is deliberately, albeit reluctantly, staging a performance in this trial, as is made clear to us by the second witness, Dr. Overholser.

Overholser is obviously aware of and complicitous in the drama being staged here. During the recess, he confers privately with Muncie, "mostly for effect" (46), to worry the prosecutor. He complains to Muncie, "I did not like your performance this morning" (47). Muncie responds: "I said the words. I don't have to win a goddamn prize for how I said them" (48). Overholser also employs game-playing metaphors in his critique of Muncie: "you will tip our hand, however inadvertently, and give us all away" (49). Overholser himself commits perjury on the stand when he denies knowledge of the findings of three psychiatrists who examined Pound in Italy and found him sane and fit to stand trial (72–73).

This play emphasizes speech acts as performance and power. "Your husband is insane because I say so," Overholser tells Dorothy Pound (56). The prosecutor's awareness of the power of spoken words is evident in a caution to Overholser: "As a result of what you say next, Ezra Pound will either spend the rest of his life in an insane asylum — or he will hang" (58). The case against Pound emerges from and comes down to spoken words: his radio broadcasts, his doctors' diagnoses, the jury's verdict (orally confirmed at the end of the play).[10] Insanity, with its attendant social consequences, is presented as authoritative pronouncement. The work's tribunal play format emphasizes the performative nature of such pronouncements. It is also clearly indicated that such pronouncements can be politically motivated. Muncie is horrified to discover that Overholser's diagnosis and his determination to protect Pound, even to perjure himself, comprise "a political decision" based on his agreement with Pound's fascist ideology (48).

Pound admits to being "not so sure" that he has won when the jury finds him to be of unsound mind and not fit to stand trial (77). He is disturbed by the image of himself that has been presented by others: "I have not enjoyed the silence. My silence. And I have not enjoyed the spectacle, here, of my portrait" (73). His self-portrait is clearly different yet still apparently intact: "To be called mad — madman — to be called insane, when I am not insane but only Ezra Pound" (73). The play ends with his reiteration of his name and his self-appointed role: "Pound. Ezra Pound. Custodian" (78).

Like Raymond in *The Stillborn Lover*, Pound resists the bureaucratic imposition of a role upon him. Pound's sense of his sanity, and hence of his self, seemingly survives any public perception or judicial pronouncement to the contrary. However, unlike *The Stillborn Lover*, this play questions Wilshire's and its own protagonist's convictions about the transcendent self. It does so by highlighting the performance of Pound's self-portrait in two ways: through the metadramatic tribunal format and through the placement of Pound's declarations of his self ("I am Ezra Pound! I am Ezra Pound!" [73]) within a long, increasingly hysterical, and highly melodramatic monologue that is the emotional climax of the play. In contrast to Wilshire, David George, in "On Ambiguity: Towards a Post-Modern Performance Theory," proposes that "The self arises and is experienced not in opposition to role-playing but co-incidentally . . ." (77).

Pound is hereby presented simultaneously as a performing *and* performed self.

The Trials of Ezra Pound ends where *Can You See Me Yet?* begins: in an insane asylum. This congruence, however, does not necessarily signal a return to the primarily personal, nonpolitical, performance issues addressed in Findley's first published play. In spite of its emphasis upon the performance of self, *The Trials of Ezra Pound* reiterates *The Stillborn Lover*'s demonstration of the often huge gap between self-portrait and official portrait and reveals the constructed enactment of each. Pound's presentation of himself may go unacknowledged by the other characters in the play, but it is heard by Findley's audience, who can recognize therein what Randy Martin identifies as the inherent resistance of performance. Carlson outlines Martin's theory that performance is "by its nature involved in resistance to what he calls the 'symbolic', the attempt of authority in art or in politics to enforce a unified and monolithic structure opposed to the 'overflowing' quality of the moving, acting, and desiring body" (141). The tribunal play format, furthermore, positions the audience of *The Trials of Ezra Pound* as jury, invited to pass judgement on — and then to resist — not the accused protagonist but the social system enforcing its "unified and monolithic structure" upon him. Thus, the play both investigates the performance of self and critiques the authoritative structures that attempt to direct and control that performance.

NOTES

[1] As noted in the introduction to this volume, at the end of her critical overview of Findley scholarship in her essay in *Canadian Writers and Their Works*, Lorraine York cites both performance and dramatic criticism as possible areas for future studies (86). In a recent interview with Laurie Kruk, Findley states, "I'm still fascinated by that idea: that writing is a performance art" (116). A number of the papers presented at the October 1997 Findley conference at Trent University addressed his portrayal of gender as performance. See also Gabriel. York discusses race as performance in the final essay in this volume.

[2] *The Wars*, likewise, begins with photographs, which serve as a bridge between the outer, present level and the past (11).

[3] See Weiss; as its title indicates, his play has a similar setting.

[4] At the beginning of a study entitled *Metafictional Characters in Modern Drama*, June Schlueter observes that "The absolutes which once informed mankind with a sense of certainty have dissolved into relativistic vision,

relegating reality to a position as subjective as the individual perceptions now believed to create it" (5). She goes on to cite Joe David Bellamy's question, "If reality becomes surrealistic, what must fiction do to be realistic?" (6). Elsewhere, she argues that Weiss's play "suggests, finally, that the art of madmen may be our only definition of reality" (78).

⁵ Another proponent of this view of self within Findley's work is Fabiana Holbach in *Headhunter*, who, Marlene Goldman notes in her essay in this volume, insists "that there can be no unveiling of an essential truth because identity itself is nothing more than a fiction — a performance" (50).

⁶ The play's portrayal of sexuality as performance, and the participation of the government (via the RCMP) therein, undermine the natural/unnatural binary of sexuality assumed in Cold War discourse. See Edelman for a discussion of the representation of and official attitude toward homosexuality in Cold War America.

⁷ Contemporary Canadian examples include John Coulter's *The Trial of Louis Riel*, George Ryga's *The Ecstasy of Rita Joe*, and portions of James Reaney's trilogy *The Donnellys*.

⁸ Findley employs the theatre of fact technique of incorporating parts of the transcripts from the actual hearings and Pound's broadcasts into the play.

⁹ A "stand" is also a term for a stop on a theatrical tour, as in "one-night stand" (*Gage Canadian Dictionary*).

¹⁰ The power of the spoken word is particularly obvious in radio productions of this play.

WORKS CITED

Berger, John. "Uses of Photography." *About Looking*. New York: Pantheon, 1980.

Burns, Elizabeth. *Theatricality: A Study of the Convention in the Theatre and in Social Life*. New York: Harper, 1972.

Carlson, Marvin. *Performance: A Critical Introduction*. London: Routledge, 1996.

Edelman, Lee. "Tearooms and Sympathy; or, The Epistemology of the Water Closet." *Homographesis: Essays in Gay Literary and Cultural Theory*. By Edelman. London: Routledge, 1994. 148–70.

Fein, Melvyn L. *Role Change: A Resocialization Perspective*. New York: Praeger, 1990.

Findley, Timothy. *Can You See Me Yet?* Vancouver: Talonbooks, 1977.

——. "I Want an Edge: An Interview with Timothy Findley." With Laurie Kruk. *Canadian Literature* 148 (1996): 115–29.

——. *The Stillborn Lover*. Winnipeg: Blizzard, 1993.

——. *The Trials of Ezra Pound*. Winnipeg: Blizzard, 1995.

——. *The Wars*. Markham, ON: Penguin, 1977.

Foucault, Michel. *Discipline and Punish*. Trans. Alan Sheridan. New York: Pantheon, 1977.

Freed, Donald. *Inquest*. New York: Hill, 1970.

Gabriel, Barbara. "Performing the *Bent* Text: Fascism and the Regulation of Sexualities in Timothy Findley's *The Butterfly Plague*." *English Studies in Canada* 21 (1995): 227–50.

George, David. "On Ambiguity: Towards a Post-Modern Performance Theory." *Theatre Research International* 14 (1989): 71–85.

Goffman, Erving. *The Presentation of Self in Everyday Life*. New York: Doubleday, 1959.

Goldman, Marlene. "The End(s) of Myth: Apocalyptic and Prophetic Fictions in *Headhunter*." *Paying Attention: Critical Essays on Timothy Findley*. Ed. Anne Geddes Bailey and Karen Grandy. Toronto: ECW, 1998. 32–55. Also published in the *Timothy Findley Issue*. Ed Bailey and Grandy. Spec. issue of *Essays on Canadian Writing* 64 (1998): 32–55.

Hunter, Catherine. " 'I Don't Know How to Begin': Findley in the Sixties." *Paying Attention: Critical Essays on Timothy Findley*. Ed. Anne Geddes Bailey and Karen Grandy. Toronto: ECW, 1998. 13–31. Also published in the *Timothy Findley Issue*. Ed Bailey and Grandy. Spec. issue of *Essays on Canadian Writing* 64 (1998): 13–31.

Isaac, Dan. "Theatre of Fact." *Drama Review* 15 (1971): 109–35.

Lane, Harry. " 'Not His Own Person': Questions of Betrayal in *The Stillborn Lover*." *Queen's Quarterly* 100 (1993): 441–56.

Laurence, Margaret. Introduction. Findley, *Can You* 9–13.

Mason, Gregory. "Documentary Drama from the Revue to the Tribunal." *Modern Drama* 20 (1977): 263–77.

Nye, F. Ivan. *Role Structure and Analysis of the Family*. London: Sage, 1976.

Sacks, Oliver. *The Man Who Mistook His Wife for a Hat and Other Clinical Tales*. New York: Harper, 1970.

Sanderson, Heather. "(Im)Perfect Dreams: Allegories of Fascism in *The Butterfly Plague*." *Paying Attention: Critical Essays on Timothy Findley*. Ed. Anne Geddes Bailey and Karen Grandy. Toronto: ECW, 1998. 104–24. Also published in the *Timothy Findley Issue*. Ed Bailey and Grandy. Spec. issue of *Essays on Canadian Writing* 64 (1998): 104–24.

Schlueter, June. *Metafictional Characters in Modern Drama*. New York: Columbia UP, 1979.

Sontag, Susan. *On Photography*. New York: Farrar, 1973.

Stern, Carol Simpson, and Bruce Henderson. *Performance: Texts and Contexts*. New York: Longman, 1993.

Turner, Victor. *From Ritual to Theatre: The Human Seriousness of Play*. New York: Performing Arts Journal, 1982.

Warnock, Mary. *Memory*. London: Faber, 1987.

Weiss, Peter. *The Persecution and Assassination of Marat as Performed by the Inmates of the Asylum of Charenton under the Direction of the Marquis de Sade*. Trans. Geoffrey Skelton. London: Calder, 1965.

White, Hayden. *The Content of the Form: Narrative Discourse and Historical Representation*. Baltimore: Johns Hopkins UP, 1987.

Wilshire, Bruce. "The Concept of the Paratheatrical." *Drama Review* 34 (1990): 169–78.

York, Lorraine M. "Timothy Findley and His Works." *Canadian Writers and Their Works*. Fiction Series. Vol. 12. Ed. Robert Lecker, Jack David, and Ellen Quigley. Toronto: ECW, 1995. 69–120. 12 vols. 1981–96.

"A White Hand Hovering over the Page": Timothy Findley and the Racialized/Ethnicized Other

LORRAINE YORK

NEAR THE END of *Headhunter*, the Berrys' maid, Orley, muses on the strange theatricality of her position in the affluent Berry household: "Here I sit in a white man's kitchen, she thought, playing the black servant. Just the way I would in a white man's book" (417). She is not the first black maid so seated — racially situated — in Timothy Findley's fictional kitchen, but she is the first to muse upon her place at the table in so self-conscious a manner. Orley even supplies the reader with a short intertextual survey of the other black maids sitting in other white writers' kitchens:

> The one . . . in *The Member of the Wedding*. Berenice. . . .
> And that Dilsey. Everybody knew about her. The servant of servants. Cook of cooks. Mammy of mammies. Coloured of the coloured. Negro of Negroes. Black of black.
> But written white. William Faulkner.
> Black — with a white hand hovering over the page. (417)

Findley, his own white hand visibly hovering over this passage, has just opened up for self-conscious examination his oeuvre, written white.

* * *

Critics of Findley have been slow to initiate this discussion of the racialized or ethnicized other, though a number of us (see Ingham; Pennee; and York) have thoroughly examined the thematics of racism in his works. Those readings, like the analysis of *Not Wanted on the Voyage* that appears in Bill Ashcroft, Gareth Griffiths, and Helen Tiffin's *The Empire Writes Back: Theory and Practice in Post-Colonial Literatures*, have focused on Findley's texts as revelatory and critical of the othering practices of Western societies. But what of Findley's own inevitable participation in the signifying systems operating in the construction of race and ethnicity? How has Findley himself written race and ethnicity? There have been, till now, only gestures made in these directions by critics concerned with postcolonial and gendered subjectivities, gestures that I have found most valuable. In a 1986 article, " 'It Could Not Be Told': Making Meaning in Timothy Findley's *The Wars*," Diana Brydon — drawing on a comic episode in that novel in which Robert responds to an angry Flemish farmer, *"Je ne suis pas français! Je suis canadien!"* — explores how Robert's national identity as a "Canadian" "disguises divisions within the country and the original fact of conquest on which that apparent unity is based" (63). She similarly locates Robert's fleeting glimpse of Indians and his worship of the runner Tom Longboat as shadowy, hushed traces of another "taboo" narrative of conquest in the history of Canada's formation (69). Focusing on another silenced drama, that of dissident sexualities, Barbara Gabriel interrupts her analysis of the ending of *The Last of the Crazy People* to note that

> this passage reminds us that Findley's own text is also written over bodies, embedded in relations of power as well as meaning. In this case, the body is recognizably that of the black mammy figure of Southern literature, the repository of tropes of suffering and endurance made legible by a discourse of nature. ("Staging Monstrosity" 193)

It's time, I think, to move the writing of race and ethnicity into a position of direct inquiry, just as Findley himself has done — and has invited us to do — in *Headhunter*.

In order to begin this process, I will engage notions of cultural difference and representation drawn from the fields of postcolonial and African-American theory, for I think that they are best suited to help me deal with some of the questions that arise when I read Findley writing race and ethnicity. How does he represent constructions of racial or ethnic otherness? What relation do these constructions bear to those of his own (WASP) ethnicity? How does the race-sex analogy work in his representations of oppressions and hegemonies? And how might we sort out his recent concern with the white authorial hand hovering over the page and his long-standing public stance on cultural appropriation, his liberal humanist defence of the freedom of the writer's imagination?

Most relevant to these concerns is performative race theory, which is well summarized by Aldon Nielsen, commenting specifically on black-white racial dynamics in the United States:

> "Black" and "White" do not designate discrete territories of clearly definable, essential racial being in America, or even essential cultural histories and traits. They often serve as terms to obscure the operations of a deeper racist signifying practice, a practice that produces race and difference in a constantly fluctuating mechanism of oppression. But they also have a historical existence as strategic terms of resistance. Race serves simultaneously as the means by which hegemonic discourse organizes its policing functions, erecting boundaries that define and oppress an other, *and* as the ever-shifting strategic locus from which others assault and reterritorialize American identity. (3)

Nielsen's understanding of race owes a great deal, I think, to Homi K. Bhabha's notion of cultural difference as "uncanny" and undecidable (312–13) and his analyses of imperialism in general. Following this theoretical move away from concepts of imperialism and difference as dualistic, I will explore race and ethnicity, as they are performed in Findley's works, as polyvalent constructions that undertake the cultural work both of critique and of repetition or echoing of hegemonic discourses.

The overdetermined figure of the black maid triggered a crisis of racial representation by the time that Findley wrote *Headhunter*. He draws attention to the scenario of the black maid and the white child in the kitchen repeatedly in interviews, each time relating it intertextually to Carson McCullers's play *The Member of the Wedding* and to his own childhood relationships with maids employed by his Rosedale family. In these discussions, Findley expresses amazement that the text of his own childhood and that of a Southern white writer could overlap with such eerie exactitude — that they could *repeat* each other: "Carson McCullers's imagery delivered me. That was me, that little girl in the kitchen with the maid — that was me" ("Masks" 34); "it [McCullers's play] just cut through me like a knife, because after all the theatre that I had loved and lived with in this other dimension of reality and movies, the two realities were suddenly one" ("Interview" 108). But in order to reinforce this cherished notion of experiential-literary identity, Findley must reracialize the maid. As he recalls to Barbara Gabriel, there was one respect in which the scenario at the kitchen table in McCullers wasn't identical to his own childhood experience:

> they [the maids] weren't black, in my case. There were mostly farm women, because in those days — the '30s and '40s — it was always the woman off the farm, the extra woman who could no longer be supported in the home, who went to the city to try to get work and since she was not educated often got domestic work. ("Masks" 34)

His black maids, then, offer a point of departure for a study of racial signification in his work in general, because their constructedness is so intensely highlighted; they reveal, in Nielsen's words, "the resignifying minstrelsy in which whites dress up their language in blackface to represent their own representations of blackness to themselves" (7).

What the black maid resignifies to Findley — via McCullers — is strength and maternal protection. Iris Browne, in *The Last of the Crazy People*, answers Hooker's questions as best she can (showing a willingness that others in his life, except perhaps Gilbert, lack), protects him from painful awareness of family conflicts, draws him up on her knee, comforts him, feeds him, embraces him. She is, explicitly, the mother surrogate; returning from the last day of school, Hooker truculently thinks that "he would not even ask for her [his mother, Jessie]. He would talk, instead, to Iris in the kitchen" (16). Bertha Millroy from "Lemonade" performs many of the same functions as Iris and is just as explicitly figured as a caregiver; she is, in Harper Dewey's eyes, "like a nurse" (*Dinner* 9). Even in *Headhunter*, in spite of its air of taking leave of the black maid of Findley's past fictions (*"From now on*, Orley decided, *I will write myself"* [418]), Findley gives readers another caretaker-mother black maid. Even as Barbara Berry churlishly accuses Orley of paying attention to her because her parents pay Orley to do so, "already she did not believe it.... Orley could not love anyone she had been paid to love. It wasn't in her" (165). What is "in" Orley — and Bertha and Iris — as racially configured essence is precisely this capacity to love and nurture unconditionally.

This myth of the all-encompassing love of the black surrogate mother has been persistent, enticing white writers long after Faulkner, so that it should repeat itself in Findley is not nearly so anachronistic as it might seem. There is, for example, Adrienne Rich's claiming of her childhood nanny as her black mother in *Of Woman Born*:

Motherhood as Experience and Institution. The controversy that ensued was both chastening and enlightening for Rich; by the time she came to write the essays in *Blood, Bread, and Poetry: Selected Prose 1979–1985,* she knew that she could never again blithely claim a mother whose history and nurturing were so clearly not hers to claim. Is Findley's Orley a sign that his perspective on race and ethnicity is undergoing a similar interrogation? To assume that it is may be problematic and may obscure the hybridity and ambiguity of his performance of race and ethnicity in his fictions.

To begin with, Findley figures this protective affection physically in terms of size. In *The Last of the Crazy People,* Iris is "not only very thin but tall" (49; by contrast, Nicholas thinks of his affection-challenged sister, Rosetta, "She was so — enormously small" [244]); Alberta Perkins, Iris's black maid friend, is "a hulk," "someone who sat in gigantic splendour" (85), bearing sorrow "across a huge and almost monstrous breadth of shoulder" (85–86). *The Butterfly Plague*'s black maid, Ida, in service to the starlet Myra Jacobs, is similarly protective of Myra, defending the increasingly depressed actor from unwanted phonecalls; she also has "large, white-shoe-encased feet," "large hands, tall legs, a long, flat body, and a small head. She looked as a giant must look to a baby lying on the floor — the top parts of her receding into diminishing perspective" (208). This tendency to inflate the body at the expense of the head is eerily suggestive of the body/mind duality that Findley re-creates in his black maid characters. As he once commented to Graeme Gibson, Iris is, like Naomi from *The Butterfly Plague,* the figure "of the brooding woman of non-intellectual sensibility," though he went on to say that "Intellectually I think they're probably smarter than anybody else, because everybody else has fallen into some kind of intellectual trap where their point of view is twisted away from reality by the brain" ("Timothy Findley" 139–40). Here is the complex ideological doubling that performative race theorists have perceived at work at various sites of representation; Findley's large, protective black maids-mother surrogates both critique an emotional dryness that he figures as WASP and become implicated in centuries-old figurations of ethnic others as brutishly physical and primarily emotional.

Indeed, in Findley, these qualities of physical prominence and nurturance are evident in other characters racially marked as other. Harold Herald, Letitia Virden's chauffeur in *The Butterfly Plague,* is a "huge and misplaced" "black of gigantic proportions," with "enormous" teeth (35, 116, 34); Dolly marvels at him as "a man so large and black" (118). In spite of this big bad wolf characterization, Harold takes Letitia's place as protector of her son, Octavius ("He's black and will protect me" [365], writes Octavius, apparently in no doubt himself about the Findleyan links between race and nurturance). In *The Telling of Lies: A Mystery*, a saddened Vanessa Van Horne watches as the denizens of the WASP enclave Larson's Neck whisper disapprovingly about a young white woman (aptly nicknamed "The Honey Girl") dancing with "a large, athletic black man" (247): "He was immense" (248). It is he who clears the crowd away from Vanessa's friend Peter Moore, who has collapsed on the floor, drunk, while the Larson's Neck crowd coolly gazes at the social outsider's pain (251). But one of the most obvious and memorable of Findley's racially othered nurturers is Lucy in *Not Wanted on the Voyage*; she is (self-)created as foreign, she is ethereally tall, and her desire is to protect and nurture, though in Noah Noyes's regime that desire can only be frustrated. In this respect, she explicitly doubles that other frustrated mother, Mrs. Noyes (and her fictional ancestor, Mrs. Ross from *The Wars*);[1] " 'If you could make him live,' " Mrs. Noyes asks Lucy of the Unicorn, " 'why couldn't you keep him alive?' 'I could ask the same of you, Mother Noyes,' Lucy said; 'of all your dead children' " (281).

Why such tracing of the associations between the racially othered and nurturance? Merely to note the intertextual pressure of McCullers, Faulkner, and others doesn't begin to answer this question; what is it that keeps this well-worn signifying minstrelsy active in the fictional world of Timothy Findley? I think that it has to do with the perceived crisis in the Canadian WASP upper middle class that haunts all of his works — both by its presence and by its racially displaced and written-over absence. Yet, surprisingly, critics of his work have had little to say about the construction of that ethnicity either; in her review of *The Wars*, Margaret Atwood made, en passant, a rather canny remark about how "it is assumed that every group but the Celts and Anglo-Saxons have loveable ethnic peculiarities" (294) — not to mention the assumptions people make about ethnicity and not-so-loveable peculiarities. Accordingly, Atwood does gesture toward a cultural reading of what she wryly calls "Ross's ingrown-toenail family," seeing in the much-discussed mother-son relationship in that novel an element of the pathological, "but it is the pathology of a society that is under scrutiny" (295). In the figure of the ethnically or racially marked and physically imposing nurturer,

Findley is representing back to himself questions about his own whiteness. And they are questions that so many of his characters phrase to those whom they see as the wielders of power. Why are you supposedly powerful, privileged people — you Winslows, Rosses, Damarosches, Noyeses — so weak, even as you hold tenaciously to the power that you have to stamp out whatever you construct as deviance? So we are taken into the ambiguity of Findley's power politics: a critique of the power brokers and a simultaneous desire for them to form a "true," difference-friendly elite. Maybe that's why so many of Findley's racialized protectors are in positions of service; they are the symbolic issuers of reformist cautions to their "betters."

There are other ways in which Findley's racialized or ethnic others are distanced from the hegemonies that construct them and that they, in turn, help to construct by their very presence in the fiction. They are frequently rendered as ancient, anonymous, and thus removed from the time and place of the fiction. In *The Last of the Crazy People*, for example, Iris is unlocatable in the history of the Winslows; she is nowhere and everywhere:

Iris had come to be part of the Winslow household — but that was so long ago that no one ever tried to count the years. . . . As long as Hooker could remember, Iris had been there in the house. She'd been there as long as Gilbert, his brother, could remember, too — and Gilbert was over twenty years old now. (17–18)

Later in the novel, Iris guards a part of her personal history from Hooker ("Why don't you walk off, then?" "I do." "Well, I've never seen it." "You've never been there" [172]). Hooker tellingly follows up with a question about her age — but disclosure is not forthcoming here either (172). In *The Butterfly Plague*, Harold Herald is thought of by various characters as "the Negro" (11–12, 116), and the story of George Damarosch murdering "one of the Chinamen" (260) is deferred, its victim encased in this racialized anonymity, for almost eighty pages. There is, of course, "the Swede," Taffler's anonymous albino sexual partner in *The Wars*, and "the dark chauffeur" accompanying Mrs. Maddox in *The Telling of Lies* (107), thought to be implicated in various deceptions. When the chauffeur receives an order from Mrs. Maddox nearly sixty pages later, the narrator highlights his preceding anonymity: "Kyle — who finally had a name — held open the door . . ." (164). Again, the signifying minstrelsy is complicated; this ancient anonymity implicitly critiques the whites who erase and forget the histories of oppression and colonization with which their own ethnic histories are imbricated. But in order to do that, the fiction must participate in those very codes of anonymity and mythic antiquity.

Not surprisingly, then, the transgressive possibilities offered by these othered figures are subject to modification and fluctuation; their transgressions are as Foucault imagined the very nature of transgression: a crossing of a line that reinscribes the hegemony of the line. To begin with, many of Findley's racialized others are described as the property of others — a condition that necessarily circumscribes or at least mutes their transgressive powers. Iris, for instance, must descend to the indignity of asking the Winslows if she might take the night off that is already designated as hers: "Iris paused diplomatically. 'Will it be all right?' she finally had to ask" (*Last* 186). In *The Butterfly Plague*, black servants are repeatedly described as property: Letitia, in her first written communiqué to Octavius, refers to "my personal Negro" Harold, who has delivered the letter (34); Ida, we hear, "became Myra's permanent property" (209). In *Headhunter*, the Beaumorris Corporation makes a bid to own the very ethnicity of the workers whom it hires to clean the boardroom; when Hong Kong and Japanese capital becomes a force to contend with on Bay Street, Hedley Ashcroft, in a fit of sadistic revenge, fires the Portuguese maids and hires Vietnamese and Chinese men, even attempting to bribe one of the Chinese men to say that he is Japanese. This humiliating display of ownership recalls a scene from Findley's *The Stillborn Lover*, in which Harry Raymond, the ex-diplomat, remembers talking peace to an unresponsive General McArthur and, as he was leaving, watching a Japanese gardener come out and rake away his footprints (74). In such situations, the transgressions are usually small ones; Iris in *The Last of the Crazy People* indulges Hooker in forbidden coffee (18), and they both escape the house to indulge in their separate pleasures (" 'I'm going to smoke now,' she would say, 'and you may chew' " [50]). The only space wherein she can effect transgression of a more dramatic sort is in narrative; she (re)tells the ballad "Frankie and Johnnie" to Hooker and Gilbert, significantly changing the ending so that Frankie's transgressive rage — shooting her mulatto lover Johnnie for consorting with a white prostitute — is forgiven by a (white) jury.[2] An ethnically constructed other, it seems, can only transgress explicitly — in the main frame of the story and in larger matters — if she or he is a member of some other elite — a higher class, for instance. The heiress Mercedes Mannheim in *The Telling of Lies*, for example, has broken "the colour bar" at Larson's Neck (248), but she routinely uses her connections with the wealthy and powerful to obtain what she wants. Yet, as Vanessa reflects when she sees the continuing racism at Larson's Neck, "Nothing changes. Nothing will" (248). Apparently, there will always be gardeners waiting in the wings to erase the footprints of dissenters.

In Findley, these problematic transgressions may assume the dramatic modes of comedy or tragedy, but they are, in any case, highly performative. In "Hello Cheeverland, Goodbye" from *Dinner along the Amazon*, the black maid Rosetta is virtually a walking satire on the pretensions of her ultra-WASP Long Island employers. When Ishmael asks for tea instead of the expected scotch, Rosetta pours out his portion of liquor and thinks of her boyfriend's advice to "Rob 'em blind": " 'But Sweet Jesus, how I hates this crap . . .' and throws it down her throat. . . . [A]nd she pours another jigger and lifts it to the window and thinks: I can't do this — and pours it down the drain again and caps the bottle" (155; first ellipsis in original). In *The Butterfly Plague*, published just five years before "Hello Cheeverland, Goodbye," Myra's maid, Ida, frustrates unwanted telephone callers by performing a tap dance version of "moving-all-over-the-house-looking-for-Myra noises" (208). At the other end of the generic scale, we have the "tragic Negro" figure most amply figured in *The Last of the Crazy People*. Iris partakes in this representation, yet she also resists its implications. Near the beginning of the novel, we read a long litany of her dead relatives; we also hear that, by disobeying her father and taking work on the trains, she "survived. She was not too proud to work" (17). When Hooker's cat Clementine dies, Iris advises Hooker that "I have always respected the laws of give and take" (171). But when her friend Alberta gives her nearly identical advice in the guise of a card game, Iris chafes at what she perceives as the quietism of the tragic Negro stance: "I don't wanta sit around the lousy dinin'-room table, playin' cards — forgotten! I want Hooker, and I want peace, and I want to *know*" (93). Whether or not she refuses this role, it does, as she despondently realizes, partly compose her: "But I have to 'cause I have to. And there isn't anything I can do" (93).

This spectre of an overdetermined character both resisting and bowing to her racialized representation foreshadows the more explicitly self-conscious drama that erupts when *Headhunter*'s Orley refuses to be always the represented and never the representer. Yet something of Iris's quiet desperation remains, if implicitly; Orley is, even in the act of uttering those defiant sentiments, being written white. But what the more implicit drama of recognition and resistance from *The Butterfly Plague* suggests is that Findley's racialized characters may have been performing race in his fictions for some time. In *The Last of the Crazy People*, Iris wryly thinks at one point, "I play the colored maid — 'who said she wasn't afraid.' Hah!" (95). Ida's tap dance phone-answering routine is described as "a performance," "a large-footed imitation of Eleanor Powell" (portrayer of the much-invoked Berenice in *The Member of the Wedding*) (*Butterfly* 209). Orley's awareness of "playing the black servant" role in *Headhunter* (417), then, needs to be seen in the context of Findley's other racial performers.

A fascinating variation on racial or ethnic performance is the refusal to perform — a refusal that is, as I've said, in Orley wryly ironic and impossible in a racializing text. Lieutenant Freyberg in *Famous Last Words*, insulted by Quinn and moved to rage by the Holocaust, tries *not* to perform an ethnicity; he denies being Jewish. Yet such denial is, in turn, denied him. As Quinn, the focalizer of this episode, notes in *his* ethnicizing text, "Freyberg had fallen — tripped — but not where Quinn thought he would. He thought the good Captain would deny being anti-social" (221).

A configuration that, like Orley's musings, highlights the constructedness of race in Findley's fictions is the radical change of skin colour. Critics of *Not Wanted on the Voyage* have said little of substance about Japeth's turning blue at the hands of the Ruffian King and his followers,[3] implicitly accepting it as an eccentric element of Findley's playful text, but this bizarre episode also burlesques colour-associated racial labelling. Japeth, the self-styled warrior who wishes to be the wielder of the oppressive sword, cannot bear to be coloured as the other; "It's because I'm blue," he complains when even the peacock in the yard is unruffled by his display of macho vigour. "And that isn't fair! I didn't ask to be blue . . ." (16). Nor did Lotte and Adam ask to be unwanted Ape children, but that doesn't stop Japeth from upholding Noah's species-cleansing initiatives. A telling Findleyan intertext is Dolly Damarosch's first conversation with Octavius in *The Butterfly Plague*:

"You're an incredible color, if I may say so."
. . . "What do you mean by incredible? Have I gone blue by any chance?"
. . .

"Once, I did turn blue and I was very ill and had to be put in an oxygen tent and treated by many, many doctors. . . ."

. . .

"What color am I, then?"

"Just white. Sort of yellow, maybe." (307)

As this text seems to ask, just what *is* an incredible colour? In this case, it is defined by viewers who construct Caucasian features as just white — just normative, that is. In fact, race as constructed by the gaze of the Caucasian is increasingly scrutinized in Findley. When Vanessa Van Horne outlines her plan to dress Mercedes's Philippine maid Imelda as a Pine Point Inn maid, Mercedes stops her with the objection that everyone knows about the colour bar — extending even to the hired staff. "I am not coloured," protests Imelda, much as Freyberg wishes to correct and re-create ethnicity, but Mercedes, with her own experience of performing race, laughs, "Yes, you are. As long as you're in this building!" (*Telling* 308).

This problematic construction of whiteness as normative, as "not coloured," has at times been highlighted in Findley too, though it comes to the fore, I think, only in his later work, such as *Headhunter*, *Stones*, and *The Piano Man's Daughter* — perhaps a sign that, with the awareness of Orley's position in a white man's text, Findley has turned more decisively to a self-conscious dissection of what Atwood called "Southern Ontario Gothic — Rosedale variation" (295). In *The Wars*, though, as Atwood sensed, the dissection had begun. I have written elsewhere about Robert learning, through his experiences at home and at the front, to perform masculinity, but I think that he also learns, in this process, to perform WASP. One warning sign, surely, is the reading material of a cabin mate, Captain Ord, on the SS *Massanabie*: G.A. Henty's ultraimperialist series of novels: *With Clive in India, With Wolfe at Quebec,* . . . (58, 59). The list goes on, just like the litany of Rosedale names that plagues Mrs. Ross outside the church: "The Bennetts and the Lawsons, the Lymans and the Bradshaws, the Aylesworths and the Wylies . . ." (52). How interesting that the Wylies make a return appearance in *Headhunter*; it's as though WASP society is, for Findley, another construction — a textual web. In spite of this highly worked construction, though, in Findley WASP ethnicity is also, paradoxically, the most hidden and secretive; as Robert thinks when the Flemish farmer yells "*Maudit anglais!*" at him, "he imagined he was being accused of something he hadn't done. He thought if he could identify himself, it might explain his innocence" (73). Canadian WASP identity — being just white — is thought to explain and to exonerate — to whitewash a host of historical sins.

In later works, if Rosedale makes a resounding return performance, Findley also shifts his study of the racialized other to a more Orientalizing strain — and the two tendencies are closely related. In *Not Wanted on the Voyage*, Lucy, the Orientalized other, is without question a consummate performer: "And such a great actress too; 'with all them funny voices!' which Mrs. Noyes — from time to time — would try to imitate" (249). But among those voices, Findley does not count any sort of stage Oriental ventriloquism; as both Barbara Gabriel and Cecilia Martell have pointed out, the language of Lucy is that of North American — specifically Hollywood — camp. A similar type of ethnic cross-dressing occurs in a more recent fiction, *The Piano Man's Daughter*; there Lily and her two girlhood friends cross the ocean to another (British) culture and culturally cross-dress when they don Japanese kimonos. But, like Lucy's performed Orientalism, these kimonos are themselves "dressed" in British Orientalism: they become stage props in the girls' performance as "*Yum-Yum, Peep-bo* and *Pitti-Sing* — Gilbert and Sullivan's 'three little maids from school'" (310). By crossing cultural and ethnic codes, and staging performances of hybridized, ventriloquized Orientalism in his later fiction, Findley explicitly critiques WASP performances and appropriations of Eastern cultures.

As with his critique of the "white hand hovering over the page" in *Headhunter*, though, Findley's relationship to the Oriental is not quite this simple. Complicating his Said-like criticism of Orientalism is an occasional reliance on overdetermined notions of Oriental sangfroid and obsessive self-control. In *Inside Memory: Pages from a Writer's Workbook*, for example, Findley opens an article about the death of Ken Adachi with "The complexities in Ken Adachi were entirely Japanese" (297), and then he imagines Adachi laughing quietly at his words. But Findley goes on to elaborate what are less complexities than generalizations about Japanese character and culture: "the balances on which he weighed his gestures were decidedly Japanese: the disciplined demeanour fronting for the passionate enthusiast; the sense of discretion which acted as the governor of rage and laughter alike. He was one of the most remarkably self-controlled people I have ever known" (297–98). Discipline, discretion, self-control; they and the prices they exact are at the heart of his characterization of Vanessa Van Horne, the admirer of Japanese culture in *The Telling of Lies*. They are also at the heart of a 1974 story, "The Book of Pins," in which the self-controlling, inwardly passionate writer Annie Bogan is figured as Japanese: "Kabuki Bogan" (*Dinner* 207). And that consummate controller, the Duchess of Windsor in *Famous Last Words*, is repeatedly described in terms of her kabuki-like cosmetic mask. Once again, clearly, race may perform remarkably diverse ideological work in Findley; if he is eager to criticize WASP performances of the Orient in his later fiction, he has also drawn substantially in his writings on Western stereotypes of Orientalism.[4]

Some of the racially implicated ideas I've been exploring here — construction and performance of race, the Findleyan crisis of WASP ethnic subjectivity — are brought into crisis in one of the most prominent racial scenarios in Findley's works: the desire/sexualization of the ethnically or racially defined other. Often, in Findley, characters desire to be their others or to possess them sexually — and the two desires often overlap. In *The Butterfly Plague*, for instance, Dolly Damarosch gazes longingly at Harold Herald (still anonymously labelled "the Negro") and explicitly categorizes his desire in racial terms: " 'Here I go again,' he thought. He was enchanted with Negroes. One of his fantasies . . ." (116; ellipsis in original; even Dolly cannot quite visualize what consummation with his ethnic other might be — it is silenced, beyond representation). And later, when Dolly sexualizes the similarly taboo act for him of driving a car, he thinks of, among other drivers whom he has watched, "Men with Negro hands" (290), as though he cannot visualize this time the bodies — historical, material — that belong to those hands. In *The Wars*, Tom Longboat, the Native runner, is the object of young Robert's hero worship — another desired material body that lies beyond access and representation. As Findley tellingly recounted, try as he might, he could not bring himself to represent Longboat as an active character in the novel:

> I kept trying to bring them together, and I wrote these things where Longboat would be seen running in the distance, in France and so on — Robert would see this figure passing through the landscape, and it would dawn on him, "My God, it's him," and he'd go over and shadow him in some way, and I thought, this is great drama, and it should, it's got to work, why not? . . . No way. It just simply wasn't right. That man had to maintain his mythic distance. The mythic distance

between Longboat and Robert's mind could not be broken by introducing the real Longboat. ("Long" 81–82)

I am particularly struck by Findley's description of the relationship as being between Longboat and Robert's *mind*; Longboat as racial other must remain a performance, a construction of Robert's mind, much as Dolly's mythic men with Negro hands must remain fantasies.

What makes this eroticization of the racial other important in Findley is the desire that Robert feels for the ethnicity, and specifically the skin colour, of Longboat. His desire to be another Longboat (as, for instance, when he tries to run a marathon of his own around his Rosedale home block) is tied to a desire *not* to be/perform WASP: "He'd go upstairs into the attic, when he was ten, and take off his clothes in front of an old, dark mirror and wish that he was red. Or black. Or yellow. Any colour but pink. Smiling and silence didn't seem to go with pink" (48). In *The Wars*, this desire to be other is further eroticized in Robert's close relationship with Harris. Harris, like Robert, has wished to be other — in his case, another species; he describes swimming in the sea with whales, wishing to be in their element and not in his socially uncomfortable one. Robert's love of Harris, then, encodes but dares not speak the desire for transgression — of ethnicity, humanity, and heterosexuality. What's more, this portrait of overlapping codes of racialized or ethnicized desire is not singular in Findley's canon; Lucy from *Not Wanted on the Voyage* is racialized by performing Oriental; sexualized when she is described variously as a courtesan and a whore; transgressive of heterosexual codes in that his/her marriage with Ham is apparently satisfying sexually; and desirous of another element: the drama of the Earth rather than the blandness of heaven.[5] In Findley, then, WASP identity is apparently as blandly undesirable as Milton's heaven; it's the ethnicized "underworld" that is the object of desire. Once more, we run up against the ideological instability of Findley's ethnic dramas: in hastening to critique WASP complacency, created ethnic otherness may become exactly that — other — and so, exoticized, sexually desirable and demonic.

In *Headhunter*, there is an uneasy alliance between art and capitalism in exploiting this sexualized demonic otherness. One of Julian Slade's series of paintings, *Shreds*, depicts a Goyaesque victim, "a beggar, perhaps, or a slave," who is both racially and sexually othered: "His skin had an olive complexion," and his clothes have been shredded with a terrifyingly clinical sexual sadism (182). What difference, Findley seems to ask, between this racialized and sexualized torture scene and the Benetton ad that pushes Orley to her final determination to *"write myself"*? *"The United Colours of Benetton,* it said. And it showed a lot of black children. Africa. Somewhere. Except that one of them was an albino. White" (418). The aptly surnamed Griffin Price is implicated in this commodification of racial difference; as the novel draws to its horrific close, he is planning "an 'Oriental' gift line," and this is why he is touring the Royal Ontario Museum's Far Eastern rooms — to implicate them in his white capitalist initiative. But Price's Orientalism is only the latest in a series of assembly line ethnicities for sale: "He now had two such factories in operation — the glass factory in Prague, where the Inuit art was imitated, and a plaster factory in Warsaw where Aztec and Inca imitations were manufactured. Both operations were doing a roaring trade — and soon Griffin would have the Romanians thrown into gear" (422). As with Benetton's shakily united colours, the setting is unimportant — somewhere. Capitalist whitewash — the blanding of the globe by the apparent celebration of colour — is at work here too.

This desire for the commodified, sexualized other brings me to the problematic of racial representation in Findley that I think requires concentrated analysis: the use of analogies of racial oppression. Many of his WASPs desire and sexualize their racialized others, and this desire occurs in the context of an identification: they want to *be* their others. To be a dissenting WASP and/or a sexual dissenter, then, is to align oneself with an othered ethnicity. Thus, in *The Butterfly Plague,* Ruth Damarosch and the "dreamers" — European Jews, various dissenters from Nazism — are one, she thinks (106), even though she can hide in her performance as a famous ballerina while the likes of Jakob Seuss die in the camps. Dolly, sexually dissident, is explicitly compared to Jakob on a couple of occasions ("In some ways he was rather like Dolly . . ." [73]; "The condemned, you see? Born that way. Like Adolphus" [352]). In *The Telling of Lies,* Vanessa, because of her artistic otherness as a cool photographic dissector of the surfaces of life, can repeatedly claim to understand her Japanese captor, Colonel Norimitsu. The fortunes of Myra Jacobs and her maid, Ida, are parallelled in *The Butterfly Plague;* Ida's status as Myra's property overlaps with Myra's slavish contractual responsibilities to the studios, Findley punning on the concept of actors as Hollywood properties: "Ida had been with Myra ever since her rise to the top, '34, and she always talked about 'us killing Mr. Danton' (a perfectly ordinary scandal) in 1936 (hushed up) and 'us being counteracted to the new studios' (whichever, whenever) and now 'our trembles' (presumably troubles) in October 1938" (209). But the most explicit example of bonding of racially and/or sexually othered characters in Findley is Octavius's seeking protection with Harold Herald in the same novel. As Findley explained to Graeme Gibson,

> Somebody said that they thought it was tremendously signifi-
> cant that the homosexual and the black man went off together,
> whereas I had meant something entirely different, which is the
> weak depend on the strong — it's that simple. The weak who
> are beautiful, that's Tennessee Williams, "All ye weak and
> lovely people", whatever that thing is of his, "Don't fall behind
> with the brutes — go forward with the poets". The symbol to
> me is that that kid went off with the one person who is going
> to survive come hell or high water because that is the black
> man's tradition — he must. Whereas the kid mustn't. I mean,
> he doesn't feel he must. He hasn't got the ability, no. He's queer.
> His genes won't survive. ("Timothy Findley" 143–44).

Oddly enough, Findley ends up arguing the countercase: that the racialized and sexualized identities of Harold and Octavius are, indeed, tremendously significant, if not in precisely the way that that somebody meant: weakness becomes sexualized and strength racialized. Barbara Gabriel calls this end-of-novel pairing "comic," "re-cast in a patently incongruous normalizing frame: 'The strange thing is — I love him' " ("Performing" 246). What both exceeds and respects this frame is the interracial bonding — both indicative and transgressive of a firm belief, at this early point in Findley's career, in the capacity of the racialized and sexualized "weak" and "strong" to come together. (Tellingly, when Findley revised the 1969 text for 1986 publication, he omitted the last scene, in which a white heterosexual romance — that of Ruth's daughter and Noah's son — provides closure.)

Findley's belief that different histories and ethnicities can be associated, even reconciled, has been motivated by a humanist framework. Repeatedly, when discussing difference in interviews or in his fiction, Findley uses the phrase "joining the human race." As he told Peter Buitenhuis,

> "Gay" is a word I loathe and detest. As a homosexual, it offends
> me deeply and it offends me twice deeply when other homo-

sexuals choose that as an appellation — as an "us against them" word. It's so confining. The point is to join the human race, as my mother would say. ("Return" 20)

Difference, then, is constructed as ghettoization, and joining humanity is the remedy. For Findley, identifying with another ethnic group's difference and history is one way of dealing with the loneliness of sexual dissidence. In his revealing lecture to the Trent University Philosophical Society, "My Final Hour," given a prominent place as the conclusion to *Inside Memory*, he speaks frankly about the overwhelming sense of ostracism and monstrosity that he felt as a homosexual adolescent; at the end of his address, he dramatizes a scene in which access to another ethnic group's oppression delivers an "epiphany"; gazing at photographs from the liberation of Dachau, Findley realizes that, "at last, I had been joined — through a unique revelation of horror — to the rest of the human race. I was never to see myself as a being apart. How, after all, can you be *apart* when everyone else is standing *apart* beside you?" (311). This is the vision that informs his public stand on cultural appropriation: as an anti-censorship humanist, he has always maintained the right of the artist to create freely — a position, critics have argued, that rests on European-grounded notions of rights and freedoms.

This act of desiring and (thereby) joining all the fragmented others receives an Orientalizing cast in the short story "Foxes," from *Stones*. Glenn Gould-like communications expert Morris Glendenning leaves his Rosedale home to examine the Japanese theatrical masks encased in the WASP-identified Royal Ontario Museum. His walk, from Rosedale to the ROM, becomes a (WASP-contained) walk on the wild side; the narrator constructs "the icons and symbols" of East and West as "opposites" (65), and the mask that particularly intrigues Morris similarly constructs and then deconstructs the opposition human/animal: it is one theatrical mask in a series showing the transformation of a fox into a man. For Morris, placing the mask over his face is an act both of "trespassing" and of joining: "Now — at last — he was not alone" (70, 73). It becomes, that is, the racially figured antidote to his terrifying Eliotic vision of Bloor Street — a moving mass of human isolates. In this story, it is almost as though Findley acknowledges — as he would do in *Headhunter* — the cultural trespass involved in healing WASP anomie by a walk on the racialized wild side, but he makes it equally clear that WASP need overrides this trespass, just as his liberally defined notion of creativity overrides, in its needs and desires, the complicated issue of cultural appropriation.[6]

* * *

What has this to do, finally, with Orley, still trapped in the white man's kitchen, where I left her at the opening of this article? Have cracks appeared in Findley's apparently firm belief in humanist representation, or is it as solid as my reading of the cultural problematics of "Foxes" suggests? It would seem from reading *The Piano Man's Daughter*, the next work to appear after *Headhunter*, that Findley has determined to write his own ethnicity; there he turns to his own ancestry, tracing its fault lines, its complexity, its *constructedness* with the kind of critical care that Jane Urquhart does in *Away* and Carol Shields does in *The Stone Diaries*. In *The Piano Man's Daughter*, Findley deracializes his black maids, reethnicizing Freda as German. But — and this is the more recent ethnic politics in Findley coming to the fore — the narrator himself, occupying that Findleyan never-never land of bland WASP homogeneity, is reethnicized. At the end of the novel, the identity of his father is finally uncovered — and that identity is German. Racial or ethnic othering in Findley has just gotten more risky; the bland "norm" is revealed as what it has always been — unstable, hybridized.

So, perhaps, amid his public stance on appropriation and his defence of putting on masks of difference in order to join the human race, Findley has — to put it ironically — somewhat reconciled himself to difference. I'll conclude with an anecdote that Findley told to Alan Twigg in an interview, an anecdote that reveals both his acknowledgement of ethnic difference and — in the very words with which he introduces it — his continuing attraction to sexual-racial-ethnic identifications and analogies:

> But, about being male: it's like a wonderful confrontation between a white woman and a black woman on a television programme. The white woman, with *dreadful* condescension, says to the black woman, "But my dear, I understand, and I've always understood, that you're just like me." And the black woman says, "But honey, you don't understand. I'm not like you at all. I'm *black*!" ("Timothy Findley" 86)

So *that's* where Orley went when, like the literary figures conjured up by Lilah Kemp, she escaped from the pages of *Headhunter*.

NOTES

¹ Compare Mrs. Ross to Robert: "Birth I can give you — but life I cannot. I can't keep anyone alive. Not any more" (*Wars* 28).

² Thanks to my fellow contributor Marlene Goldman for suggesting that I draw this fascinating retelling of the ballad into my argument.

³ An important recent exception is Peter Dickinson's astute reading of Japeth's blueness as strategic camp counterdiscourse in his essay in this volume, " 'Running Wilde': National Ambivalence and Sexual Dissidence in *Not Wanted on the Voyage*."

⁴ Many thanks to fellow contributors Marlene Goldman and Catherine Hunter, whose perceptive comments about this section on Findley and the East helped to give it greater focus and direction.

⁵ As Dickinson points out, ". . . Findley's deliberate orientalizing of the transvestite figure in his text . . . adds another element of national ambivalence to Lucy's already evident sexual dissidence" (137–38).

⁶ Thanks to Marlene Goldman for suggesting that I include a discussion of "Foxes" in this paper.

WORKS CITED

Ashcroft, Bill, Gareth Griffiths, and Helen Tiffin. *The Empire Writes Back: Theory and Practice in Post-Colonial Literatures*. New Accents. London: Routledge, 1989.

Atwood, Margaret. "Timothy Findley: The Wars." *Second Words: Selected Critical Prose*. 1982. Boston: Beacon, 1984. 290–95.

Bhabha, Homi K. "DissemiNation: Time, Narrative, and the Margins of the Modern Nation." *Nation and Narration*. Ed. Bhabha. London: Routledge, 1990. 291–322.

Brydon, Diana. " 'It Could Not Be Told': Making Meaning in Timothy Findley's *The Wars*." *Journal of Commonwealth Literature* 21.1 (1986): 62–79.

Dickinson, Peter. " 'Running Wilde': National Ambivalence and Sexual Dissidence in *Not Wanted on the Voyage*." *Paying Attention: Critical Essays on Timothy Findley*. Ed. Anne Geddes Bailey and Karen Grandy. Toronto: ECW, 1998. 125–46. Also published in the *Timothy Findley Issue*. Ed Bailey and Grandy. Spec. issue of *Essays on Canadian Writing* 64 (1998): 125–46.

Findley, Timothy. *The Butterfly Plague*. 1969. Harmondsworth, Eng.: Penguin, 1986.

——. *Dinner along the Amazon*. Harmondsworth, Eng.: Penguin, 1984.

——. *Famous Last Words*. Harmondsworth, Eng.: Penguin, 1982.

——. *Headhunter*. Toronto: HarperCollins, 1993.

——. *Inside Memory: Pages from a Writer's Workbook*. Toronto: Harper-Collins, 1990.

——. "Interview with Timothy Findley." With Eugene Benson. *World Literature Written in English* 26.1 (1986): 107–15.

——. *The Last of the Crazy People*. 1967. Harmondsworth, Eng.: Penguin, 1983.

——. " 'Long Live the Dead': An Interview with Timothy Findley." With Johan Aitken. *Journal of Canadian Fiction* 33 (1982): 79–93.

——. "Masks and Icons: An Interview with Timothy Findley." With Barbara Gabriel. *Canadian Forum* Feb. 1986: 31–36.

——. *Not Wanted on the Voyage*. 1984. Harmondsworth, Eng.: Penguin, 1985.

——. *The Piano Man's Daughter*. Toronto: HarperCollins, 1995.

——. "The Return of the Crazy People." Interview with Peter Buitenhuis. *Books in Canada* Dec. 1988: 17–20.

——. *The Stillborn Lover*. Winnipeg: Blizzard, 1993.

——. *Stones*. Markham, ON: Viking, 1988.

——. *The Telling of Lies: A Mystery*. Markham, ON: Viking, 1986.

——. "Timothy Findley." Interview with Alan Twigg. *Strong Voices: Conversations with Fifty Canadian Authors*. Madeira Park, BC: Harbour, 1988.

——. "Timothy Findley." Interview with Graeme Gibson. *Eleven Canadian Novelists*. Toronto: Anansi, 1973. 115–49.

——. *The Wars*. 1977. Harmondsworth, Eng.: Penguin, 1978.

Gabriel, Barbara. "Performing the *Bent* Text: Fascism and the Regulation of Sexualities in Timothy Findley's *The Butterfly Plague*." *English Studies in Canada* 21 (1995): 226–50.

——. "Staging Monstrosity: Genre, Life-Writing, and Timothy Findley's *The Last of the Crazy People*." *The Gender Issue*. Ed. Gabriel and Lorraine M. York. Spec. issue of *Essays on Canadian Writing* 54 (1994): 168–97.

Ingham, David. "Bashing the Fascists: The Moral Dimensions of Findley's Fiction." *Studies in Canadian Literature* 15.2 (1990): 33–54.

Martell, Cecilia. "Unpacking the Baggage: 'Camp' Humour in Timothy Findley's *Not Wanted on the Voyage*." *Canadian Literature* 148 (1996): 96–111.

Nielsen, Aldon L. *Writing between the Lines: Race and Intertextuality*. Athens: U of Georgia P, 1994.

Pennee, Donna Palmateer. *Moral Metafiction: Counterdiscourse in the Novels of Timothy Findley*. Toronto: ECW, 1991.

York, Lorraine M. *Front Lines: The Fiction of Timothy Findley*. Toronto: ECW, 1991.

Contributors

Anne Geddes Bailey, University of Western Ontario
    and Brescia College
Peter Dickinson, Vancouver
Barbara Gabriel, Carleton University
Marlene Goldman, University of Toronto
Karen Grandy, Mount Saint Vincent University
Tom Hastings, York University
Catherine Hunter, University of Winnipeg
Heather Sanderson, University of British Columbia
Lorraine York, McMaster University